Long-Range and Short-Range Planning for Educational Administrators

James Lewis, Jr.

71989

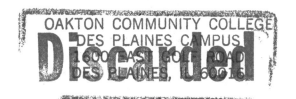
Allyn and Bacon, Inc.
Boston   London   Sydney   Toronto

TO EDITH REISNER

A warrior in public education whom
I will surely miss.

Library of Congress Cataloging in Publication Data

Lewis, James, 1930–
    Long-range and short-range planning for educational
administrators.

    Bibliography: p.
    Includes index.
    1. Educational planning.   2. School management and
organization.   I. Title.
LB2805.L415   1982   371.2'07   82-11509
ISBN 0-205-07756-0

Printed in the United States of America

10 9 8 7 6 5 4 3 2   87 86 85

CONTENTS

iii

6 SELECTING PROGRAM STRATEGIES 109

7 DEVELOPING OPERATIONAL PLANS 124

8 PREPARING SHORT-RANGE OBJECTIVES 135

9 ESTABLISHING PERFORMANCE STANDARDS 150

10 ESTABLISHING AN ACTION PLAN 161

11 REPORTING OPERATIONAL PERFORMANCE RESULTS 171

12 PROBLEM-SOLVING PLANNING 181

Defining a Problem-Solving Plan 181, When Is a Situation a Problem? 182, Advantages of Preparing Problem-Solving Plans 184, Understanding the Three Essential Phases of Problem-Solving 184, Implementing Problem-Solving Planning 188, Salient Points 189, Application Strategy 12 189

13 UNDERSTANDING PLANNING CONTROLS 191

Defining Planning Controls 191, The Planning Control Cycle 193, Some Advantages of Planning Controls 195, Defining Management by Exception 195, Implementing Management by Exception 195, Advantages of the Planning Exception Report 197, The Planning Exception Report Illustrated and Explained 198, Identifying Planning Controls 203, Causes of Variations in Standards 204, Salient Points 205, Application Strategy 13 205

14 IMPROVING THE PLANNING PROCESS USING A COORDINATOR 206

The Role of the Planning Coordinator 207, Qualifying for the Position of Planning Coordinator 210, To Whom Should the Planning Coordinator Report? 213, Using an Outsider or Insider to Fill the Position of Coordinator 214, Training: The Primary Function of the Planning Coordinator 214, Salient Points 217, Application Strategy 14 218

15 EFFECTING THE PLANNING PROCESS 219

Getting the Planning Job Done 219, Planning Staffs in Large Planning Units 221, Selecting a Planning Consultant 222, The Traditional Function of School Administration 223, The Theories behind Job Enrichment 224, Making School More Meaningful for Teachers 226, Using Job Enrichment to Effectuate the Planning Process 226, Defining Job Enrichment 227, The Objectives of Job Enrichment 228, Some Assumptions about Job Enrichment 229, Guidelines for Using Job Enrichment in the Planning Process 230, Salient Points 232, Application Strategy 15 233

16 GUIDING HUMAN EFFORTS USING A PLANNING MANUAL 234

Defining the Planning Manual 234, Functions of a Planning Manual 234, Criteria for an Effective Planning Manual 236, Developing the Planning Manual 238, Dealing with the Size of Plans 239, The Planning Manual 239, Salient Points 242, Application Strategy 16 242

17 EVALUATING PLANNING EFFECTIVENESS 243

Human Problems Associated with Planning 244, Gauging the Effectiveness of the Planning System 245, Why Planning Has Failed 249, Pitfalls to Avoid 252, Measuring Planning Effectiveness 256, Assessment Instruments of Others 260, Evaluating the System Against its Objectives 261, Assessing the Planning System against Pitfalls 261, Salient Points 262, Application Strategy 17 262

FOREWORD

In our modern, technological, and dynamic society the life of organizations is directly dependent upon their sustaining the public's perception of them as serving some "useful to people" purpose, both today and in the future. Tenure of managers and other persons in both public and private organizational leadership positions is contingent upon a thorough knowledge base and understanding of this phenomenon. Additionally, managers and leaders must be able to demonstrate knowledge of and develop designs essential to goal identification. They must be able to conceive systematic and scientific plans through which organizations will make significant movement toward goal obtainment, and to do so in a humane manner within constraints imposed by political, economic, and other factors.

The author has written this book, calling upon his extensive and vast experiences as an educational leader. It will be most useful to "firing line" managers and organizational leaders in recognizing the value of goal identification, planning, and the planning process. Moreover, many specific suggestions in the form of detailed narrative, charts, diagrams, and location of additional help are provided throughout the volume.

As the "sustaining public" becomes more sophisticated, as well as impatient, more critical questions are asked, and more stringent limitations are placed on the institutions they support. These very strong concerns are coming at a time of inflationary cost increases, declining enrollment, and general unrest in the ranks of the employee groups. In light of these problems, this volume is most timely. The author presents a handbook which will help managers or organizational leaders master goal-setting and problem-solving techniques through the strategic long- and short-range planning processes. Successful administrators or organizational leaders, however, must understand much more than the concept of the planning process. In order to enhance the reader's understanding of practical application, the author provides well-conceived and designed models for developing, implementing, and evaluating strategic and operational plans in the field of education. In spite of the highly complex nature of the subject matter, the reader is given, through clarity of thought and examples, many reasons to understand that persistent organizational problems in this dynamic society are not insoluble. Change will come, and the leader must be able to manage this change in a manner consistent with the perceptions of the sustaining public. The careful reader will find many suggestions of this book helpful in developing the understanding and knowledge base which are prerequisite to the achievement of this goal.

Ulysses Byas, Ed.D.
Superintendent of Schools
Roosevelt, New York

PREFACE

This book will assist school administrators to understand the mechanics of the total planning process, apply the systems approach to planning and management, simulate the future, and measure performance results. Through utilization of this "operating manual," administrators and supervisors will learn what they *can* and *must* do to deal with pressing educational problems. It will also provide a framework for decision-making purposes, induce goal- and objective-setting, reveal and classify future opportunities and threats, act as an effective communication to enhance the implementation of a viable training program for administrators, and provide staff with an opportunity to participate in the important planning affairs of the district.

Long-Range and Short-Range Planning for Educational Administrators is not meant to be a "magic formula." It is obvious that no single plan is appropriate for all schools. The information that has been included results from the author's ten years of practical experience in educational planning, as a superintendent in two school districts, a department chairman in higher education, and a director with a state department of education. This book is fundamental, and can be utilized by *all* educational administrators in their efforts to make well-founded decisions concerning today's and tomorrow's problems. In addition, this book will serve as a handy reference guide for state department of education officials when establishing state-wide policies and procedures to govern the planning process, and as a basic text to introduce administrative education students to the concepts, methods, and procedures for engaging in long-range strategic and short-range operational planning.

Every school administrator must be conscious of the immense changes that have affected management of public education in this country. School district improvement does not depend merely on administrators taking advantage of technological or instructional advances, but on making an organized effort to explore and evaluate opportunities made available within the school-community complex by new concepts and ideas. It is more important today than ever before for school administrators to possess a thorough understanding of the school organization's environment. Advanced instructional techniques, improved technologies, new state and federal legislation and validated programs, and increased costs and community needs demand more and more attention, yet resources—funds, machines, and humans—are limited. In order to meet the challenges of this changing environment, school administrators must be able to:

- Assess opportunities within and without the school environment so that goals and plans are based on well-defined and realistic objectives.
- Predict the major economic, technological, political, and other factors that are likely to have a significant impact on the district.
- Examine alternative courses of action to achieve long-range goals.
- Convert strategic plans into operational plans.
- Integrate planning and budgeting systems for an effective overall managerial system.
- Organize a competent team of administrators and teachers to help implement long-range and short-range plans.

Most informed school administrators will agree that planning is a good thing. Only a small number of districts, however, have effectively incorporated long-range planning into their decision-making process. This fact is substantiated by the author's recent study, which concluded that while all of the state departments of education in the United States require a prescribed plan for illustrating the budget, less than 30 percent of these mandate some form of long-range planning. How funds can be wisely spent without long-range planning points to a serious public education problem.

A recent edition of the *New York University Education Quarterly* reported that most school districts do very little long-range planning. The article maintained that the mission of school districts is often assumed, programs are stabilized, and performance results are subject to very little scrutiny. Short-range planning results have been of questionable value because the "top-of-the-head" approach to planning still prevails in many school districts, while the "seat-of-the-pants" approach evolves around the line-item budgeting process, and they often produce devastating effects when implemented without long-range plans.

Another problem that seriously hampers the growth of long-range planning is that fewer than twenty American universities and colleges have included this vital process in their curriculum for training school administration students.

For a number of years, the term "long-range planning" referred to planning of facilities. This book does not help the reader to prepare plans for constructing a new school building, but serves as a guide for establishing comprehensive plans for making current decisions about the future. Today, the term "long-range planning" is being replaced in business and industry by "strategic planning." However, because the latter term is relatively new in public education, it is best to continue with the old term and, when appropriate, to include both terms. Therefore, when strategic long-range planning is mentioned, it is done so to emphasize the advanced stage of long-range planning, giving emphasis to both the macro- and micro-environments. I have also thought about using the term "education planning"; however, this term has been mistaken for facilities planning.

Any critical comments concerning long-range planning as it currently exists are not meant to offend any individuals or administrators involved in a formal planning process. Weaknesses in the present models are highlighted in order to suggest ways to strengthen individual components and the process as a whole.

I am indebted to a few organizations that helped to make this book a reality: to Harvard University and the Massachusetts Institute of Technology, where I received my first meaningful training experiences in educational management and planning; to the Conference Board, a management research organization whose research and informative documents helped to crystallize my thoughts and ideas; to the Department of Educational Planning at the University of Toronto, Canada, the first higher-educational institution in North America to offer a full-time graduate program leading to a terminal degree in educational planning, and where planning has become an integral component of the curricula for school administrators; and to several state departments of education and numerous school districts around the nation that shared their planning documents, guidelines, plans, training manuals, and comments so that this book could be comprehensive in scope and concept.

Limited space does not permit me to acknowledge all of the noted personages who shared their experiences and ideas either personally or through printed words, thus providing the necessary impetus for this manual; however, I would like to give credit to those who played a primary role in my development as a strategic planner: to M. Scott Myers, who acted as my mentor while I attended MIT; to George S. Odiorne, who provided the momentum for further exploration in the area of planning; to George A. Steiner, whose comprehensive approach to strategic planning helped to clarify several important points; to William E. Rothschild, who really delved into the strategic thinking process and helped make it possible for me to arrive at a systematic plan for performing this complex process; and to H. Igor Ansoff, whose analytical and creative thoughts and ideas triggered a number of useful concepts and methods mentioned in this book, which will be of some value to those in public education.

I am indebted to Ms. Susan Bergen, whose patience as an editor and typist helped produce this book without separating the words, thoughts, and ideas from the person.

Finally, I would like to extend my appreciation to Ms. Afrodite E. Lewnes, who artistically developed the many charts and forms contained in the book.

$\boxed{1}$

THE STRATEGIC PLANNING
PROCESS

Everybody talks about planning, but few are able to put it into successful practice. Take, for example, the results of a recent nationwide survey to determine the extent to which state departments of education mandate long-range planning. Of the forty states responding to this survey, only fourteen, or roughly one-third, required any kind of long-range planning.[1] These states are to be commended for their efforts, but a review of their planning models revealed serious flaws or planning gaps. This statement is not intended to downgrade those states that are engaged in long-range planning, but to point out that much more is necessary if maximum benefits are to be realized from a comprehensive planning process.

As an introduction to strategic planning, the author briefly discusses the purposes of the school district. He then comments on the nature and purpose of planning to pinpoint the rationale for the planning process, and focuses on the definition and characteristics of planning. Guidelines for facilitating, managing, and organizing the planning process are suggested. The three types of planning are discussed, as are differences between strategic and long-range planning and the advantages of the former planning process over the latter. The instructional long-range planning model and the comprehensive strategic planning model are defined and clarified. A ten-step process to install the stra-

---

[1] State Departments of Education that have mandated some form of long-range planning for local school districts include: California, Hawaii, Idaho, Iowa, Maine, Massachusetts, Minnesota, Oregon, Pennsylvania, Rhode Island, Texas, Washington, Wyoming, Virginia.

tegic planning process with minimum difficulty is outlined. The chapter concludes with some truisms about the planning process.

WHY A SCHOOL DISTRICT EXISTS

A school district does not exist merely to increase student achievement. But using a student achievement platform for the maintenance of public education is a sound posture. Theoretically, student learning serves four purposes: (1) as a way to help produce productive members of society, (2) as a means to gain a better understanding of people and the world around them, (3) as a means to increase literacy, and (4) as a process to inculcate the country's political beliefs. The purpose of public education, however, is twofold, serving both conscious and subconscious ends. Ideally, in the conscious state, the public schools exist primarily to increase student learning and growth, and this should be the foundation for funding the public education system. However, although they haven't been voiced publicly, there are a host of other reasons school districts exist that fall under the subconscious state. Under this category would be an administrator's wish to maintain his or her employment, or the public's expectation that the community foster public education or that the school system make a social contribution. The reasons for the school district's existence are complex and interwoven with the personal goals of many individuals and groups within the school-community environment. Changing times and conditions affect the purposes of the school district, which become more varied among the different groups involved, so that the educational system may be of social value to some and economic value to others, and either may be implicitly or explicitly stated.

Although the synthesis of the purposes of public education is permissible for some individuals and groups, the superintendent of schools cannot afford to accept this philosophical approach to the educational system without compromising his or her true role as an educational leader. Dalton E. McFarland is talking about the duality of purposes when he refers to personal goals:[2]

> One important element of complexity with respect to goals is that of determining real or legitimate goals. Within the goal repertoire of a manager, for example, a mixture of goals is affirmed and desired that will bring agreement and recognition by others. The manager may also have goals which are hidden beneath the surface, for they are not acceptable personally or by colleagues or by society in general. Consequently, to the extent that one's true goals are less

[2] Dalton E. McFarland, *Action Strategies for Managerial Achievement* (New York: AMACOM, 1977), p. 18.

than fully acceptable in a public way, goals will be covered, hidden, and not made explicit. Likewise, there may be "pseudo goals"—ones that operate like real goals but are understood to be only for show or talk, not for real action.

In strategic planning, a certain amount of risk is involved in setting long-range goals and in establishing strategies and pursuing short-range objectives. If a planning unit administrator begins to compromise the direction in which the planning unit is heading by forgoing increased student learning and growth for, say, employment maintenance or for other reasons, the school district as a whole will neither prosper nor grow.

THE NATURE AND PURPOSE OF PLANNING

When an innovation is installed, many persons often become disappointed because they expected too much to be accomplished too soon. This is also the case with planning. Long-range and short-range planning are not panaceas. They will not solve all educational ills, predict the future accurately, or prevent mistakes. Planning will, however, minimize the degree to which administrators and teachers will be caught by surprise and enable them to revise goals and objectives by reacting to dynamic variables within the school-community environment. The board of education should no longer judge the effectiveness of school personnel solely on the basis of their having reached an objective, but rather on how well they have performed during changing times and conditions.

Developing a plan of action is a way to respond to changes within a school organization. However, the most important reason to plan is to build a process for reaching a mutual agreement in setting and revising goals and objectives. The following four interrelated variables or forces directly affect the nature, purpose, and techniques of planning.

Difficulty in Predicting the Future

The American public educational system is rapidly evolving through changes brought on by the intellectual, emotional, physical, and social differences in students, the demographic shifts in ethnic populations, state and federal legislation mandating certain programs, economic conditions limiting use of resources, and alterations of the internal and external school environments that affect the entire school organization.

Recognizing the dynamic forces of change in public education, three assumptions can be made about the future:

1. It will differ from the past.
2. It will be difficult to predict.
3. The rate of change will be faster than ever before.

When Professor Forrester of MIT was asked to explain how the future can be predicted with more accuracy for planning purposes, he stated that never, in his experience, had there been a larger number of unpredictable events; therefore, a planning process should be developed that would enable the planner to get better results in spite of the difficulty in predicting the future with accuracy.

The Knowledge Explosion

Television and the computer are two major technological advancements that have enhanced the knowledge explosion. Much more information has been made available within the last fifty years than in all of the preceding years. As a result, administrators must begin to organize information differently by zeroing in on the purpose and use of an extensive data base. They must be able to distinguish between meaningless and meaningful information and be able to retrieve pertinent data quickly and at a minimum cost. Effective planning is dependent primarily on the availability of current, useful, and accurate information. Proper planning helps to clarify decision-making responsibility and to provide the essential and critical information when and where needed.

The Changing Role of School Administrators

Today's educational leaders can no longer lead by virtue of their official power and authority. School employees are too sophisticated during these contemporary times and are neither impressed nor inspired to perform because of a title or position that once was able to energize human effort. This is not to say that the influence of power and authority is unimportant, but to indicate that the most important qualification for the position of school administrator is competence. The term competence refers to an administrator's ability to enable the staff to fulfill the school's organizational goals while they are pursuing their personal goals. When this occurs, they have earned the acceptance and respect of their staff and actually have transferred official power into unofficial acceptance. The process of planning is a worthwhile endeavor to begin this new role.

Management Effectiveness

The traditional definition of management is the art of getting things done *through* people. A more contemporary definition is getting things done *with* people. With this shift in administrative style, today's administrators must employ a participatory approach to making decisions. They should no longer rely solely on power or authority to obtain maximum performance from their staff, but instead should recognize, accept, and apply current motivational theories to encourage their staff to want to perform well. They must also open up the communication channels through an effective and systematic planning process that will help optimize performance in the ever changing school environments.

DEFINING AND CHARACTERIZING PLANNING

Planning may mean different things to different people; however, from an analysis of definitions in planning books, guidelines, and statements in interviews with planners in education and other fields, certain key concepts have emerged.

Planning
- Maintains that plans must be long- and short-range in duration with short-range plans being implemented to attain long-range results.
- Relates to a comprehensive and systematic strategy for the effective and efficient use of human and nonhuman resources to effect change and improvement in the best interest of the school organization.
- Means that performance gaps must be eliminated and opportunities must be explored to improve on the overall performance of the school district.
- Maintains that internal and external variables that may affect planning decisions must be determined as accurately as possible so that they can be considered in the overall planning process.
- Recognizes that the process is incomplete if it does not include a systematic method for evaluating performance results toward long-range goals, short-range objectives, performance standards, and the execution of plans. Plans often have to be altered, sometimes on very short notice, in view of changing times and conditions.
- Is a continuous process, not a once-a-year or quarterly exercise, that involves representatives from all areas of the school district.
- Is distinctly different from forecasting. Forecasting is one essential element of planning, which predicts what will happen on the basis of certain assumptions. Planning is an attempt to determine what should occur and what steps must be taken to make it happen.
- Requires that crucial areas of the school organization be pinpointed so that plans can be initiated to improve results in these areas.

- Views strengths as internal variables and opportunities as external variables that may affect planning positively. Likewise, weaknesses are viewed as internal variables and problems as external variables that affect planning negatively unless corrective actions are taken. The interrelationship of these variables must be understood to arrive at an information base to make adequate planning decisions.
- Means that problem-solving planning must take place before strategic and operational planning, and long-range planning should take place before short-range planning.

Therefore, educational planning is the process of identifying, collecting, and analyzing essential and critical internal and external data about a school district to arrive at current and useful information for preparing and executing long- and short-range plans in an effort to help realize the district's basic purposes, mission, and operational goals.

GUIDELINES FOR EFFECTIVE PLANNING

The following suggestions will make the planning process more effective. They are prerequisites for installing and maintaining any kind of planning system. Most of these guidelines have been drawn from planning programs that have worked well in any kind of school organization.

- Make certain an adequate data base is available for formulating plans. This information should be of two types: (1) essential information about the school organization and (2) critical data that will enable planners to prepare plans.
- Keep the planning process as simple as possible, so that school administrators can use it despite the day-to-day pressures of operating a school. One way to simplify the process is to design forms that are easy to complete, and that facilitate monitoring performance results.
- Maintain flexibility in the planning process. School administrators who are planning for the first time may have to experiment a bit to arrive at the correct process. Without flexibility, the planner will not be able to respond to the dynamic requirements of the planning process. Flexibility may be augmented by preparing a planning manual in a looseleaf notebook with each page containing essential descriptive data. Another assurance of flexibility in planning is to store information about the school organization in a computer so that it can be retrieved quickly.
- Designate a planning coordinator. In a small school district a superintendent may serve in this capacity, whereas in a larger district the position may be filled by an individual in the central

administration. The planning coordinator will not devise the school district's planning program, but will assist in training staff in planning techniques, ascertain that the planning process is being correctly carried out, and be responsive to the planning needs of the staff.

- Keep paperwork to a minimum. Nothing can kill a new concept more quickly than requiring a great deal of paperwork. The following steps should help minimize paperwork:
  1. At times, an idea can be more effectively expressed in words or phrases than in complete sentences.
  2. Store only essential information that will assist the planner in making decisions. Do not include supporting documents in the planning manual.
  3. Include only important information in the plan.
  4. Ask planners to identify ways to reduce the amount of paperwork required in the process.
- Make planning a well-coordinated and integrated process. Problem-solving planning should be coordinated with operational planning and the latter should be coordinated with strategic planning. Financial planning should be incorporated into all kinds of planning. To ensure coordination, each major strength, weakness, problem, opportunity, and threat should be keyed to a goal, objective, performance standards, and activity. If the planning process is not properly coordinated and integrated, time will be wasted, performance gaps may result, confusion may occur, and the process may be doomed to failure.
- Maintain an updated information data base. The information used for planning purposes must be current and reliable. Although the future cannot be accurately predicted, every attempt must be made to forecast using current and reliable information to arrive at the best possible hypothesis.
- Conduct planning meetings away from the school district. The planning process is too important to be interrupted by the day-to-day operations of a school. A quiet place in the country or at the shore may be an excellent location for meetings.
- Implement planning in the humanistic mode. Planning is a "people" activity, and as such, the concerns, needs, and interests of those who will be affected by the plans must be considered. A mechanistic planning process has no place in public education.

ORGANIZING FOR PLANNING

To facilitate the planning process, it is best to decentralize management authority by dividing the school organization into units or divisions. Each school in a small or medium-size school district (15,000 or fewer students), would become a planning unit. In a larger school district teams or departments may be identified as planning units. Planning units are often determined by administrative or operational practices. For the purpose of developing a suitable planning strategy, the planning unit should have generally uniform qualities so that a common policy can be applied to it. Thus, there are basically two planning units of a school organization:

1. Central planning unit. The central planning unit incorporates all members of the central administration staff including the superintendent, assistant superintendents, directors, and other individuals in positions reporting directly to the chief school administrator.
2. School planning units. The school planning units include all schools within the school district: preschool, primary, middle, junior high, and senior high. School planning units also include innovative programs, such as alternative schools.

Planning subunits are sometimes organized to involve staff in the planning process. These subunits, called planning teams or task forces, are usually subsumed under school planning units. Planning teams that may be used by the central planning unit consist primarily of school planning unit administrators (principals and headmasters). School planning unit teams usually include department chairpersons or team leaders. When planning subunits are used, staff involvement is organized using the Likert Concept, whereby planning unit administrators and team leaders are also members of the preceding and succeeding organizational levels. In this way, the communication network has proper linkage to ensure a greater flow of information for effective planning.

SUGGESTIONS FOR SCHOOL ORGANIZATION PLANNING UNITS

Following are some guidelines for enhancing the effectiveness of the planning process and planning units:

- Each school planning unit should have the same written information, such as the district's mission or educational goals, as the central planning unit. This information should be disseminated to and clarified for everyone in the school organization.
- The central planning unit should be knowledgeable about the internal and external school environments as they relate to the total effectiveness of the school organization.

- Each school planning unit should collect, analyze, and record all critical data about the internal and external environments so that it can prepare its unique plans to accommodate its unique environments.
- The central planning unit staff should be as small as possible—but avoid an "ivory tower" approach to planning.

UNDERSTANDING THE THREE TYPES OF PLANNING

The basic distinction between the three types of planning processes is the time phase. Activities or objectives are set in problem-solving planning to return performance to a routine level, objectives are set in short-range planning to achieve goals in long-range planning, and goals are set in long-range planning to achieve the mission and operational goals of the school organization. Each type of planning moves the planning process toward the fulfillment of the school district's mission. Table 1–1 clarifies the differences among the types of planning. A more detailed explanation follows.

Table 1–1   Contrasting the Three Types of Planning

Item	Problem-Solving Planning	Operational Planning	Strategic Planning
Time Span	One to two months	Usually one year	Three to ten years
Risk Factor	Extremely high	High	High
Purpose	To restore performance back to a routine level	To improve on routine performance or to reach an aspirational performance level	To improve performance in order to reach the mission and educational goals of the school district
People Involvement	Team involvement and responsibility for executing; high involvement by individual planning units	Greater number of people involvement than other kinds; to some extent all staff members are involved	Planning committee involvement comprised of a cross section of the school district. High involvement of central planning unit administrators
Consonance with	Operational Planning	Strategic Planning	Mission and educational goals of the school district
Cost	Low	Moderate	High
Contemporary Budgetary Process	Line-item Budgeting	Zero-Base Budgeting	Program, Planning and Budgeting Systems
Priority Rating	First	Second	Third

Problem-Solving Planning

A problem-solving plan should have a life span of no more than two months. The process involves: (1) identifying a problem that adversely affects the routine performance of a school district; (2) selecting an appropriate strategy for resolving the problem; (3) outlining controlling and evaluating activities; and (4) carrying out the plan within thirty to sixty days. Planning unit administrators who permit a problem to last for more than two months have outlived their usefulness within the school organization.

When strategic long-range planning and operational short-range planning have become well entrenched, there should be less need for problem-solving planning. It will usually take from two to three years to phase out problem-solving planning. The effectiveness of the entire planning process should be based on the degree to which this phasing out is realized.

Operational Planning

Operational, tactical, or short-range planning covers a period of several months to a year and is implemented to improve routine conditions in the school district. It is the process of identifying a need, setting short-range objectives, detailing performance standards, and describing an action plan. This type of planning usually involves a greater number of school personnel than problem-solving or strategic planning.

Strategic Planning

Strategic or long-range planning has a longer time phase than the two previous types, and may cover a period between three and ten years. Strategies are matched with needs (strengths and weaknesses) to arrive at the best approach to the mission and educational goals of the school district. Basically, strategic planning is the process of realizing the school organization's mission, long-range goals, and strategies governing use of human and nonhuman resources needed to achieve the mission. This type of planning is much more dynamic than operational planning, and much more in need of revisions if drastic changes in the internal or external environment of the district occur. It deals with more uncertain variables about the future of the school district, and therefore requires a more in-depth study of planning variables and new opportunities than either problem-solving or operational planning. Strategic planning calls for subjectivity in analyzing trends and opportunities, as well as creativity in determining the most effective use of resources.

The budget is an integral element of each kind of planning. Therefore, resource needs should be included in some manner in the system for detailing plans. The cost for solving problems should be a part of the operational budget. The projected long-range budget in the strategic plans should make allowances for each year of operational planning.

THE ESSENTIAL DIFFERENCES BETWEEN STRATEGIC AND LONG-RANGE PLANNING

Long-range planning as implemented in public education is based on the static theory of the school district, which is based on the assumption that conditions currently affecting the school district will be similar in the future. Under these conditions, planning is merely a matter of selecting the most appropriate activities from those available. In this view, long-range planning is a problem of determining the plan that will maximize student achievement.

However, the static theory is an unrealistic way to view the school district. There is sufficient evidence to convince most planning unit administrators that the external environment can have a profound impact on the school district, necessitating plans to cope with the unpredictable future. There is no possible way for present and future conditions to be the same.

Strategic planning is based on the dynamic theory of the school district. This theory rests on the assumption that, regardless how uncertain the future may be, plans must be developed considering all conditions or factors that may have an impact on the school district. The difficult problem in strategic planning is the determination of outside factors, such as dissident parents, shifts in enrollment, competition with the parochial schools, school budget, and the like. Quite often it is a matter of forecasting and determining probabilities.

Much of the early thought concerning long-range planning revolved around the need to formulate plans for more than one year to improve the instructional program. These beliefs have basically ignored the changing needs of students and the critical school environments.

Essentially, strategic planning adds the following strengths to long-range planning:

1. It recognizes that school organizations should be concerned not only with measuring student learning and growth, but also with achieving social acceptance within the community, influencing policies, and ensuring that teachers as well as administrators are motivated and committed to the school district and its policies.
2. It recognizes that school administrators cannot afford to focus their attention solely on satisfying the needs of students and

parents, but must also consider the demands of other powerful groups or stakeholders within the community. The strategic planner is very much aware that it is usually necessary, at one time or another, to give priority to the needs of one interest group over another, depending on the problems of the school organization and that all of the stakeholders have the power to damage or help the school district.

3. It recognizes that no matter how ably one may try, very limited student learning and growth will result from focusing mainly on the instructional program. Other key phases of the school organization must be analyzed and considered in the planning process, and unless improvement occurs in these areas, only limited progress will occur throughout the school district.

4. It recognizes that environment can have as much of an effect on the progress of a school district as teachers, programs, and services. Unless the "total school" is reflected in the planning process, progress will be slow or nonexistent.

Unfortunately, many school administrators do not view long-range planning as a requirement for effective decision making, but as a luxury on which they cannot afford to spend the time or money. Any administrator in an urban school district will readily indicate that because of the complexity of the ghetto child or the multifaceted problems in an urban community, survival, not long-range planning, is the order of the day. As a result, administrative efforts are intended not to make waves and to avoid risks to maintain a state of equilibrium. In reality, the school as an organization begins to control the school administrator. As a result, the administrator becomes a reactive-oriented leader or maintenance keeper.

The ideal situation is one in which the school administrator is in control of the school, and through planning brings staff together to work cooperatively to eliminate problems or threats, to make the most of opportunities, to improve on strengths, and to avoid weaknesses.

School administrators who constantly engage in reactive planning in reality give up their rights to decide which problems school personnel will attempt to solve. The reactive administrator typically waits for problems and threats to occur before taking either preventive or corrective action, does not learn from past experience, and ignores most opportunities. Usually, new problems are the direct result of previous encounters. Obviously, a reactive administrator can have some serious consequences on the effectiveness of the school and school district as a whole, as described by Thomas J. Sergiovanni and Fred D. Carver:

1. *Stability is prized.* Reactive behavior is inertia-based. Periods of inaction are welcome, for they resemble equilibrium and satisfy

the need to eliminate uncertainty. Stress is kept to a minimum. Innovation and change are not encouraged because they upset the state of equilibrium, result in stress, and require efforts to bring about a new level of equilibrium. The location, intent, or effect of this new level is often not as important as reaching some level somewhere.

2. *Defensive management is encouraged.* Reactive strategies often result in school executives evaluating decision alternatives in terms of their own safety, security, and status. One who continually responds to stress which is beyond his control soon becomes obsessed with his own survival. The school executive is pitted against hostile organization and unsympathetic environment in a win-lose contest.

3. *Paternalism is encouraged.* Defensive management leads to the establishment of alliances. Decisions are often made on the basis of favoritism and protective trade-offs. Kingdoms are encouraged and special interest groups emerge as protective lobbies. Since little attention is given to future planning, uncertainty is actually increased. Information is scarce and prized. In effect the communication network becomes a control mechanism and reward-granting device, with school executives buying loyalty from subordinates by permitting them some access to the network. People feel safer when they have some notion of what is going on and will pay for this safety with loyalty.

4. *Long-range planning is forfeited.* Reactive strategies are short-term survival- and maintenance-oriented. Little attention is given to long-term goals and directions. Thus while the elimination of uncertainty is important for today, tomorrow's problems are guaranteed because no deliberate attention is given to the future.

5. *Educational goals assume the lowest status.* The most serious result of reactive planning and decision-making is implicit in each of the dangers discussed above. In each case educational goals and the welfare of students are displaced by organizational and administrative needs, goals, and demands. School executives and teachers become defense bound and react to stimuli primarily in terms of promoting their own safety, security, and status. Self-actualization of students and commitment to other educational goals are indeed luxuries under such conditions.[3]

[3] From pp. 214–215 in *The New School Executive: A Theory of Administration* by Thomas J. Sergiovanni and Fred D. Carver. Copyright © 1973 by Harper & Row, Publishers, Inc. Reprinted by permission of the publisher.

One of the most prophetic statements ever written against reactive planning and for long-range planning was stated three and one-half centuries ago by Spanish Jesuit Baltasar Gracian:

> Think in anticipation, today for tomorrow, and indeed, for many days. The greatest providence is to have forethought for what comes. What is provided for does not happen by chance, nor is the man who is prepared ever beset by emergencies. One must not, therefore, postpone consideration till the need arises. Consideration should go beforehand. You can, after careful reflection, act to prevent the most calamitous events. The pillow is a silent Sibyl, for to sleep over questions before they reach a climax is far better than lying awake over them afterward. Some act and think later—and they think more of excuses than consequences. Others think neither before nor after. The whole of life should be spent thinking about how to find the right course of action to follow. Thought and forethought give counsel both on living and on achieving success.[4]

TWO BASIC APPROACHES TO STRATEGIC PLANNING

There are basically two approaches or models that can be used to implement strategic planning.

Instructional Program Model

This model tends to dominate in public education. All of the reporting states that mandate some form of long-range planning used this model to some degree. With the instructional program approach, planning consists of setting educational goals and objectives, conducting a needs assessment, selecting or modifying the instructional program as determined by needs, and evaluating the effectiveness of program change or modification. All activities revolve around an instructional program to improve performance results. Figure 1–1 is an example of an instructional program model for long-range planning.

Comprehensive model

This model is most frequently used in industry, business, and nonprofit organizations. Certain aspects of this approach are used in some of the larger school districts, such as Washington, D.C. and New York

[4] Baltasar Jeronimo Gracian y Morales, *The Science of Success and the Art of Prudence*, trans. Lawrence C. Lockley (Santa Clara: University of Santa Clara Press, 1967), p. 45.

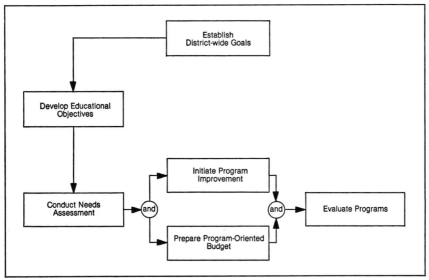

Figure 1–1 *An Instructional Program Long-Range Planning Model*

City. As the model name implies, an attempt is made to consider the internal and external school-community environments during the planning process. With the comprehensive approach, the network of aims of public education, consisting of a mission statement, basic purposes, and educational goals, are a guidance system for conducting a critical analysis of the internal and external school environments, preparing planning assumptions, selecting long-range goals, and identifying program strategies in order to initiate operational planning. The strategic planning components, as illustrated in Figure 1–2 are discussed in individual chapters in this book.

COMPREHENSIVE MODELS OF STRATEGIC PLANNING

The following list shows some distinct differences between the instructional program model of long-range planning and the comprehensive model of strategic planning. A review of these differences reveals that the comprehensive model is more desirable for improving all aspects of a school organization, and that overall performance results are more difficult to achieve with the instructional program model.

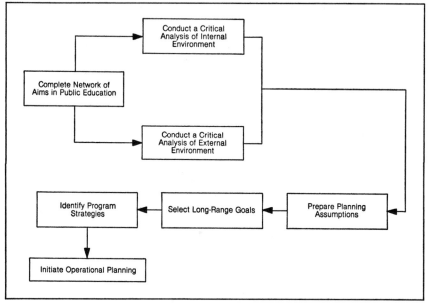

Figure 1–2 *A Comprehensive Strategic Planning Model*

Instructional Program Model

1. Needs assessment usually determines needs or performance gaps on the instructional program level only.

2. Planning assumptions are usually not included in the strategic planning process.

3. Proper controls are usually not incorporated as an essential feature of the planning process; therefore, plans are seldom updated.

Comprehensive Model

1. Critical analysis covers all major key result areas of the school organization, recognizing that the lack of performance in one area can adversely affect other areas.

2. Planning assumptions are essential elements of the strategic and operational planning processes.

3. Proper control procedures are built into the planning system. A planning exception report is required whenever there are deviations in the information data base, goals, objectives, standards, or activities. These items are keyed to each other throughout the planning process.

Instructional Program Model	*Comprehensive Model*
4. Long-range goals and educational goals are used as synonymous performance indicators.	4. Long-range goals are set to realize the educational goals and mission of the school district.
5. The planning process does not include a means for solving critical short-range problems that may be hampering achievement of goals or objectives.	5. Problem-solving plans are considered during the strategic planning process as a means to tackle problems that may hinder progress toward either short-range objectives or long-range goals.
6. The total planning process is seen either consciously or subconsciously as a one-phase process with five to seven subprocesses.	6. The total planning process is viewed as a three-phase process (strategic, problem-solving, and operational planning) with numerous subprocesses.
7. The planning document contains more information than is necessary to make planning decisions; therefore, it is seldom read from cover to cover.	7. The planning document contains only essential information that is tersely written and can be read in one sitting.
8. Budget, at times, tends to be treated separately from the planning process.	8. Budget tends to be treated as an essential component of strategic, problem-solving, and operational planning processes.

INSTALLING THE STRATEGIC PLANNING PROCESS

Although there are numerous ways to install a strategic planning process, one model that is recommended for both large and small school districts is shown in Figure 1–3.

Stage I—Prepare and Disseminate Planning Guidelines or Manual

The central planning unit should construct planning guidelines for two reasons: (1) it has the labor to perform this task; and (2) the task provides an ideal opportunity for its members to become knowledgeable about and committed to the strategic planning process.

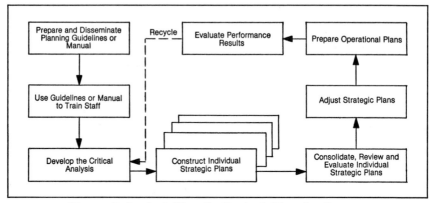

Figure 1–3 *Installing the Strategic Planning Process*

The Mechanics. This segment of the guidelines should contain the scope and format in which plans should be presented, such as subjects to be covered, time schedule, supporting data required, forms to be completed, and the like. Planning guidelines or manuals will usually cover the following items:

1. A critical analysis of the school district, both internal and external factors.
2. Past performance results.
3. Planning assumptions.
4. Long-range goals.
5. Program strategies.
6. Long-range budget.
7. Operational plans.

In some of the more creative guidelines, planning unit administrators are requested to project certain features of the school districts in ten years. In addition to the items listed above, the guidelines should also contain a time schedule for planning, explanation of planning concepts, glossary, and forms and instructions for completing them.

Stage II—Use the Planning Guidelines or Manual to Train Staff

Once the planning guidelines or manual have been developed by the planning coordinator, they should be used as a basis for the staff to carry out all of the major aspects of the strategic and operational planning processes. During the training, actual problems or situations should be used to make the learning process more meaningful.

Stage III—Develop the Critical Analysis

Preparation of the critical analysis will involve the recording of essential data about the school district, which will be used as a starting point for planning. These data should include a description of the school district, the network of aims of public education, a demographic profile, faculty profile, student achievement and growth, and the like.

Critical Data. This phase of the critical analysis should provide key information about the internal and external environments of the school district. An analysis of strengths/opportunities, weaknesses/problems, threats, stakeholders' expectations, and competition should be included.

A letter from the superintendent of schools that addresses the kickoff of the planning cycle should be included or submitted with the guidelines.

Stage IV—Construct Individual Strategic Plans

Using information supplied by the central planning unit, as well as information prepared (see Stage I, The Mechanics) for individual school planning units, each planning unit administrator constructs strategic plans. Sensitive or critical comments should be discussed with the central planning unit administrators before they are included in the plans.

Stage V—Consolidate, Review, and Evaluate
Individual Strategic Plans

At this stage, individual school planning unit strategic plans are collected by the planning coordinator, who reviews and analyzes them for content, comprehensiveness, and completeness. Satisfactory plans are sent to the central planning unit for further examination. Unsatisfactory plans are used to conduct planning conferences with individual planning unit administrators to discuss problems with specific plans and provide assistance to improve on them.

When plans are received by the central planning unit, the following critical questions should be used as a guide for examining each individual strategic plan:

1. Was sufficient information submitted to planning unit administrators for them to make proper planning decisions?
2. Have threats and opportunities been satisfactorily addressed?
3. Are goals, objectives, assumptions, and other pertinent information in the critical analysis keyed appropriately?

4. Will the goals help fulfill the mission of the school district, and are these goals measurable and challenging?
5. Are operational plans realistic, and will they help accomplish the school district's mission?

Also accomplished during this step of the planning process are:

1. Tracing the financial and other implications of the plans.
2. Recommending substantive comments and criticisms of the plans.
3. Stating how the plans can be improved.

Stage VI—Adjust Plans

During this stage, the central planning unit administrators suggest changes to be made in the individual school planning unit plans. Additional information may be provided on opportunities, threats, planning assumptions, goals, budget, and so on. This stage may also involve some strategies for utilizing resources.

Stage VII—Obtain Final Approval of Plans

The superintendent presents the central planning unit plan and all school planning unit plans of the district to the board of education for approval. The necessary changes are made, and the final school district strategic plan is distributed to each planning unit administrator. Sometimes, central or fiscal approval is reserved for a separate meeting.

Stage VIII—Prepare Operational Plans

Once the strategic plans have been finalized, each planning unit administrator and staff member is responsible for preparing an operational plan which will help to meet the strategic plan. A copy of this operational plan should be submitted to the central planning unit for approval. Any exceptions noted during the planning cycle are indicated on a planning exception report and submitted to the appropriate central planning unit administrator for approval. Changes are recorded accordingly.

Stage IX—Evaluate Performance Results

A monthly or quarterly report is completed by each planning unit administrator and submitted to the central planning unit. These reports are the basis for controlling and evaluating performance in an effort to determine if the short-range objectives and activities will help eventually to reach the long-range goals in the strategic plan.

Stage X—Recycle Planning Cycle

Information gathered in Stage I is updated on an annual basis, and modified plans are proposed to carry out the school district's mission. Refer to Table 1–2 for an example of a schedule for installing the planning process.

Table 1–2 Schedule for Installing the Planning Process

Phases	Objectives	Activities
1. Awareness— July 1, 19xx to Sept. 30, 19xx	1. To collect and compile information on planning	1. a. Obtain books and articles b. Attend one-day seminars and conferences conducted by the American Management Association c. Visit appropriate school districts d. Accumulate materials from state departments of education and local school districts across the nation e. Discuss with noted personages f. Converse with practitioners g. Speak to planning consultants
2. Understanding— Oct. 1, 19xx to Dec. 31, 19xx	2. To obtain training	2. a. Read appropriate books and articles b. Attend five-day workshop conducted by the American Management Association or others offered by state departments of education c. Enroll in planning course at a college or university d. Appoint a planning coordinator e. Search for and select a planning consultant f. Conduct briefing session between consultant and central planning unit administrators g. Present planning proposal to central planning unit administrators

Table 1–2 *Continued*

3. Commitment— Jan. 1, 19xx to March 31, 19xx	3. To develop planning system and prototype	3. a. Design planning units b. Convene meeting with central planning unit administrative staff and school planning unit administrator to explain planning design c. Produce illustrative draft of Central Unit Strategic Plan d. Produce illustrative draft of School Unit Strategic Plan e. Produce illustrative draft of operational plan
4. Implemen- tation— April 1, 19xx to	4. To educate key personnel	4. a. Involve key school personnel b. Conduct seminar for planning unit administrators c. Appoint planning coordinator d. Train planning coordinator
	5. To implement planning process within each planning unit	5. a. Obtain mutual agreement between planning coordinator and planning unit administrator of any planning process b. Continue further briefing of key personnel c. Organize planning subunits d. Conduct workshops for planning subunits
	6. To complete plans	6. a. Complete all essential and critical data collection and plans b. Prepare a draft of all plans c. Reach mutual agreement between planning unit administrators and superintendent
	7. To finalize district-wide plan (central and school unit plans)	7. a. Coordinate/consolidate all unit plans b. Draft district-wide plans c. Present plans to board of education for approval d. Revise plans as directed by board of education

SOME TRUISMS ABOUT PLANNING

The way a planning program is implemented within a school organization depends upon the knowledge, training, and experience acquired by those involved in the process. These variables will produce either a negative or a positive impact on the total planning process. To help steer planning efforts in the appropriate direction, the following truisms are included:

1. Planning is difficult. Planning is one of the most complex and difficult mental activities in which school administrators can engage. Therefore, training and developmental activities must be systematically planned and implemented before and after plans are developed and executed. The talents required for producing exemplary plans are not plentiful, since few colleges and universities include this topic in their curricula. As a result, school districts and the state departments of education *must find ways* to provide a variety of training activities to improve the planning capabilities of school administrators.
2. There will be resistance to change. Some school personnel will complain about either the mechanics of the system or the process itself. Experience has shown that the greater the resistance to planning, the greater the need for such a program. In addition, larger school districts seem to resist change more forcefully than smaller ones.
3. Planning takes time. Planning is a process that takes from three to five years to be fully implemented. During this period, old ways must give way to new ideas, techniques, and methods. Because any process as intricate as planning deserves thawing-out time, school administrators must be patient and allow those, including themselves, who are involved in the process adequate time to iron out the wrinkles.
4. Planning reveals and clarifies opportunities and threats. If an analysis of the internal and external environments to determine future opportunities and threats is not included in the planning process, the success of the plan will be limited. School planners will not be able to make adequate decisions without having synthesized their intentions with the available data. The significance of this act should not be overlooked or underestimated as it has been for so long in public education's past.
5. Good planning focuses on major needs. When an unlimited number of needs are identified, the planning process has not been carefully executed. To avoid confusion and frustration, and to make planning a viable mechanism for improving the overall performance of a school organization, a limited number

of needs should be cited. One of the salient reasons many school districts have not achieved expected results from their planning processes is that they attempted to accomplish too much too soon, thus diffusing their efforts.

6. Planning is a training process. If the planning process is to be implemented successfully, the individuals involved must be properly trained. They should receive specialized training in addition to an introductory orientation to planning. The techniques and methods learned in a formal setting will take on new dimension when individuals apply them to the actual planning process and real problems that exist within their school system.

7. Planning will improve communication. Planning is more than producing a document or schedule for committing resources. It is a human experience designed to improve communication between the various levels of the school organization. This communication is achieved through the goal-setting process, selection of appropriate strategies, development of objectives, formulation of standards of performance, and finally through preparation of adequate action plans. All of these activities will involve some give-and-take on the part of those involved to lead ultimately to a mutually agreed-upon planning process.

8. Planning focuses on decisions about the future. Although the future cannot be predicted with a great deal of success, it is better to hypothesize and prepare plans to accommodate expected future events and conditions than to develop plans without considering the dynamics of change.

SALIENT POINTS

The following precepts should be adhered to when implementing a comprehensive planning program:

1. Do not initiate the planning process by involving everyone at one time. Not only would this be an impossible chore to perform, but it would create havoc among the planning units and subunits. A more appropriate approach would be to begin the planning process with the central administration and one elementary school. Problems encountered by these two units could be used as a basis for installing the process on a district-wide level.

2. Concentrate primarily on the needs of the school district first, and then accommodate individual planning units. It is important to remember that there is no perfect planning system that can solve the needs of all school organizations.

3. Keep the planning process simple. Prepare tersely written statements, and make certain that new terms are defined and located in the planning manual.
4. Practice the principle that every employee is a manager. As a result, all personnel will be given an opportunity to be involved in the planning and controlling aspects of education, greatly benefiting from a commitment to the planning process. In addition, when maximum involvement occurs, much more information is readily available to be analyzed and utilized during the process.
5. Involve and commit the superintendent to the planning process. Without his or her support, the program is doomed to fail.
6. Prepare all plans in writing to ensure honest evaluation of the results. Plans that are not formally written down can be altered to suit the actual outcome.
7. Proceed in an aggressive and optimistic manner. Only through taking risks will public education forge ahead in these dynamic times.
8. Face reality. Avoid cognitive dissonance. Do not be afraid to face up to problems, issues, and concerns regardless of how much they may hurt.
9. Value the planning process. Keep in mind, however, that plans are only sometimes useful. The importance of the planning process is that it encourages everyone to think creatively, project the future, and air his or her views so that the school organization as a whole can agree on its purpose and how conditions can be improved. Remember that the most successful and important part of planning is the *process* and *dialogue* that ensues. The actual production of the plan is of least importance.
10. Understand the dynamics of change. Because times and conditions change, plans must change. A plan that works today may not work tomorrow.

APPLICATION STRATEGY I

Acquire a commitment to strategic planning by performing the following phases:

Phase One—Awareness Phase

1. Read two of the following: "Planning Handbook," California Department of Education, Sacramento, 1978; "Performance Planning in Action," Board of Education of the City of New

York, 1975; "Long-Range Planning—Guidelines and Instructions, Parts I and II," Pennsylvania Department of Education, 1978.
2. Read two of the following books: George A. Steiner, *Strategic Planning—What Every Manager Must Know* (New York: The Free Press, 1979); Ray A. Lindberg, *Long-Range Planning* (New York: American Management Association, 1979); Gerald Zaltman, David Florio, and Linda Sikorski, *Dynamic Educational Change, Models, Strategies, Tactics, and Management* (New York: The Free Press, 1977); Mary R. Caroll, David L. Clark, Anne S. Huff, and Linda S. Lotto, *New Perspectives on Planning in Educational Organizations* (Santa Barbara, Calif.: Far West Laboratory, 1980).
3. Subscribe to one or more of the following: *Managerial Planning,* Planning Executives Institute, P.O. Box 70, Oxford, Ohio 45056; *Long-Range Planning,* published by Pergamon Press, Ltd., Maxwell House, Fairview Park, Elmsford, N.Y. 10523; *Planning Review,* Crane Russack Co., Inc., 347 Madison Avenue, New York, N.Y. 10017; *Educational Planning,* Michigan State University, 424 Erickson Hall, East Lansing, Mi. 48824.
4. Become a member of the following planning associations: The American Society for Corporate Planning, Inc., 1406 Third National Building, Dayton, Ohio 45402; Planning Review, Crane Russack Co., Inc., 347 Madison Avenue, New York, N.Y. 10017.

Phase Two—Knowledge and Training Phase

1. Attend the training activities of any two of the following: International Society for Education Planning, Ontario Institute for Studies in Education, Department of Education and Planning, 252 Bloor Street West, Toronto, Ontario, Canada M5S 1V6; Center for Planning and Implementation, American Management Association, Box 88, Hamilton, N.Y. 13346; NTL Institute, P.O. Box 9155, Rosslyn Station, Arlington, Va. 22209; The Mader Group, Inc., One Station Circle, Nasberth, Pa. 19072; Applied Management Institute, 555 East Ocean Boulevard, Long Beach, Ca. 90802. Although four of the above organizations do not sponsor workshops on strategic planning specifically designed for public education, the concepts, techniques, and programs covered can easily be adapted to school districts.

Phase Three—Commitment Phase

1. Read the following from research series N of the Planning Executives Institute: "Strategic Managerial Planning," by George

A. Steiner, Professor of Management and Public Policy, Graduate School of Management, University of California at Los Angeles; "Pitfalls in Comprehensive Long-Range Planning," by George A. Steiner, Professor of Management and Public Policy, Graduate School of Management, University of California at Los Angeles; "An Overview of Corporate Planning with Staff References," edited by Sabhash Join, University of Dayton, and Sarendra Sinshri, Armeo Steel Corporation; "So You Want to Have a Long-Range Plan?" by W. W. Simmons, President of Applied Futures, Inc.

2. Acquire the planning models of a minimum of two school districts from four different states. Identify the similarities of these planning models, and evaluate them with the one used in this book. Prepare a short analysis contrasting the essential differences between long-range planning and strategic planning.

Using the knowledge gained from all of the activities in this Application Strategy:

1. Prepare a comprehensive long-range strategic planning model.
2. Develop a time schedule for implementing the model.
3. Implement the model in a school district on a partial basis, if possible.
4. Evaluate the effectiveness of the model.

2

CONDUCTING A CRITICAL ANALYSIS OF THE SCHOOL DISTRICT

In education, the critical-analysis stage of the planning process is usually called needs assessment or self-study. In industry it is referred to as the situation analysis or appraising the business. This phase should involve the collection and analysis of vital data about all facets of the internal and external environments of the school district to make decisions about the future. Using this information as a base, plans involving the identification, employment, evaluation, and analysis of the school district's capabilities are developed. This will require a review and analysis of strengths, weaknesses, opportunities, and problems, in order to build on strengths, eliminate weaknesses, benefit from opportunities, and avoid threats.

This chapter begins by defining a critical analysis. To help clarify the definition, the purpose and dimensions of the process are explained, and the process is conceptualized from the developmental to the implemental stage. The needs assessment process and the critical analysis process are compared. The two important phases of critical analysis and the internal and external environments are also discussed, enabling the reader to identify factors or forces that may have an impact on the progress of the school district. The chapter concludes by citing techniques for recording information in the critical analysis and listing some salient points about this process.

DEFINING THE CRITICAL ANALYSIS

A critical analysis is the process of collecting, organizing, assessing, and synthesizing past, present, and future information to provide a foundation or base for preparing, implementing, and evaluating long-range and short-range plans. It is not an easy chore and will no doubt be one of the most time-consuming elements of the planning process, particularly when long-range plans are being developed for the first time. In addition to providing a comprehensive data base, the critical analysis serves several other functions:

1. To present a comprehensive picture of the planning unit's history and current condition.
2. To understand the internal and external environments of the school organization, so that planners are aware of all of the factors and variables affecting progress.
3. To provide a basis for other elements of the planning process, such as objectives, strategies, and the like.
4. To provide planners with significant information about the past, current, and possible future conditions.
5. To identify strategic issues relevant to the fulfillment of the school district's mission.

Determining the extent to which a school district is fulfilling its mission and reaching its educational goals will require an assessment of those facets of the external environment that may affect the school organization and an analysis of the internal environment, which includes an appraisal of strengths, weaknesses, opportunities, and threats. The examination of previous plans is an additional feature of the critical analysis. The proper analysis and application of this information will be the foundation on which long-range goals and short-range objectives are set.

The critical analysis process will involve the precise selection and delicate organization of pertinent information taken from a vast amount of available data, which may or may not be stored in a computer. Although forecasting may or may not be included in this section, it is certainly an important component of planning, which must be realized either concurrently with or prior to the completion of the critical analysis.

UNDERSTANDING THE DIMENSIONS OF THE CRITICAL ANALYSIS

Following are several dimensions, associated with a critical analysis, that will help to clarify issues usually related to this process.

1. Although there is no recommended format for recording a critical analysis, the content and forms contained in this book have been found to reduce unnecessary paper work, to expedite the

implementation of the process, to highlight essential and critical information, and to arrive systematically at significant information to render major decisions concerning the strategic planning process. Regardless of the forms, content, and format used, the important point to remember when developing a collection and reporting process is that the content should be readable and understandable within a time period of one sitting.

2. The range of critical analysis is unlimited. This is the essential reason care should be given to the format for displaying information and the areas which should be covered. Trivia should not be included. In order to ensure continuity in scope and content, the major key result areas, discussed in chapter 4, provide the basis for guiding the analytical study.

3. The content will vary depending on the planning unit responsible for conducting the analysis. This variation occurs because of differing internal or external environments in each planning unit and the individual characteristics of its members.

4. The critical analysis should not be expected to be completed in one or more formal settings, but should be used by individual planners to exchange ideas between and among staff members and maintain data bases for surveillance of the school environment.[1]

5. The critical analysis should be updated annually whenever possible. If properly constructed forms are used to collect the data, and a computer is used to analyze them, updating will not be a lengthy process. If, on the other hand, the critical analysis is in narrative form, preconstructed forms are not used extensively, and updating generates more than a hundred pages, the critical analysis may be too time-consuming. If strategic plans are going to help to make decisions about the future, the information should be as current as possible, because only then can decisions be made to change plans and activities when conditions warrant.

6. The cost for conducting a critical analysis will vary according to the size of the school district, the kind of information needed, and the method of collection and analysis. Obviously, a larger school district will need more information than a smaller one, and more personnel will be needed to collect and analyze the data. It appears that school districts with one hundred thousand students or more usually require more sophisticated informa-

[1] Reprinted with permission of Macmillan Publishing Co., Inc. from *Strategic Planning —What Every Manager Must Know* by George A. Steiner. Copyright © 1979 by The Free Press, a Division of Macmillan Publishing Co., Inc.

tion. As the informational needs become more complex, it becomes more costly to meet them. In addition, it is impossible to meet the information needs of a larger school district without a computer. The cost for either leasing or purchasing the needed software will add to the cost of the critical analysis.

CRITICAL ANALYSIS VERSUS NEEDS ASSESSMENT

Most school districts that have attempted long-range planning have used the needs assessment process for generating an information data base for setting goals and objectives. A needs assessment is basically "the difference between what is and what should be."[2] A basic definition of critical analysis is the difference between what is and what is feasible. The key term here is "feasible," for this term differentiates strategic planning from long-range planning and makes critical analysis a potent process.

Any assessment or analytical process that is used to generate an information base for improving performance results requires that those implementing the process take a critical look at the school-community environments. The process also requires an intelligent appraisal of the school organization's own conditions.

Using the needs assessment process to develop an information data base to set goals and objectives began in the 1960s when the long-range movement started. During this period the classical or traditional long-range planning process, which focuses on the gap between what presently exists and what should be as illustrated in Figure 2–1, came into vogue for businesses around the country. Recently, however, most corporations and business firms have abandoned this approach to planning and have focused instead on what is feasible in view of the ever changing internal and external environments. It is high time that members of the public education field began to realize how long-range planning can be improved. The school district must be viewed as an organization that may be affected either positively or negatively depending on the forces interacting with it.

COMPARING ESSENTIAL FEATURES OF THE NEEDS ASSESSMENT AND CRITICAL ANALYSIS PROCESSES

The following comparison highlights some of the distinct differences between the traditional needs assessment process and the contemporary critical analysis process. A review of these differences will reveal

[2] W. Robert Houston, Len Faseler, Sarah C. White, Priscilla Eanders, Joy Senter, and William Butts, *Assessing School/College Community Needs* (Omaha: The Center for Urban Education, The University of Nebraska at Omaha, 1978), p. 3.

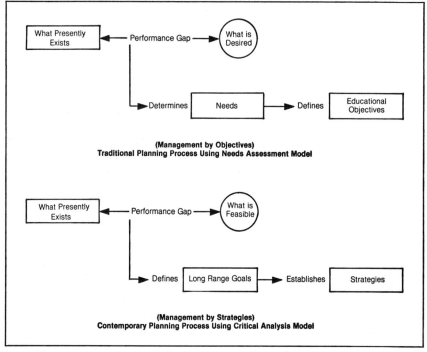

Figure 2–1 *Comparison Between Needs Assessment and Critical Analysis*

that the latter is more desirable in meeting the challenge of assessing the whole school district to obtain maximum results.

Needs Assessment	*Critical Analysis*
1. Tends to focus on the instructional program to the exclusion of other critical areas of the school district, such as financial resources and capital facilities.	1. Tends to focus on all of the critical factors of a school district that have been identified prior to the assessment.
2. Major key result areas of a school district have not been defined.	2. Major key result areas are stated and clarified.
3. Focuses most often on strengths and weaknesses of the instructional program.	3. Focuses on major strengths and weaknesses, opportunities, problems, and threats related to the instructional program as well as other critical areas of the school district.

Needs Assessment	Critical Analysis
4. Tends to focus on factors involving the internal school environment.	4. Tends to focus on the internal school environment as well as the external school environment.
5. Long-range forecasting in areas other than declining enrollment is usually omitted.	5. Forecasting is an essential component of the planning process and involves a multitude of areas.
6. No mechanism exists for reporting "planning exceptions."	6. A "planning exception" reporting form usually accompanies the planning process. Any exceptions in planning data, such as opportunities, threats, planning assumptions, goals, objectives, and activities, are noted on this form and disseminated to the appropriate parties. Changes are made accordingly.
7. Report tends to consist of more than a hundred pages.	7. Report tends to be confined to between fifty and seventy-five pages.
8. Final report tends to include the collection, recording, and analysis of data information for dissemination.	8. Final report tends to include only essential information necessary to make a planning decision.

UNDERSTANDING THE TWO ENVIRONMENTS OF A SCHOOL DISTRICT

Once upon a time school administrators could engage in long-range planning merely by determining the performance gap and using human and nonhuman resources to remedy the situation. The school-community complex was relatively static. Today, however, a host of technological developments have helped produce a dynamic school-community complex that must be carefully scrutinized during the planning process. One of the world's most adept planners, H. Igor Ansoff, supports this premise: "For the non-profits, it has meant a transition from centuries'-old introverted perspective to opening of the doors to the environment. The view through the window is on a society that is challenging the social relevance of non-profits on the one hand, and demands expan-

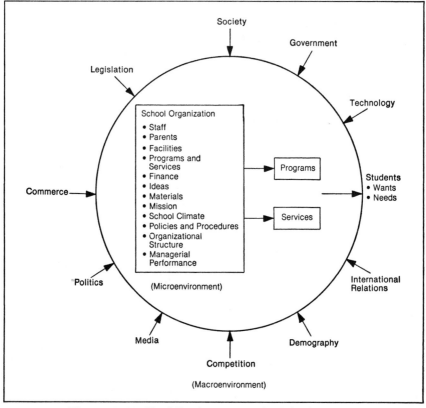

Figure 2–2   *Dual Environments of a School District*

sion of their services and increased effectiveness on the other."[3] Every school district functions in two environments, as illustrated in Figure 2–2. There is the internal or microenvironment, which involves the internal operations of the school district, and the external or macroenvironment, which consists of external or outside forces or factors that may affect the educational system.

Recognition of the macroenvironment as an important consideration of the planning process and the actions initiated to effect plans by analyzing, synthesizing, and evaluating this environment are two essential features of the strategic planning process that separate it from long-range planning. Anyone who feels that the internal and external environments are not important considerations when developing the planning process should read the following headlines taken from a New Jersey newspaper:

[3] H. Igor Ansoff, *Strategic Management* (New York: Wiley, 1979), p. 31.

"Falling Enrollments Boost Tensions as Parents Battle School Shut-
tings"
"NEA Influence Seen as Threat"
"A New Agency Must Be Vetoed"
"Public School Malaise Boosts Private Sector"
"Teachers Reject Bloomfield Pact"
"College Admission Plan Will Affect High Schools"
"Woodbridge Dispute Could Set Precedents for Future Beginning"
"Politics Faulted on Education Chief"
"State Board is Upheld in Closing Plan"

It is appropriate to emphasize this point by indicating why the environments have progressively increased in turbulence and demand careful consideration during all phases of planning:

1. The important events that affect school districts are progressively disconnected from past experience.
2. More attention is being focused on the effectiveness of school
   districts by stakeholders.
3. The macroenvironment is growing and changing at an acceler-
   ated speed.
4. As the macroenvironment grows with such intensity, it becomes more complicated.

CONCEPTUALIZING AND IMPLEMENTING THE
CRITICAL ANALYSIS PROCESS

The following is an approach to systematizing the development and
implementation of the critical analysis as illustrated in Figure 2–3.

The Rationale for the Critical Analysis

The role of the critical analysis is to identify, analyze, and evaluate
the key trends, factors, forces, and phenomena having a potential impact on the formulation and implementation of long-range goals and
strategies. This is extremely critical and an important step in strategic
planning, because many changes in the school organization's environments may have a direct impact on the district. Maximum results will
be achieved if these variables are identified and planned for before they
occur.

Item
A perfect example of this is the declining rate of SAT scores. For
more than ten years, SAT scores across the nation have been de-

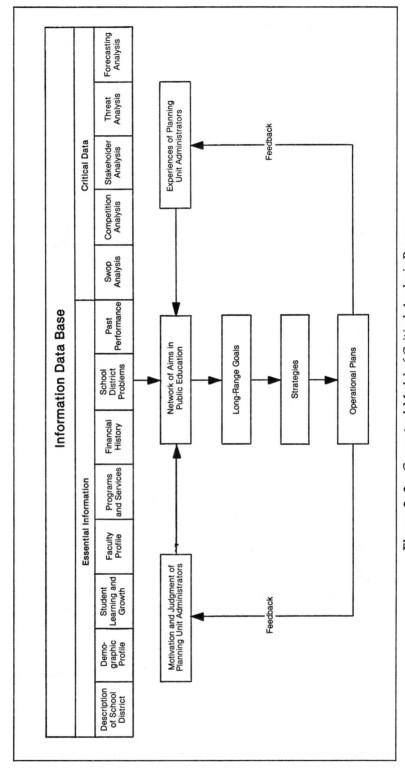

Figure 2–3 *Conceptual Model of Critical Analysis Process*

clining steadily. If a mechanism for either forecasting or assessing the SAT situation had been implanted in the long-range planning system, it is probable that an appropriate intervention strategy could have been implemented to offset this decline. However, because no such mechanism existed at the time, the American public educational system has declined. It took several newspaper reporters and a few researches to determine that the decline was due to numerous factors, but chief among them was that students were opting for more social science courses rather than enrolling in basic skills courses, such as English and mathematics. Another point to consider is that while the needs assessment process movement began more than ten years ago, few school districts detected the SAT phenomenon. The chief reason is that the needs assessment process tends to focus too narrowly in the educational process by concentrating primarily on the instructional program with little regard for the external environment.

To ensure that all of the elements of the critical analysis are developed and contained in the plan, a title page which specifies all sections of this component of the planning process should be used.

Identifying Two Main Sections of the Critical Analysis

The critical analysis is composed of two main sections.

Essential Information Phase
The essential information phase provides pertinent facts about the school district which act as a foundation for decision-making purposes when considered with the critical data phase. However, unlike the latter phase, this information can usually stand alone and is suitable for planning purposes in its original form.

Past performance. No plans should be developed without first assessing past performance. Past performance records provide a springboard from which to revise long-range goals and set new short-range objectives. An assessment of past performance also affords the planning unit administrator an opportunity to determine if current goals will lead to the attainment of the school district's mission. A form that can be used to facilitate this process is illustrated on page 292 of the Appendix.

Description of the school district. This description should include a brief history of the district, its scope, organizational structure, and activities. Also included in this section should be a description of each building within the district.

Network of aims of education. This network should include a description of the mission, basic purposes, and operational goals of the school district.

Demographic profile. The demographic profile identifies major trends of the past and makes projections for the future. It should include: (1) population of the community, (2) race, (3) occupations, (4) family income, and (5) number of foster and welfare children. A form that can be used for displaying these projections is illustrated on page 271 of the Appendix.

Student learning and growth. This section should include a description of student achievement by grades, median SAT scores, number of students receiving awards and honors, and the number of students entering college, the armed forces, businesses, and so on. A form that will prove helpful for displaying this type of information is illustrated on page 272 of the Appendix.

Faculty profile. Faculty profile is a description of training, educational background, and experience of the teaching and administrative staff. Also included in this section should be a list of awards, honors, and other accomplishments of the faculty. Page 274 illustrates an example of a form that can be used for recording this information.

Programs and services. These items or activities are related to programs and services offered for students and members of the community.

Financial history. Using a program-oriented format, identify quantitatively the fiscal history of the school district for the past four years up through the current year. A suggested format for this information is illustrated on page 276 of the Appendix.

School district problems. This section should be a summary of school-related problems, such as the absentee rate of students and faculty, staff turnover, pregnancy rate, vandalism rate, accident rate involving students, the number of teachers and students assaulted, and other useful information pertaining to the problems besetting school districts. A suggested format for recording this information is illustrated on page 278 of the Appendix.

Critical Data Phase

The critical data phase involves the selection and organization of pertinent data culled from the essential information phase. In addition, it includes forecasted projections for and judgmental decisions about both environments. It is during this phase that strategic thinking is first applied.

The terms selected for describing each section of the critical data phase have been chosen to stimulate thinking in an analytical and evaluative mode. One fault of many long-range planning models used in education is that planning is only viewed in terms of "problems," or internal "strengths and weaknesses." A problem, when observed from another viewpoint, might be considered an opportunity or internal weakness.

The critical data phase should only be completed when there has been a thorough investigation and development of "hard facts." If plans are developed without comprehensive data, they will not produce viable strategic and operational plans.

Swop analysis. For simplicity and brevity, a situational analysis form is recommended to record most of the critical data phase of the critical analysis. This is a general form for recording *swop* (strengths, weaknesses, opportunities, and problems) and designating the action to be taken. For an example, refer to page 279 of the Appendix. One or more of these forms should be prepared for each major key result area. After all forms have been reviewed to understand the "total picture" of the situation, they should be ordered by priority. To make certain that each aspect in *swop* is covered, a reference section should be included in the planning process.

The integrals of *swop* are:

1. Major Strengths. These include those services, products, programs, and activities that the school district currently provides, performs well, or effects by complying to an expected standard of measurement.
2. Major Weaknesses. These are those services, products, programs, or activities that the school district provides, performs poorly, or effects in a manner that fails to meet the expected standard of measurement. They are internal and controllable variables that have a negative impact on some aspect of the school district, and should be either corrected or avoided. Major strengths and weaknesses deal primarily with the capabilities and/or capacity of school personnel, departmental functions, organizations, facilities, procedures, finances, and the like. Strengths and weaknesses should be evaluated internally, while the standard of measurement should be created to meet the expectations of the board of education, students, and state department of education.
3. Opportunities. These are areas in which favorable circumstances provide the potential for improving various aspects of

the school district. They are activities or services that the district could or should be performing, or areas that provide possible solutions to other important problems. Opportunities frequently result from a recognition of strengths. Weaknesses, on the other hand, should lead to the introduction of plans for resolution. Opportunities and needs also offer a chance to capitalize on strengths and convert weaknesses into assets.

4. Problems. Problems revolve around external factors that may or may not be partially controllable. These are outside conditions or obstacles that may prevent the school district from reaching its mission and educational goals.

5. Action to be taken. This category includes a statement concerning what the planner intends to do about the problem, how strengths will be built upon, and how opportunities will be utilized to their utmost.

Competition analysis. Does a school district have competition similar to that which is found in industry? If so, does the competition pose a serious threat? Several years ago this author would have answered this question with an emphatic no. However, because of recent declining enrollment, the budget crunch, and a number of other factors affecting every public school district in the nation, the answer to this query is yes. Unless administrators become more conscious of the threat of competition, they may soon find themselves out of a job. Table 2–1 illustrates the various competitors of a public school district.

1. Enrollment. Student enrollment is declining in almost every community across the nation, affecting public as well as private schools. A number of private schools have developed marketing strategies to attract a greater number of students, and in

Table 2–1   Public School Districts' Competitors

Competitor	Compete for	Threats Negative Consequences	Opportunities Positive Consequences	Effects
Private Schools	• students	• Decreased student enrollment	• Increased student enrollment	high
Commerical Schools		• Decreased or stabilized budget	• Increased budget	low
Parochial Schools		• Adverse public relations	• Improved public relations	moderate
Armed Services		• Decreased programs and services	• Increased programs and services	low
Public Schools	• funds • programs • services • staff	• Decreased programs and services • Decreased or stabilized budget • Decreased staff	• Increased programs and services • Increased budget • Increased staff	moderate

some communities private school enrollment is actually increasing. Two examples of this trend can be found in Alpine, New Jersey, and Tuskegee, Alabama. For the most part, public school administrators have ignored marketing as a tool with which to compete with private institutions.

2. Budget caps. In some states, there are limitations on how much money can be spent for education. New Jersey, for example, has enacted a cap law that defines the budget limitations of school districts to regulate discrepancies between affluent and less-affluent school districts. This cap law is actually advantageous for private schools, because it does not apply to them, and, therefore, they can accelerate budget expenditures as they wish.

3. Programs. Because staff salaries are lower in private schools than in the public sector, these schools can often afford additional programs denied to public schools due to prohibitive costs. Many private schools also have a cadre of voluntary professional staff help to enlarge program offerings.

4. Discipline. Outstanding educators are often attracted to private schools because they have stricter regulations regarding student discipline. Disciplinary problems that occur in private schools are handled more expeditiously than they would be in public schools. This is especially true in regards to expulsion, as it is much more difficult to expel a disruptive student from a public school than a private one.

5. Staff. The majority of students enrolled in better private schools are from either middle- or upper-class families, and thus represent a higher proportion of "cream of the crop" students than would be found in public schools. Exemplary teachers who are challenged by this type of student are naturally attracted to schools that enroll the highest percentage of them. It should be noted, however, that the threat of private schools is not restricted to school districts of wealthy constituents.

Item

The author was engaged to speak to a long-range planning group regarding a serious declining enrollment problem in their district. Prior to the meeting, he received a copy of their long-range plans. While the plans shed much light on the needs of the community, they did not address the problem. The school district was located in a small upper-class community. Each year, more students were being enrolled in six private schools, located in the periphery of the district, than in the public ones. The planning group was concerned that if the trend continued, the school district could not survive. The author took a simple approach by requesting that group members regard their district as a business that wanted not only to survive, but to thrive. Taking this new posture, they could think differently about resolving the problem.

He said that private schools could either be viewed as a threat or an opportunity, and that they would have to decide which definition would best suit their purposes. If the private schools were treated as a threat, the district would be compelled to combat it in the best manner possible and hope for the best. On the other hand, if the private schools were seen as an opportunity, the following three steps should be systematically performed for each one:

1. Analyze their past performance results.
2. Study their successful strategies.
3. Evaluate their resources.

From this analysis, they could learn why the private schools are successful in capturing additional students each year. The planning group was instructed to assess the external as well as internal environments. This dual study could provide them with the basis for comparing the schools and establishing strategies for initiating changes. By analyzing the external environment, they could identify other factors that adversely affect the district. One such example is real estate brokers. If real estate brokers are telling prospective clients that the public schools are inferior to the private ones, this would have a serious impact on the survival of public education in the community. The planning group was requested to designate an individual to pose as a prospective home-buyer and visit each real estate broker for the purpose of analyzing his or her approach to the district's educational system and determining how the threat of negative attitudes could be turned into a positive opportunity.

The meeting lasted for nearly four hours. Many of the ideas shared during this time were used to stimulate further discussion among committee members and for purposes of planning.

The incident cited above is only one of countless numbers of similar ones occuring every day in public education. Yes, school administrators and planners must give more credence to competition as a serious factor that must be considered in developing strategic plans. A form for analyzing the school district's competition and describing what action should be taken is illustrated on page 287 of the Appendix.

Stakeholders analysis. Stakeholders are those individuals, groups, or organizations who have an interest in the school system. Their missions, objectives, and concerns should be taken into consideration in an informal or formal manner. Although the dominant stakeholders of an educational district are the citizens and parents, within these two groups are numerous other interest groups. Some of the groups that can have a positive or negative impact on plans are:

Internal	*External*
Student Groups	Teacher Union/Associations
Other Unions	(state and national)
Teachers	Politicians
Professional/Associations/Union	Social Service Agencies
Support Staff	Chamber of Commerce
School Administration	Business Firms
Board of Education	Corporations
	Irate Parents
	Citizen Groups
	Statespeople
	U.S. Government
	State Department of Education
	Local Colleges and Universities
	Local Newspapers

A stakeholders' analysis form, as illustrated on page 288 of the Appendix, is used to assess the attitudes and expectations of the major stakeholders so that the concerns of powerful groups can be considered when preparing planning assumptions, setting goals, identifying strategies, and the like. A key element of this form is that the attitudes and expectations of each major stakeholder are keyed to appropriate goals, objectives, and standards to prevent omissions during the planning process.

Threat analysis. Threats are potential future problems or weaknesses that may have a serious negative impact on the school district if preventive measures are not taken. Each strength and weakness is in a sense also an opportunity or threat, the distinction between them being that opportunities and threats represent advantageous and disadvantageous conditions that could develop as a result of changes in strategy or the environment.

The threat analysis chart, illustrated on page 289 of the Appendix, is used to identify pictorially those events or conditions that may threaten the normal operations of the school district. The vertical axis represents the degree to which the threat will have an impact on the school, ranging from none to catastrophic. The horizontal axis identifies the probability of threats that will occur ranging from zero to 100 percent. Threats must be considered when preparing plans either to prevent them from occurring, as in the case of a student riot, or to plan around them.

Item
One contemporary administrator organized an eight-member team to identify possible threats to the school district. The team identified not only individuals, groups, and organizations, but also the demands made by these stakeholders. The list of demands were ranked according to the degree to which they would have a major impact on the school district. Another list was developed in terms of how much pressure each stakeholder group would use to get its demands heeded. Results of the committee's efforts were then used in the long-range planning process.

A situation analysis form is also included on page 290 of the Appendix, to identify major threats and devise a plan of action to change them into opportunities. As with other forms, a reference section should be included.

Forecasting analysis. Forecasting is the process of making a current decision about the future. There are a number of forecasting methods, each of which has its own advantages and disadvantages depending upon the kind of information desired. Chapter 5 on planning assumptions goes into greater details about forecasting. However, there are a few guidelines that planners might consider in making a decision on a forecasting method.

1. Although forecasting can be a difficult and time-consuming concept to master, there is some easy-to-read literature that approaches understanding forecasting in a simple way.
2. The forecasting system should not be so expensive as to cause the entire process to be dropped from the planning process. Instead of utilizing a computer, it may be more desirable to use a less technical forecasting procedure to generate the desired information.
3. The planning unit administrator and staff must be properly trained to use forecast information. If a formal training program has not been organized and instituted, maximum effectiveness from the forecasting will not be realized.
4. Planning unit administrators and board members must realize that forecasting is not a pure science, and, therefore, a method that has produced accurate information in the past may fail in the future.
5. A format should be developed to record forecast information. At times, it may be desirable to divide the data under probabil-

ity ratings such as low, medium, and high. The planner may wish to use a "low probability" rating for one critical area and a "high probability" rating for another area.

TECHNIQUES FOR RECORDING INFORMATION IN THE CRITICAL ANALYSIS

The critical analysis presents information in a precise manner to expedite decision-making during the initial stages of strategic planning. To this end, the following techniques are recommended when preparing the critical analysis:

1. Use forms that have been tried and found to be effective in highlighting essential information about the situation of the school organization.
2. Limit the length of the text to fifty to seventy-five pages.
3. Use charts, diagrams, and tables to shorten the text and to facilitate interpretation.
4. Do not include supportive documents as part of the original text, but attach them under separate cover as an appendix.
5. Avoid verbose terms, jargon, and long drawn-out statements. At times, it may be more desirable to use incomplete sentences if the gist of the statement can be easily understood.
6. Update the existing critical analysis, instead of developing a new one from scratch.
7. Use summaries of conditions, and avoid detailed expositions of them.
8. Be thorough, but avoid including information twice.
9. Do not repeat items adequately covered under one major key result area in another area. The planning unit administrator should locate the most accurate or suitable viewpoint and highlight the subject once.
10. Do not list obvious terms, but include only those items that help to explain strategic and operational decisions.
11. Identify the major fundamental factors of each statement, but not all of their symptoms and causes.

REDUCING GAPS IN THE PLANNING PROCESS

When completed properly, the critical analysis contains a wealth of information about the school district. Because of the abundance of this information, some important planning details may go unnoticed. As a result, serious gaps may exist in the planning process. To minimize

STRATEGIC PLANNING

Reviewer __Dr. James Wilkinson_____ Date __August 15, 19XX__

Position __Assistant Superintendent of_____ Page __1__ of __1__

Planning Unit __Central__ Administration and Personnel

Planning Component: Strategic Planning Highlights

Page	Para.	Information Description
381		Teachers in grades 7 to 12 received less training than those in other grades.
384	14	Number of students entering private schools increased by nearly 25 percent this year.
384	10	Incidence of pregnancy is increasing at the rate of 10 percent per year.
	12	The number of students killed in school has increased to an alarming seven this year.

Figure 2–4 *Strategic Planning Highlights Form*

these gaps and to ensure a complete planning spread, a strategic planning highlights form should be used. The form illustrated in Figure 2–4 relates to information contained in the critical analysis in the Appendix on pages 274 and 278.

1. A central planning administrator identifies planning highlights that are not covered in either strategic or operational plans and indicates the page number, paragraph, and a description of the information on the strategic planning highlights form.
2. The completed strategic planning highlights form is forwarded to the responsible planning unit administrator, who, in turn, makes certain that plans are developed to cover each item described on the form.

One of the problems superintendents are bound to face is whether or not all vital information contained in the critical analysis is covered by adequate plans. When the strategic planning highlights form is used this no longer poses a problem. If any gaps exist in the planning process, the reason will probably revolve around insufficient information about the subject or condition.

SALIENT POINTS

Most needs assessment processes can be substantially improved to include many of the important components of the critical analysis if the following steps are achieved:

1. The amount of paperwork associated with the process is reduced, and only that information that is absolutely necessary to make an important decision about a major aspect of the school organization is included.
2. The needs of the instructional program level are continuously identified, with a recognition of all internal and external forces that may have an impact on the school district.
3. The major key results areas of the school organization are identified, and assessed to the same extent as the instructional program.
4. Planning decisions are based not on what is desired, but on what is feasible depending upon the school environments.
5. Past performance is included in the essential information phase of the process.
6. A system is developed for identifying and recognizing possible threats to the school district, and stakeholder's attitudes and expectations are considered depending on the extent to which they will have an impact on the school district.
7. A forecasting system for all factors affecting the school district is organized, and the information gathered is included as an integral part of the strategic planning process.

8. The mission statement for the school district, as well as for each planning unit, is prepared, disseminated, and clarified to the staff.
9. The use of the educational goals ascertained from community input is maintained, and the utilization of long-range goals, short-range objectives, and performance standards is considered, keeping in mind that they are dynamic indicators of performance results.

APPLICATION STRATEGY 2

For further study pertaining to needs assessment, read Fenwick W. English and Roger A. Kaufman, *Needs Assessment: A Focus for Curriculum Development* (Washington, D.C.: Association for Supervision and Curriculum Development, 1975).

For further information on the need for considering the environment when engaging in long-range planning, read: H. Igor Ansoff, *Strategic Management* (New York: John Wiley & Sons, 1979).

Acquire a needs assessment that has been completed by a school district. Using this document as a guide, convert it into a critical analysis by assessing all critical elements of the school district, considering both the internal and external environments.

3

ESTABLISHING THE GUIDANCE SYSTEM FOR STRATEGIC PLANNING

The first and most important step in the strategic planning process is the establishment of a guidance system to direct human efforts in the school district. The guidance system is a network of aims which spells out the primary reason for the school district's existence and ensures that everyone is working together. Developing a guidance system is an extremely difficult task because most school administrators take the aims of public education for granted. They have either oversimplified this task, failed to perform it satisfactorily, or completely ignored it during the planning process.

This chapter assists planning unit administrators in producing a satisfactory guidance system as a foundation for implementing the strategic planning process. A basic understanding of the network of aims of public education is initially presented, along with an illustration to help clarify this concept. Some attention is given to the basic purposes, philosophy statements, and educational goals of the school district. Additional discussion translates the guidance system into policies and procedures that can stabilize human efforts and maintain policy validity. The chapter concludes with comments and questions that will further clarify the guidance system.

UNDERSTANDING THE NETWORK OF AIMS OF PUBLIC EDUCATION

There is no uniformity in the structure of the network of aims of public education. Therefore, the only way to identify the network components is to describe what school districts around the nation have produced on

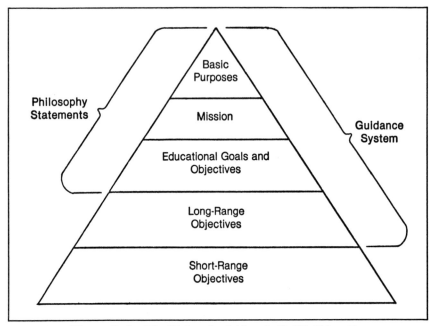

Figure 3–1 *The Network of Aims in Public Education*

a piecemeal basis. Figure 3–1 depicts the network in a pyramid, illustrating that the number of statements increases as the pyramid is descended. The statements at the pyramid's top are usually short, broad, and abstract and related to mission, basic purposes, and educational goals. The statements at the pyramid's bottom are lengthier, more specific and concrete, and related to long-range goals and short-range objectives. The top three statement sections are usually developed by school personnel and community members, whereas the bottom two statement categories are usually prepared by school personnel alone.

The network of aims begins with individual beliefs but is expressed and implemented within the larger educational framework. The aims must relate to the school district's situation, and they must support and be supported by the economic system and community the district serves. Thus, the network of aims must be responsive on four levels:

1. Individual. Each school employee should understand and accept *what* the school proposes to do and why. The network of aims should be in accord with individual beliefs so that the personal goals of the staff are integrated with the goals of the organization.
2. School district. The network of aims must be reflected in poli-

cies, procedures, and actions. They should promote harmony, achievement, and success.
3. Community. The network of aims should reflect the needs and expectations of the local citizens and taxpayers served by the school district. Only through this consideration will the school district grow and prosper.
4. State education system. Every school district's reason for being should be equally applicable to the state-wide system of education of which it is a part. All school personnel must believe that they are involved in a state-wide as well as a local system. Thus, the network of aims should be accepted and supported by the whole educational system.

A BASIS FOR ACTION: SCHOOL DISTRICT'S PHILOSOPHY

Philosophy statements usually express the school district's mission and basic purposes or roles. However, some districts have been known to include only the basic purposes, while others include only the mission.

There are numerous reasons for developing philosophy statements. The most important ones are listed below.

The philosophy statements:

1. Describe the school organization or unit's reason for existence.
2. Provide a logical starting point for determining goals and validating objectives.
3. Are a communication link along the school organization lines that helps to clarify job responsibilities.
4. Provide a means by which planning unit administrators can evaluate their efforts toward meeting goals and objectives.
5. Provide a basis for determining where human and nonhuman resources should be invested.
6. Help keep track of where the school district should be heading.
7. Provide a basis for measuring the school organization's effectiveness.

THE BASIC PURPOSES OF THE SCHOOL DISTRICT

There are two common methods used to describe the basic purposes of the school district.

"We Believe" Approach

In this approach, each category begins with a "we believe" statement followed by individual purpose statements separated by the word "that," as illustrated in the example below.

Instructional Program and Services
WE BELIEVE that the instructional program and services should reflect the learning needs of individual students; that it should include assessment, clear objectives, a variety of learning experiences, evaluation, and provision for special needs; that the objectives should build toward excellence; that the activities should ensure opportunity for success; that the evaluations should reduce wasted effort and keep the instructional program and services moving in the desired direction; that the instructional program and services should encourage the development of warm human relationships, which are an essential element of daily living; that it should allow the individuals opportunities to discover their talents and freedom to explore areas of special interest.

Performance Evaluation and Development
WE BELIEVE that when educators are given opportunities to participate in consistent and regular evaluations, they will be more inclined to improve their performance; that the need to make evaluation as positive an experience as possible suggests that clear, objective procedures be carefully developed; that performance evaluation results should be given to educators in written form as a basis for improvement; that there should be mutual agreement between the administrative and teaching staffs on the procedures to be employed.
WE BELIEVE that the school district must provide the time, resources, and opportunities for staff development; that the training and development program should be aimed at improving the professional skills of school personnel; that these programs should be based upon a careful indentification of professional needs; that evaluation data can serve to identify strengths and weaknesses, providing the basis for planning specific types of training and development programs; that other data sources may include classroom visitations as well as consultations.

Community Involvement and Relations
WE BELIEVE that schools should depend on the support of the local citizens; that good interest and support depends on the citizens' understanding of school affairs; that this communication between laypeople and educators will help to produce an improved

educational system; that the school has the responsibility for making information about educational opportunities and services available to all citizens within the community.

Role Statement Approach

In this approach, a paragraph is used as a basis for a series of statements which describe the various reasons the school district exists. Following are two examples:

1. To ensure that every student receives a quality education and a meaningful growth experience by:
   a. helping to prepare each student to become a productive member of society;
   b. providing students with a variety of classroom and class-world experiences to help them become well-rounded individuals; and
   c. providing students with assistance to discover their own talents, skills, and abilities.

2. To create an educational environment that will foster an ever-improving instructional program for students through:
   a. determining where performance gaps exist in educational programs and implementing innovative program methods or techniques to effect program improvement;
   b. maintaining an adequate number of programs and appropriate services to produce a meaningful educational process;
   c. implementing appropriate financial programs and procedures to operate a cost-effective school district;
   d. ensuring cost-effective use of available resources in pursuit of the school district's mission;
   e. making certain that the community is adequately informed and involved in the affairs of the school district;
   f. implementing a participatory decision-making and result-oriented staff evaluation program in an effort to determine performance needs and install viable performance improvement activities; and
   g. providing a healthy school climate through proper planning, adequate staff involvement, and the application of effective motivational techniques.

The basic purposes should relate to the whole school district. In addition to the major key result areas, each group who has a stake in the educational progress, such as students, community members, teachers, and administrators, should be considered. Unfortunately, basic purpose statements are usually written in two or three paragraphs and confined to students, as indicated in the first set of statements appearing under the role statement approach section. Using the major key result areas and including staff and community members could solve this problem and provide planning unit administrators with comprehensive directions for guiding the planning process. The second set of role statements highlights this feature.

PREPARING EDUCATIONAL GOALS AND OBJECTIVES

The third component of the network of aims is the development of educational goals and objectives to guide and direct the human effort in the planning and execution of plans.

An educational goal is a broad, written statement which describes a desired outcome in student learning and growth. It is designed to provide a focus for the planning actions of school personnel. An educational goal should be written on the following levels:

- State-wide.
- District-wide.
- School.
- Programmatic.
- Instructional.
- Learner.

The following is an example of a state-wide educational goal that is used as the umbrella for developing the district-wide educational goal:

- State-wide educational goal: To acquire basic skills in obtaining information, solving problems, thinking critically, and communicating effectively.
- District-wide educational goal: To develop mathematical understandings and skills that enable the learner to solve problems of a quantitative nature, such as personal and family finance and time and space relationships.

For educational goals to be valid, they must meet certain criteria:

1. They must be developed involving a cross-section of the school-community.
2. They must touch upon all areas of the curriculum.
3. They must be consonant with the state-wide educational goals.
4. They must be approved by the board of education.
5. They must be proposed in writing, and disseminated and clarified to the staff in a timely manner.

The two educational goals above are expressed in broad and general terms, making an accurate assessment of their attainment difficult or impossible. Therefore, in an effort to improve the measurability of educational goals, objectives should be included with goals. An educational objective is a statement that contains an act or performance (sometimes referred to as an indicator), a standard of proficiency (usually higher than that required by the state), an assessment tool to determine if the projected level of proficiency has been met, and a time frame that indicates the maximum period allotted for achieving the objective. Following is an example of an educational objective used to qualify the previous district-wide educational goal:

- District-wide educational objective: The student demonstrates proficiency in computational skills as indicated by a grade equivalent of 10.0 on the California Achievement Test by the end of grade twelve.

Because the district-wide educational goal is broad in scope, only a portion of it would be achieved when the educational objective has been attained. All of the educational objectives subsumed under the educational goals have to be met before the goal is satisfactorily achieved.

The goal tier in Figure 3–2 shows the continuum of goals and objectives that constitute the educational goals and objectives portion of the pyramid in Figure 3–1. Because each school is a separate and unique entity, an educational goal and objective continuum must be produced by each planning unit.

It is appropriate here to point out that some variations in the goal tier may exist within some schools:

- School goals may appear as program goals.
- School objectives may appear as program objectives.

Figure 3–2 illustrates that a complete goal tier will include goals and objectives up to and including the sixth or learner's level. Note that long-range goals are set to meet the first (district-wide) level requirements and short-range objectives are established to achieve the requirements of either the fourth (program) or fifth (instructional) level.

DEVELOPING MISSION STATEMENTS

The mission statements describe the reason the school district exists. They should be stated in terms of student achievement. Developing mission statements without stating a goal is like filling a bottomless pitcher with water. Without goals the school district personnel will wander aimlessly through the educational process without achieving

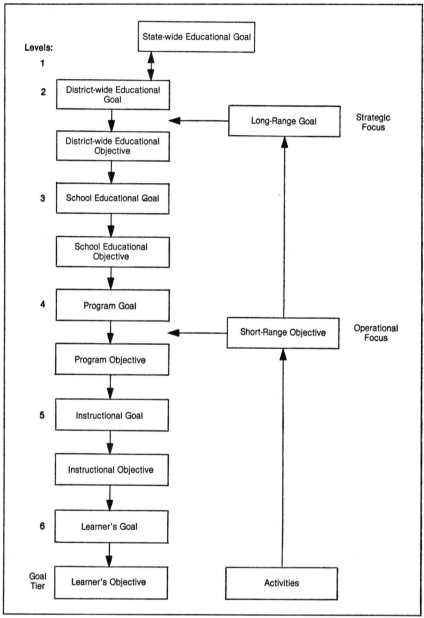

Figure 3–2   *Goals and Objectives Relationships*

anything of significance. Socrates said, "For a man without an intended port, no wind is favorable."

Mission statements traditionally have been written in broad and abstract terms; however, recently there has been a trend to produce mission statements in results-oriented terms. More information about this matter is included later in this section. There is no set pattern for developing mission statements, but three examples are listed below.

The mission statement may be expressed by:

1. A single phrase, such as, "Quality education for all."
2. A simple sentence, such as, "Our primary goal is improved student learning and growth."
3. A more complex sentence such as, "Our primary goal is to provide all students with a cost-effective, high quality education and a meaningful growth experience while attending school."

There are a number of ways to develop mission statements. The following represents several successful methods used by school administrators. These techniques can also be applied to preparing basic purposes and educational goals.

1. The superintendent can prepare a mission statement, receive input from his or her staff, modify the statement, if need be, and disseminate it to all staff members.
2. A committee composed of representatives from the school and community can be organized into subcommittees to identify acceptable mission statements from a sample of several. A spokesperson from each subcommittee indicates which statements have been selected by his or her group, and a tally is taken to determine which statement received the most votes. This mission statement is adopted as the school district's mission.
3. The superintendent selects a cross section of school personnel and community members to form a special task force. This group attends a two- or three-day retreat to discuss and determine the mission of the district. Working in groups of six to eight, task force members define the characteristics of a successful school district. This information is then used to develop a comprehensive mission statement.

REASONS FOR DEVELOPING A MISSION STATEMENT

When mission statements have not been formally drawn up, implied missions evolve out of the developmental process of the school organization. In most instances, implied missions are activity- or process-oriented and school personnel determine their effectiveness based on the activity or process rather than on the actual results of students. The effects of an implied mission are:

1. Overlapping of responsibilities.
2. Duplication of efforts.
3. Frustration of goal seekers.
4. Poor utilization of resources.
5. Wasted time and money.

Item

The commissioner of education ordered a review of the state-wide educational network system because of his staff's varied impressions of the role and function of each component within the network, which consisted of twenty-one county superintendent offices, four regional service centers, and several education consortiums. The results of the study revealed that because missions were never officially developed for each component of the network system, duplications in the delivery of services existed. In addition, the study revealed that no more than two persons, among the several who were interviewed, had the same perception of the role and responsibilities of the network system. The county superintendents' offices were monitoring and delivering technical services to school districts, the regional service centers were delivering technical assistance and reducing service costs of the local school districts, and the education consortiums were reducing service costs of the local school districts. The formulation of an official mission for each component on a results-oriented basis established the county superintendents' responsibility for ensuring that local school districts comply with the state education laws, the regional service centers' responsibility for improving student achievement, and the education consortiums' responsibility for reducing and saving delivery of services costs for the local school districts. Personnel members who were duplicating services were transferred to the appropriate component or dismissed from the system.

The mission statement provides general guidelines for preparing strategic plans and also serves other useful purposes, particularly if it is written in results-oriented terms.

Mission statements:

1. Facilitate the task of identifying opportunities and threats that must be responded to during the strategic planning process.
2. Determine how resources will be allocated to accommodate needs.
3. Reveal new opportunities and threats when charged to respond to the ever changing school district environments.
4. Prevent efforts being wasted on strategies and plans that may be considered inappropriate by the superintendent.

PREPARING THE MISSION STATEMENTS IN
RESULTS-ORIENTED TERMS

A few planners are beginning to stress that mission statements should be results-oriented. Results-oriented missions provide a basis for measuring the school district's effectiveness and guidance for making changes in plans and activities.

George S. Odiorne identifies the activity trap, the substitution of an activity for a goal, which often occurs when staff members become so involved in a program activity that they lose sight of the goal.[1] A. Etzioni stipulates that in order to avoid the activity trap, certain terms, such as "to," should be deleted.[2] In this way the result will state the condition which will rest outside the school organization as advocated by Peter Drucker.[3] For an example, an activity-oriented mission statement would be:

> The mission of the Alpha School District is to improve student learning and growth.

In results-oriented terms, the mission statement would read:

> The mission of the Alpha School District is improved student learning and growth.

Some readers may judge this example as a waste of time; however, as stated by Drucker, the mission should be viewed outside of the organization. The activity-oriented mission statement looks in at the school district, while the results-oriented mission statement looks outward from the school district. No one can fault either an individual or school district that *attempts* to improve student learning. However, accountability is truly established when improved student learning occurs through a results-oriented mission statement.

TRANSLATING THE GUIDANCE SYSTEM INTO
POLICIES AND PROCEDURES

The guidance system of a school district must be developed with good intentions. The system should not mislead its teachers, parents, or students, or be claimed as representative of something it is not. The development of such a system solely for the sake of having one available or for accreditation purposes serves no useful function. The guidance system must have the support and commitment of the superintendent and

[1] George S. Odiorne, *Management and the Activity Trap* (New York: Harper & Row, 1974).

[2] A. Etzioni, *Modern Organizations* (Englewood Cliffs, N.J.: Prentice-Hall, 1964), p. 10.

[3] Peter F. Drucker, *Management, Tasks, Responsibilities, Practice* (New York: Harper & Row, 1973), p. 61.

his or her administrative staff, who will translate it into active policies and procedures for creating strategy and operating the school district.

STABILIZING HUMAN EFFORTS USING POLICIES

Policies are intended to stabilize the school district's administration and to create a climate in which personnel will feel comfortable and confident. They are also intended to secure maximum performance and to provide the impetus and direction for the guidance system in the strategic planning process. Policies can also:

1. Help to prevent errors and avoid stumbling blocks that might prevent the school district from reaching its mission.
2. Provide guidelines that discourage extreme changes.
3. Encourage ingenuity and initiative to attain goals.
4. Encourage achievement and excellence.
5. Provide limits that discourage decisions, direction, and activities that would be detrimental to the school district's mission.

MAINTAINING POLICY VALIDITY

The development of the guidance system must be viewed as a dynamic process that should change with changing times and conditions. Because of the changeable aspects of the internal and external environments, policies must be adaptable to the interacting forces that affect the educational process.

The superintendent of schools is primarily responsible for reevaluating the guidance system. Some questions he or she may consider when performing this task are:

- Are the current basic purposes, mission statement, and educational goals and objectives still valid?
- Are all of the current policy statements necessary?
- How long has it been since they were changed?
- How should they be changed?

Policy statements are only important and useful if they are valid and correctly administered to give impetus to the guidance system as the strategic planning process is implemented.

CLARIFYING THE GUIDANCE SYSTEM

The guidance system must be formulated first by the central planning unit and subsequently by each school planning unit. The following questions are intended to assist central planning unit administrators in preparing the guidance system for the central planning unit:

1. What should the school district provide and why does it exist?
2. Who are the primary and secondary beneficiaries of the school district's services?
3. What are the primary services?
4. How does the district differ from its status of ten years ago?
5. What should be different about the district ten years from now?
6. What are the primary and secondary sources of funding?
7. What are the expectations of all stakeholders in regard to the philosophical issues facing the school district?

The following questions are intended to assist school planning unit administrators to prepare a guidance system:

1. What should the school provide and why does it exist?
2. Who are the primary and secondary beneficiaries of the school's services?
3. What are the school's primary and secondary services?
4. How do these services contribute to the overall school district guidance system?
5. How does the school differ from its status of ten years ago?
6. What should be different about the school ten years from now?
7. To what extent is the school budgeted?
8. What is unique about the school that separates it from others in the district?
9. What are the concerns of all stakeholders in regard to philosophical and other issues facing the school?

SALIENT POINTS

In the final analysis, the guidance system of the strategic planning process relies on individuals. The success of the system is measured by the contribution it makes to the effective operation of the school district. If individuals view the guidance system purely as "words," without substance, then the internal components are poorly worded or erroneously understood by the planning unit administrators. The guidance system is relevant and effective to the degree that it fulfills the following requirements:

1. Is it acceptable to teachers, administrators, and parents? The basic purposes, missions, and educational goals and policies must be reasonable and acceptable.

2. Is the meaning understood? All components of the system should be developed using the entire school-community complex. The language should be easily read and understood.
3. Is it effectively communicated? One frequent problem in public education is the school district's philosophy statements and educational goals, which are prepared with little input from staff and community and seldom communicated or clarified to the school personnel.
4. Is it effectively promoted? One way to promote the guidance system is to demonstrate how human activities and efforts are influenced by the system and what results are possible when this takes place.
5. Does it contribute to positive results? This is the guidance system's moment of truth. Its practical application must influence human efforts as they strive to implement the strategic planning process.

Each school personnel member must be able to relate personally to the guidance system. This system must be able to be altered, adapted, improved, and constantly updated to serve changing needs. When a viable guidance system is translated into action through the planning process, the school organization becomes its living projection.

APPLICATION STRATEGY 3

Begin by writing a policy statement on the network of aims in public education for a local school district. Design a plan for involving a cross section of the community in the process of constructing the guidance system. Implement the plan, if possible. If this is not possible, complete all sections of the network of aims in public education for a school district by using any existing relevant information.

4

SETTING LONG-RANGE GOALS

The third step in strategic or long-range planning is clarifying long-range goals for the central planning unit and each school planning unit (department or individual school). Long-range goals help to clarify the mission of the school district, describe the results to be achieved, and indicate where the primary focus should be placed. Long-range goals are also guidelines for human efforts. They are statements expressed in quantitative and measurable terms that identify what is to be achieved by the system's network of policies, procedures, administrative edicts, rules, budgets, programs, and strategies inherent in the planning process. The planning unit administrator who is involved in setting long-range goals should ponder the questions, "What should be accomplished that will have a significant impact on the school, and when should it be done?"

This chapter begins by defining long-range goals. Assumptions to be made in establishing long-range goals are discussed briefly, as are the criteria and approaches for writing long-range goals. Educational and long-range goals are clarified in an effort to contrast them.

Also discussed is the starting point for writing long-range goals, which revolve around major key areas. Long-range goals are indicated for each major key result area.

The chapter ends with an explanation of the different approaches to setting long-range goals, identification of various levels of performance, and description of the steps to take when setting these goals.

DEFINING LONG-RANGE GOALS

Simply stated, a long-range goal is a written, specific, and measurable task assignment or result designated for an individual or group to achieve over a period of three years or more. A more complex definition of long-range goals is eloquently given by Charles L. Hughes:

> A goal is an end, a result, not just a task or function to be performed. It is a place in space and time that describes the condition we want to achieve. It is a standard of achievement, a curtain of success, something tangible, measurable, and valuable that we are motivated toward. It is concrete and explicit, definitive and desirable and predetermined. It guides our actions and helps us plan as individuals and as managers. It can be long-range or short-range goals: long-range goals help clarify our short-range goals, major goals determine minor goals, and the present is determined by the future—not the past.[1]

Long-range goals are formulated or established on the following assumptions:

1. Planning unit administrators will not know where they are as individuals or as a group until they have considered and determined what it is they are trying to become and do.
2. Planning unit administrators will know whether or not what they are doing is meaningful only after they have identified the long-range goals they are trying to achieve.
3. Planning unit administrators will know the real meaning of their individual jobs only after they have recognized the reason for coming together as a school organization.
4. Planning unit administrators are nothing more than what they do, and they will become nothing more than what they see themselves achieving in terms of long-range goals.
5. Planning unit administrators are individually responsible for what they are and what they choose to make of themselves.
6. Planning unit administrators cannot know where they are going in their personal and professional lives until they know where the school district is going.[2]

---

[1] Reprinted, by permission of the publisher, from *Goal Setting—Key to Individual and Organizational Effectiveness*, Charles L. Hughes, © 1965 by American Management Association, Inc., pages 8 & 9. All rights reserved.

[2] Reprinted, by permission of the publisher, from *Goal Setting—Key to Individual and Organizational Effectiveness*, Charles L. Hughes, © 1965 by American Management Association, Inc., pages 8 & 9. All rights reserved.

Thus, only after a school district has established meaningful long-range goals will it have direction.

CRITERIA FOR LONG-RANGE GOALS

Long-range goals are guides to help school personnel make decisions and act on all levels of the school organization. As such, long-range goals should be developed only after the following criteria have been understood and used in the validation process; they:

1. Are oriented to the basic purposes, mission, and educational goals of the school district.
2. Are time-phased for a period of three, five, or ten years.
3. Permit a reasonable amount of latitude in precise means and timing.
4. Are broad and flexible enough to be guidelines for plans and not likely to become obsolete as a result of changing times and conditions.
5. Are set in those key areas where results are essential to the continued improvement of the school district as a whole.
6. Are specific about what is to be achieved and by when.
7. State expected results, in positive and measurable terms.
8. Are sufficiently difficult to ensure a high level of human effort, but not too difficult to make them impossible to achieve.
9. Are communicated to the staff for their input and recommendations.

WRITING LONG-RANGE GOALS

There are two approaches to constructing long-range goals, the improvement-action and the prediction approach.

Improvement-Action Approach

The improvement-action approach to writing a long-range goal is to state the action required to improve on performance first, and then the time span for achieving results. When using this approach each long-range goal should:

- Begin with an action verb preceded by the word "To".
- Indicate the present and desired or projected results.
- State the time span for accomplishing the goal.

The following are two examples of a long-range goal using the improvement-action approach:

- To increase the number of primary students reading on grade level from 19 percent to 65 percent by June 30, 19xx (five years).
- To replace the current teacher evaluation program, the trait-approach, with the objective approach by September 15, 19xx (three years).

Prediction Approach

The prediction approach to constructing a long-range goal is to stipulate the time phase for achieving a goal first, then predict performance results. When using this approach, each long-range goal should:

- Begin with the time phase for achieving the goal preceded by the word "By".
- Predict performance by stating current performance and projected results.

The following are two examples for writing long-range goals using the prediction approach:

- By June 30, 19xx (five years), the number of intermediate students achieving on grade level in math will increase from 35 percent to 70 percent.
- By September 30, 19xx (three years), the line item budget will be replaced by a program-oriented budget.

EDUCATIONAL GOALS AND LONG-RANGE GOALS

Although educational goals are essentially long-range goals, there are some distinct differences between them which should be clarified.

Educational Goals	Long-Range Goals
1. Usually are set involving all elements of the school-community, such as teachers, administrators, parents, and citizens.	1. Usually are set involving only school personnel.
2. Time span tends to be unlimited.	2. Stated for a period of three, five, or ten years.

Educational Goals	*Long-Range Goals*
3. Usually set to encompass the major key result areas of instructional programs, services, and student achievement and growth.	3. Usually set to include all major key result areas.
4. Based upon the premise that improvement of the instructional program is sufficient to improve the overall effectiveness of the school system.	4. Based upon the premise that improvements must be made in all critical areas of the school organization in order to improve the overall performance of the school district.
5. Community involvement aspect makes establishing these goals a more time-consuming process.	5. Can be established in a minimum amount of time, depending upon the goal-setting process implemented.
6. At times, are commercially produced and adopted by the board of education.	6. Never commercially produced, but arrived at according to the individual needs of the school district and adopted by the board of education.
7. At times, tend to be heavily activity-oriented.	7. Usually constructed and used to reduce the effects of the "activity trap."
8. Set as guidelines for achieving performance results.	8. Set to reach educational goals on the mission of the school district.

MAJOR KEY RESULT AREAS: GUIDELINES FOR SETTING LONG-RANGE GOALS

Managing a school organization effectively necessitates the setting and achievement of long-range goals to improve on strengths and eliminate weaknesses. Therefore, long-range goals are needed in every critical area where performance and results directly and vitally affect the survival and growth of the school organization. These major key result areas are affected by every decision maker and consequently must be considered in the strategic as well as the operational planning processes. Major key result areas are also guidelines for directing performance so that a well coordinated effort will be exerted by all school personnel to meet the mission of the school district.

Long-range goals in the major key result areas should enable planners to do several things:

1. Clarify through several general statements the entire range of the planning process in education.
2. Determine if gaps exist between projected and actual performance.
3. Assess the soundness of decisions and activities.
4. Evaluate and improve on performance.

Although major key result areas will require different emphases depending on the school district and its particular stage of growth and prosperity, the major key result areas are the same, regardless of these differences.

In the public education arena, there are eight major key result areas for which strategic long-range goals can be set. Table 4–1 contrasts these areas with those used by industry, a government agency, and an educational regional service center. Each major key result area is an independent variable that affects the school organization in either a positive or negative manner; however, these areas should be viewed in a systematic manner as part of the planning process and with a realization that the breakdown of one key variable can seriously affect the total school organization.

Student Learning and Growth

No planning process in education is complete unless a direct attempt is made through the goal-setting process to improve student academic learning and growth. Learning refers here to the modification and/or change in student behavior in the cognitive domain. Growth refers to changes in the affective and psychomotor domains.

The following long-range goals measure student learning and growth:

1. To increase the number of elementary students reading on grade level from 17 percent to 75 percent by June 30, 19xx (three years).
2. To reduce the number of physical defects found in kindergarten students by the time they enter second grade from 12 per classroom of 25 students to 3 per classroom of 25 students by June 30, 19xx (four years).

Financial Resources

To set goals without planning for financing is like trying to operate a vehicle without fuel. In education, financial planning is usually thought

Table 4-1 Contrasting Major Key Result Areas

An Educational Regional Service Center	Industry	Public Education	A Government Agency
Impact Service	Productivity	Student Learning and Growth	Support of Regional Agency
Product Development	Financial Resources	Financial Resources	Strong Fiscal Policy and Procedures
Compliance Service	Physical Resources	Physical Resouces	Capital Facilities
Information Service	Innovations	Innovations	Innovations in Program
Reactive Service	Social Responsibility	Community Involvement and Relations	Public Service Facilities
Resource Development	Human Organization	Organizational Management	Sound Personnel Policy
Management and Operations	Marketing	Performance Evaluation and Training	Strong Contractual Relationship
Staff Evaluation and Training	Profit Requirements	Instructional Programs and Services	Staffing for Services to Citizens

of as a component of operational or tactical planning. This is far from the truth. Plans must be devised on a long-term basis to expend those funds in the most efficient manner.

Some long-range goals pertaining to financial resources may be:

1. To increase the funds generated from federal, state, and private foundation grants from $3,100,000 to $7,500,000 by March 31, 19xx (five years).
2. To convert the current line-item budget to a result-oriented budget by January 31, 19xx (three years).

Physical Resources

The acquisition of physical resources, such as capital facilities, equipment, and machines, is too important to be excluded from the planning process. Because physical resources can involve large sums, the strategic planning process will certainly collapse if a financial commitment is not made adequately to accommodate student and staff needs.

Two long-range goals pertaining to physical resources are:

1. To demolish the Grant Street Elementary School building and construct a middle school building housing 750 fourth, fifth, sixth, and seventh grade students by August 30, 19xx (four years).
2. To reduce the operational cost of the transportation department in the school district, without affecting student services, from $1,500,000 to $1,200,000 or by 20 percent by June 30, 19xx (three years).

Innovations

All major key result areas could be categorized under this one heading because long-range goals must be set to improve on every critical area of the school organization. However, because it can no longer be assumed that educators will innovate to improve performance results, this critical item is being given separate focus.

Two long-range goals under this area are:

1. To increase the number of students scoring 1000 or more on the SAT from 2 percent to 20 percent by June 30, 19xx (five years).
2. To revamp the current traditional high school curriculum to include a nongraded, flexible high school curriculum combined with a community college curriculum that provides students with the options of graduating within three, four, or five years,

receiving either a high school diploma or A.A. degree by June 30, 19xx (three years).

Community Involvement

Long-range goals must involve the community in the educational process and keep the public-at-large informed of the various operations of the school organization. Both of these activities are obligations of the board of education. Community involvement cannot be left to chance or it may emerge as a threat rather than a boon to the planning process.

Two long-range goals relating to community involvement are:

1. To increase the number of parents voting on the school budget from 1300 to 4000 by May 30, 19xx (three years).
2. To increase the number of community members involved in various activities of the school district from 4,000 to 10,000 during the school year by June 30, 19xx (five years).

Organizational Management

To become and remain effective a school district must set long-range goals to improve the operation of the school district through positive administrative leadership and organizational structure. Effective leadership is enhanced through an organizational structure that permits teachers to fulfill their personal goals while pursuing school organizational goals.

Two long-range goals involving organizational management are:

1. To substitute management by objectives for the traditional method of operating the school district by June 30, 19xx (three years).
2. To implement a job enrichment program throughout the school district, increasing the level of teacher decision-making involvement from "very low" to "moderately high" by June 30, 19xx (five years).

Performance Evaluation and Training

Performance evaluation is one area in education in which long-range goals are seldom established. This may be one of the reasons supervisors have not received the kind of results desired. Staff evaluation must be continuously planned and carefully executed. An important component of performance evaluation is training. The success of each of these two activities depends upon the other. Changing times and conditions have reduced the life span of the education degree to approximately five years. As a result, if long-range goals to improve performance through a variety of training and development activities are not set, obsolescence will creep into the system, and the school organization will find itself in a precarious situation, as demonstrated by hundreds of failing school systems throughout the nation today.

Two long-range goals pertaining to performance evaluation and training are:

1. To convert the current trait approach to teacher evaluation to the objective approach by June 30, 19xx (three years).
2. To implement a professional improvement program in which 75 percent or more of the staff will report that the program has been "effective" by June 30, 19xx (five years).

Instructional Program and Services

There are basically two methods by which the instructional program and services can be improved:

1. Modifying the existing program, which may involve changing procedures, abilities, products, skills, or services.
2. Changing the current program or substituting a new one, which may necessitate the acquisition of new skills, products, and services.

Regardless of the approach selected, long-range goals must be set to effect instructional improvements in either programs or services.

Listed below are two long-range goals relating to instructional programs and services:

1. To convert the current sight approach to reading to the phonetic approach, thereby increasing the number of elementary students reading on the seventy-fifth percentile (using the state-mandated reading test) from 33 percent to 100 percent by June 30, 19xx (five years).
2. To increase the number of elective courses available to high school students from 33 to 150 by June 30, 19xx (four years).

Item
Some school administrators who have not had much success in planning may complain that the long-range goal setting process is too quantitative. Although this process sets quantitative guide-

lines for human efforts on a long-range basis, the setting and achievement of short-range objectives and performance standards provide qualitative leaps toward the attainment of long-range goals.

GOAL-SETTING PROCESS

There has been a great deal of controversy over the best approach to setting long-range goals. A number of variations have emerged; however, the following three approaches have been tried or recommended by noted planners.

Top-Down Approach

The central planning unit prepares and submits its recommended long-range goals to the superintendent of the school district, who in turn modifies, deletes, or adds to the list and submits it to the board of education for approval. Revisions are made where necessary, and the approved list is disseminated to the planning unit administrators. Using these long-range goals as guidelines, along with the essential data, each planning unit administrator sets his or her own long-range goals and plans for reaching the central goals. This information is then submitted to the central planning unit for review and comment. Certain aspects of the school goals and plans may have to be renegotiated with central staff. The final list of long-range goals is the basis for performance action.

Bottom-Up Approach

Each planning unit administrator collects information for making planning decisions by constructing a data base consisting of critical information about the planning unit. Using this information along with that furnished by the central planning unit, long-range goals are prepared and submitted to the superintendent for review, comment, and recommendations. Usually the chief school officer will call on the staff to criticize the long-range goals. Sometimes, the superintendent may personally review the proposed plans with the teachers and administrators. The planning unit staff make their recommendations and comments on their reactions, changes that may have taken place in either the internal and/or external environment, planning assumptions, and the like. Revised long-range goals are submitted to the central planning unit for approval. Once approval is obtained, each planning unit administrator develops an individual plan for reaching the long-range goal and submits it to the central planning unit for review, comment, and recommendations. The approval process for plans is similar to that for long-range goals.

Although the top-down and bottom-up approaches to setting long-range goals afford a convenient way of looking at the strategic planning process, they do not do justice to the dynamics of long-range goal setting, as the following statements attest:

1. There is no indication that planning assumptions can be changed or that unforeseen events can call for alteration to update long-range goal statements.
2. The two approaches suggest that preparation, evaluation, approval, and implementation of long-range goals are tantamount to effective planning when there should be a serious move to make long-range goal setting an ongoing activity.
3. Long-range goal setting is viewed as a step-by-step process rather than a steadily recirculating one.

A more effective and contemporary way to implement an effective long-range goal-setting process is by infusing it from the start into the strategic planning process, as is exemplified in the third approach.

Participatory Approach

In this approach, an equal number of central administrators, building principals, department chairpersons, and teachers serve on a planning council not only to identify long-range goals but also to establish the strategic planning system from the onset and to determine responsibilities in the planning process. Through this arrangement each professional group is able to articulate district-wide planning needs and concerns as well as individual interests and concerns as these affect their schools. Once the planning system has been established and a data base organized and critically reviewed, the council will arrive at the long-range goals for the school district. A great deal of discussion and negotiation is to be expected throughout the long-range goal setting process. This same course is followed for all subsequent activities of the strategic planning process. After long-range goals have been agreed upon, they are submitted to the superintendent for input and approval.

It may be more appropriate to delay finalizing long-range goals until council representatives have had an opportunity to discuss them with their staffs. This will depend to a large extent on how much time is available for the long-range goal-setting process.

Once the long-range goals have been approved by the superintendent and board of education, planning unit administrators, with or without a council member, review and clarify each statement with members of their staffs.

Ultimately, this goal-setting process should function continuously, smoothly, and with so much interaction among the members of the council that top-down versus bottom-up issues will become relatively academic.

Lewis summarizes the above three approaches in *School Management by Objectives* by stating:

1. The chief school officer can initiate a freewheeling "think" session by getting the long-range goal session started. One school superintendent made arrangements for top school administrators to attend a resort in the mountains, away from the daily routines of the school system, to encourage in-thinking, dialoguing and planning of long-range goals. The summer may be a convenient time to perform long-range goal-setting.
2. The superintendent can develop a personal draft of long-range goals for the school district and then request each administrator and supervisor to comment and to make suggestions.
3. The chief school officer can ask each administrator and supervisor to draft individual and school or department long-range goals and use these drafts for formulating district-wide long-range goals and priorities.
4. The superintendent can assign an advisor the responsibility of formulating long-range goals for the school district after meeting in either individual or group sessions with administrators and supervisors.
5. The superintendent can meet with top administrators and supervisors to form a committee to prepare priorities and long-range goals for the school district.[3]

LEVELS OF PERFORMANCE

Understanding the various levels of performance is an important prerequisite for setting and attaining long-range goals. There are basically four performance levels, as illustrated in Figure 4–1, which are described below.

Minimal Performance Level

The minimal performance level is obtained when a job description has been established, and each key result area has been matched with one or more performance standards. This collection of key result areas and performance standards provides the basic and minimum job re-

[3] From the book, *School Management by Objectives* by Dr. James Lewis, Jr., © 1974 by Parker Publishing Company, Inc. Published by Parker Publishing Company, Inc., West Nyack, New York 10994.

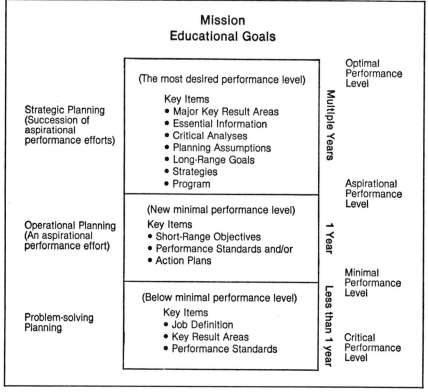

Figure 4–1 *Levels of Performance*

quirements for each school employee. When all employees perform in accordance with the key result areas and performance standards, the school district is said to be performing at a minimal level.

There are three requirements for maintaining a minimal performance level:

1. A job description must be established for each employee.
2. Key result areas must be matched with performance standards.
3. Each school employee must be performing his or her key result areas and performance standards in a satisfactory manner.

Some interesting facts about the minimal performance level are:

1. Even though the aspirational performance level may not have been reached, the degree to which it has been attained or the actual achievement level becomes the basis for the new minimal performance level. For example:

   An aspirational performance level of a planning unit administrator was to reduce the accident rate during a one-year period from 425 to 250 incidents. The actual achievement level was 292 incidents, which becomes the new minimal performance level.

2. Long-range goals are not set in order to reach minimal performance levels, but rather to effect performance results over a long period of time or across several aspirational performance levels.
3. Creative short-range objectives are set to achieve a new minimal performance level.
4. Problem-solving objectives are usually set to attain a minimal performance level because they are intended to restore performance to its minimal level before the onset of the problem.
5. The minimal level of performance will not be reached unless the three requirements described above have been met; if they are not, the planning unit may never attain a minimal performance level and will usually be operating on a level below the minimal standards.
6. Educators of high-achieving schools tend to think of their minimal performance level as their aspirational performance level (consciously or unconsciously) when, in essence, they may not even have reached the minimal performance level.
7. There is a greater risk inherent in not achieving the minimal performance level than there is in not satisfying the aspirational or optimal performance levels.

Critical Performance Level

The critical performance level exists below the minimal performance level and has occurred because one or more educators has failed to perform a routine job or task at an acceptable level. It usually has reverberating effects on the performance of others and can have serious consequences for the school district as a whole.

There are two conditions that have taken effect when a critical performance level exists in a school district:

1. Someone failed to perform in an acceptable manner in an essential key result area.
2. Short-range planning has not been properly executed.

Some interesting points about the critical performance level are:

1. An educator who repeatedly fails to perform his or her routine responsibilities in an acceptable manner risks losing employment in the school district.

2. Problems inevitably create chain reactions that can have numerous grave consequences for a department, school, or school district as a whole.
3. The magnitude of the problem is related to the organizational position of the person responsible for the problem; that is, the effects of the problem are greater for an assistant superintendent than they would be for a building principal.

Aspirational Performance Level

The aspirational performance level is reached when a creative short-range objective to improve on the minimal performance level has been set and achieved. These objectives are usually matched with performance standards and/or activities, and are used as a "road map" to achieve the aspirational performance level.

There are three requirements for reaching an aspirational performance level:

1. A creative long-range objective that is challenging, realistic, and measurable must be set and achieved either on or above plan.
2. Performance standards and/or activities must be matched with short-range objectives, which serve as performance indicators.
3. A minimum of 70 percent of the school staff must perform at a 70 percent effectiveness level.

Some interesting facts about the aspirational performance level are:

1. The aspirational level is seldom reached by a school district without a comprehensive and effective strategic planning system.
2. A planning unit administrator who aspires to improve on the minimal performance level, but fails, has not reached the aspirational performance level, but has established a new minimal performance level.
3. A new minimal performance level has also been attained when the aspirational performance level has been achieved either on or above plan.
4. A series of aspirational performance attempts provides the basis for reaching a long-range goal.
5. The risk of not reaching the aspirational performance level is greater than the risk of not reaching the optimal performance level.

Optimal Performance Level

The optimal performance level is reached when a series of short-range objectives to reach a succession of aspirational performance levels has been set and achieved. In effect, the optimal performance level means that the mission and educational goals of a particular aspect of the school organization have been realized. It is a level of performance achievement that is seldom reached; however, the attempt is well worth the effort.

There are two requirements for attaining an optimal performance level:

1. A long-range goal that is directed toward the mission and educational goals of the school district must be established and attained.
2. A number of short-range objectives must be set and achieved either on or above plan over a period of three, five, or ten years.

Some interesting points about the optimal performance level are:

1. Some educators believe that this level of performance is unattainable, and therefore they abandon the quest. (This is particularly true in lower-achieving schools.)
2. Educators who work in high-achieving schools usually feel that they have reached the optimal performance level, when they may not even have reached the minimal or aspirational level.
3. School districts that do not strive to reach their optimal performance level perpetuate mediocrity.

STEPS FOR SETTING LONG-RANGE GOALS

The techniques for setting long-range goals are very subjective. There is no scientific way to perform this task other than to make a guess based on the availability of essential information. Following, however, is one technique which has been found useful by the author, and may prove of value to the reader:

1. Read and study thoroughly all of the essential information about the school organization.
2. Using the major key result areas as a base, digest each segment of the critical analysis.
3. Make an analytic study to identify major strengths and weaknesses, considering all problems and taking advantage of all opportunities. Using Figure 4–2 as an example, the following options have been arrived at to facilitate setting a long-range goal:
   a. Install management by objectives.
   b. Implement an objective approach to teacher evaluation.
   c. Establish a trait-objective approach to teacher evaluation.
   d. Overhaul the current teacher evaluation program.
   e. Establish a teacher evaluation council.

Strategic Planning

Planning Unit: _____   Date: _____

Planning Unit Administrator: _____   Position: _____

Planning Component: Critical Analysis   Page _____of _____

Swop Analysis: _____

Major Key Result Area: |

Major Strengths/Opportunities	Major Weaknesses/Problems
Assistant superintendent for personnel is the author of several books on staff evaluation. Good relationship exists between teacher union and superintendent. For the past few years, superintendent initiated an active program for involving teachers in the decision-making process. State department of education has mandated some major changes in staff evaluation. The new state mandate on staff evaluation presents an excellent opportunity for the school district to overhaul its entire staff evaluation program. Able leadership exists in central administration and teachers union to perform this task effectively.	Current teacher evaluation program does not meet new state mandate. Teacher evaluation program has not been validated or tested for reliability. Current teacher evaluation program evolves around characteristics and traits of teachers. Teacher evaluation program does not improve instruction. The time span set by new mandate poses a serious problem for the school district because of the desegregation ruling by the federal government and the need to modify the desegregation proposal.

Action to be taken: Reference

Develop a more effective teacher evaluation program by June 30, 19XX (3 years).

Organize a district-wide staff evaluation council to assist in planning, developing, implementing, and evaluating the teacher evaluation program. (Include this proposed action as an objective, performance standard, or activity.)

Figure 4–2 *Analysis of Strengths, Weaknesses, Opportunities, and Problems*

4. Examine each proposed option to determine the degree to which it will improve performance results. After much consideration and dialogue with associates, it was decided that item (c) might be the best long-range approach to solve this particular performance problem.

Item (a) was excluded as a viable alternative because organizing a teacher evaluation council is not a terminal step to improving the performance evaluation program. Items (a) and (b) were also discarded because it was thought they might provoke a problem with the teachers unions. Item (d) was also deleted as it gave too much latitude to the planners. Using item (c) as a departure point, the following long-range goal was established:

• To convert the current trait approach teacher evaluation to the objective approach by June 19, 19xx (three years).

5. Record the long-range goal in the appropriate form and key it with appropriate critical information.

Item

Some school districts have resorted to a multiple approach for setting long-range goals. By combining several methods such as an edict from the superintendent, reliance on past performance, and an analysis of swop with the major key result area techniques, a comprehensive attempt is made to cover all areas which may be missed by using one method. There may be some validity in this method; however, it is quite possible that too many long-range goals may be generated from the multiple approach.

CODING STRATEGIC AND OPERATIONAL PLANS

To ensure uniformity in plans, key result areas, long-range goals, short-range objectives, performance standards, and activities should be constructed under a uniformed coding system. The coding system recommended by this author is designed around the key result areas. Each key result area has a permanent number assigned to it. For example, student learning and growth is assigned the code number 1. The long-range goal is usually displayed by the second code number, which is usually zero, unless there is more than one long-range goal per key result area. For example, the code number 10. would mean a long-range goal in student learning and growth; the code number 11. would indicate a second long-range goal under the same key result area. This is rarely the case, because usually no more than four or five long-range goals should be set by a planning unit, and all of these goals should be in different key result areas. The third code number relates to short-range objectives. For example, 10.1 would indicate a short-range objective set to achieve a long-range goal in the area of student learning and growth. If a second short-range objective is set in this key result area, it would receive a code number of 10.2, and so on. The fourth code number relates to performance standards. A performance standard for the second short-range objective would be coded 10.2.1. Finally, the fifth code number relates to activities of an action plan. Using the second short-range objective coded 10.2.1. as a base, the first activity would be coded 10.2.1.1. This is one reason this author is opposed to including activities in an operational plan. There are just too many numbers to work with.

Therefore, the coding system would be:

1	0.	1.	1.	1.
Key Result Area	Long-Range Goal	Short-Range Objective	Performance Standard	Activity

SALIENT POINTS

Although the issue of top-down versus bottom-up process for setting long-range goals has received a great deal of thought, it is still being debated and remains a prevailing problem in education as well as in business and industry. Because the United States is a democratic country where a strong desire exists to bring democracy into the employment area, these processes are not easily executed and may not be desirable at times. In fact, even the recommended participatory goal-setting process may not be the best approach for certain school districts. Independently, top-down and bottom-up long-range goal setting can be employed effectively in the following manner:

1. Long-range goal setting can be a bottom-up process to the extent that it requires planning unit administrators to propose where their individual planning units should be navigating, how they can best get there, and the resources that will be needed to perform the activity.
2. The review, approval, and monitoring of long-range goals can essentially have a top-down thrust. Defining district-wide planning assumptions and providing guidelines can also be a function of the top-down input process.

APPLICATION STRATEGY 4

Review the substance in the critical analysis prepared in Application Strategy 2, and construct appropriate planning assumptions for each major key result area. Critically review the planning assumptions to determine if any important points have been omitted. For example, although international relations may not appear as a factor in the critical analysis, they may have to be considered separately to arrive at a complete set of planning assumptions.

Identify six critical subject areas, and prepare scenarios using three probabilities. One technique that can be used to do this is to organize individual groups of knowledgeable persons and have them use the Delphi technique to arrive at the planning assumptions and probabilities.

5

PREPARING PLANNING
ASSUMPTIONS

No planning unit administrator should ever prepare a long- or short-range plan until a value judgment about the variables that may affect his or her performance results has been made. These value judgments are called assumptions because they identify factors that are assumed to exist when the plans are executed. If an attempt is made to plan without carefully considering variables that may have a significant impact on the progress of the school district, the plan may be of little value.

The intent of this chapter is as follows. First, planning assumptions are defined. The difference between preparing planning assumptions and developing plans is explained, because planning unit administrators often confuse the two processes. A brief explanation of the purposes, clarification, and types of planning assumptions is provided. A large segment of the chapter is devoted to the process of preparing planning assumptions. Strengthening planning assumptions using probability estimates is discussed. Consideration is also given to various methods for arriving at planning assumptions and the sources for determining them. The chapter concludes by explaining how planning assumptions should be recorded.

DEFINING PLANNING ASSUMPTIONS

Preparing planning assumptions is predicting the events and conditions that are most likely to influence the performance of individuals, departments, schools, and the school district as a whole.

There are numerous factors or variables over which planning unit administrators have no control and administrators have no assurance that they can predict these with 100 percent accuracy. To maximize the achievement of plans, planning unit administrators should prepare planning assumptions to identify these factors and the degree to which they will have an impact on the school district. Preparing planning assumptions is also referred to as forecasting or arriving at premises.

The process of preparing planning assumptions is often confused with planning. Assumptions are concerned with what the future *will* look like. Planning in either short- or long-range terms is concerned with what the future *should* look like. Preparing planning assumptions is an integral part of the planning process. The model used to arrive at planning assumptions can determine what the school-community environment will look like if left alone . . . or what it will be like if planning unit administrators make different assumptions about the future . . . or what it will look like if no change is made. The major benefits of preparing planning assumptions are realized in the development of an improved and consistent plan and from a comparison of alternative plans under a given set of assumptions about the future.

PURPOSES OF PLANNING ASSUMPTIONS

When planning assumptions are prepared, updated, or modified when necessary, and used appropriately, they can serve several useful purposes. They:

1. Help administrators anticipate likely events and conditions and plan for them rather than simply waiting for things to happen and reacting.
2. Assist central planning unit administrators to come to some conclusion on the future the school district faces and, through group deliberation, to arrive at a set of major predictions that can be generally accepted.
3. Protect the planning unit not only against undesirable changes that may be produced by grave events, but also against those arising simply from changes on the part of central planning unit administrators.
4. Permit the planning process to begin and to progress—without planning assumptions there would be so many uncertainties that planning unit administrators would not know where to begin to plan.
5. Serve as one of several checks on the validity of plans by taking a considerable amount of the guesswork out of the planning process.

6. Serve as continuing checkpoints for possible revisions to the plans; if during the school year actual events are different from predicted events, planning unit administrators are alerted immediately that corrective action is necessary to keep objectives, plans, and resource allocations realistic and current.
7. Guide and simplify the planning process by minimizing the unknown factors.
8. Provide more meaningful long-range goals and short-range objectives.

CLASSIFYING OF PLANNING ASSUMPTIONS

Planning assumptions are time-oriented, and as such they are classified into two major categories.

Long-Range Assumptions

Long-range assumptions are broad, overall predictions affecting the school district as a whole, and may cover three years or more. They provide common reference points for all planning unit administrators to whom the assumptions are pertinent. For example, an assumption on declining enrollment would involve all planning unit administrators. Other examples of long-range assumptions may deal with matters such as the rate of inflation, legislation that may have an impact on the school district, and the need for additional facilities.

Short-Range Assumptions

Short-range assumptions apply in particular to individual planning unit administrators. They are usually more specific in subject matter and cover a period of one month to one year. For example, the business manager may formulate an assumption covering collective bargaining settlements, or an assistant superintendent for curriculum and instruction may develop an assumption relating to textbook obsolescence.

INTEGRATING LONG-RANGE AND SHORT-RANGE PLANNING ASSUMPTIONS

Usually long-range planning assumptions should deal with the same conditions and events as short-range planning assumptions. At the outset these two sets of planning assumptions are identical, but from the second year onward there will be notable differences. To integrate these two sets of planning assumptions on a yearly basis, the long-range planning assumptions must be reconciled with the short-range planning assumptions. Thus, all planning assumptions should, to the best knowledge and experience of the preparer, be in tune with expected realities.

STRENGTHENING PLANNING ASSUMPTIONS USING PROBABILITY ESTIMATES

One effective technique used by business and industry, which can be adopted by school districts when preparing planning assumptions, involves the estimation of probability. Probability estimates are the planning unit administrator's best prediction, expressed in either quantitative or relative terms, of the degree to which a planning assumption is likely to become a reality. They can be used in the decision-making process to provide a more precise evaluation of factors and variables that may affect performance so that pros and cons of an event may be weighted against the advantages and disadvantages of another condition or variable. There are two methods for expressing probability estimates:

1. They can be expressed as percentages, for example, "It is assumed for planning purposes that there is a 10 percent (or 90 percent) probability that a strike will occur during the next school year."
2. They can be expressed as values, for example, "It is assumed for planning purposes that there is a high (or low) probability that a strike will occur during the school year."

Assume that the superintendent is interested in implementing an experimental program in mathematics by establishing ten control classes and ten experimental classes at a cost of several hundred thousand dollars. The results of the experimental program will be used to make a recommendation to the board of education. In view of the possibility of a strike next year, the superintendent is faced with a decision that hinges to a large degree on the probability that a strike will take place. If the probability of a strike is rated at 10 percent, there is little threat to the experimental math program. If the strike probability is rated at 90 percent, the decision might be quite different. Contrast the situation in which probability estimates were used with one with which the superintendent would be faced if they were not used. Under the 90 percent probability, the chief school administrator would have additional information to guide decision making; there could be a strike that might necessitate either modifying the program or eliminating it entirely. Reliable probability estimates can be effective in minimizing *risk*.

TYPES OF PLANNING ASSUMPTIONS

The types of planning assumptions are governed by controls. There are basically three types of planning assumptions.

Noncontrollable Planning Assumptions

Noncontrollable planning assumptions are associated with factors or variables that occur outside of the school environment, over which the school district has no control. Some examples are:

- Rising or declining student enrollment.
- Local, state, and federal legislation.
- Economic factors.
- Increase or decrease in funding level.
- Political environment.

Semicontrollable Planning Assumptions

Semicontrollable planning assumptions are factors within the school environment over which the school district has some control. Some examples are:

- Character of staff turnover.
- Staff salaries and fringe benefits.
- Direction of the school.
- Method of appraising performance.
- Projected budget increase or decrease.

Controllable Planning Assumptions

Controllable planning assumptions are the variables within the school environment over which the school district has a great deal of control. Some examples are:

- Instructional program.
- Textbook and materials allocations.
- Purchase of equipment, furniture, and the like.
- Superintendent edict.
- District-wide goals and objectives.

METHODS FOR PREPARING PLANNING ASSUMPTIONS

Planning assumptions are important in every phase of the school planning process. The chief problem for planning unit administrators will be to decide which assumptions are most important, which should be studied in depth, and how much of the school district's resources should be used to clarify them.

Planning assumptions fall into three main groups.

1. Qualitative planning assumptions are projections that have been formulated by the judgment of one or more persons.
2. Quantitative planning assumptions are forecasts that have been determined by a formula or mathematical calculation.
3. Qualitative/quantitative planning assumptions are projections that have been arrived at through both a judgmental decision and a formula or mathematical calculation.

QUALITATIVE METHOD OF FORECASTING

The following represents two qualitative methods of forecasting.

Method: Delphi

The process of collecting opinions from a group of experts concerning conditions or variables that have affected the school district is the Delphi method. The experts are requested to respond (usually through the mail) to each question more than one time (several rounds). During the second round, the experts are provided with the group responses. During the third round, those experts providing extreme answers are requested to give reasons for their answers. The reasons are summarized anonymously for the next round, and so on.

Advantages
1. Additional rounds of contact and feedback seem to contribute to accuracy.
2. The method tends to be accepted by organizations.
3. Delphi tends to be less expensive than other methods.
4. It is easier to administer (via mail).
5. Users understand the method.

Disadvantages
1. The method is time-consuming.
2. Its value tends to be overrated.

Item

The superintendent of schools is interested in identifying, for long-range planning purposes, the single most important variable affecting reading achievement. She directs the assistant superintendent of instruction to retain one of the nation's most reknowned reading experts for the purpose of preparing a questionnaire on variables affecting reading achievement. In addition, the assistant superintendent of instruction was instructed to use the Delphi method for ascertaining from a group of reading experts, half from within the school district, and half from the local college of education, what the single most important variable affecting reading achievement was.

The following is a summary of the questionnaire and results which were mailed to each reading expert on six rounds.

*Variable Affecting Reading Achievement**	*A*	*B*	*C*	*D*	*E*	*F*
1. Personalized Reading Instruction	2	2	2	2	3	4
2. Grouping Patterns	4	9	4	6	7	5
3. Sufficient Reading Materials	5	3	3	1	4	3
4. Exclusive Teaching of Basic Skills on Primary Level	1	1	1	3	1	1
5. Implementation of a Single Reading Program	9	5	6	7	6	2
6. Early Introduction to Reading	10	6	5	9	5	6
7. Committed Principal	7	7	9	4	9	7
8. Integration	8	4	8	5	2	8
9. Socioeconomic Factors	6	10	10	8	10	10
10. Assorted Reading Materials	3	8	7	10	8	9

* It is assumed that the teachers are highly trained in reading.

Extreme comments related to round 5 were as follows:

4. Too many nonbasic subject areas are taught on the primary levels, reducing the amount of time spent on formal and informal reading instructions.
7. Without a committed principal, reading achievement will suffer.

This information led the assistant superintendent for instruction to produce the following planning assumption:

It is assumed for planning purposes that the single most important factor affecting reading achievement is the exclusive teaching of basic skill subjects on the primary levels.

Method: E-T-E (Estimate-Talk-Estimate)

A group of top school administrators or experts, at a structured meeting, is asked to independently and anonymously make a prediction about the condition or variable under consideration. Without revealing their individual answers, the group discusses particulars about each response. After this initial discussion, each individual is requested again to make a prediction. Using the results of the second round of responses, the superintendent makes a prediction, which then becomes the basis for arriving at a planning assumption.

Advantages
1. E-T-E tends to provide greater accuracy than averaging responses at a traditional meeting.
2. The process can be completed expeditiously.

Disadvantages
1. Sometimes individuals tend simply to present their predictions without providing some evidence.
2. The process tends to be less accurate for long-range planning than for short-range planning.

Item
The superintendent of schools is interested in predicting the in-service needs of secondary teachers within a five-year period. A decision has been made that the E-T-E method will be used to base estimates. The following resulted:

Those Invited to Participate	First Round Discussion Results	Second Round Discussion Results
Deputy Superintendent	Making allowances for individual differences	Diagnostic-presciptive teaching
Assistant Superintendent for Instruction	Diagnostic-Prescriptive Teaching	Diagnostic-Prescriptive Teaching

Those Invited to Participate	*First Round Discussion Results*	*Second Round Discussion Results*
Director of Secondary Education	How to Use the Behavioral Objectives	Teaching Students to Use Their Whole Brain Power
Director of Elementary Education	Individualizing Instruction	Individualizing Instruction
County Superintendent	Teaching Students to Use Their Whole Brain Power	Teaching Students to Use Their Whole Brain Power
Professor of Education	How to Individualize Instruction	Individualizing Instruction
Superintendent's Decision:	Teaching Students to Use Their Whole Brain Power	

Resultant Planning Assumption:
It is assumed for planning purposes that secondary teachers are equipped to teach students to use their whole brain power.

QUANTITATIVE METHOD OF FORECASTING

The following represents three quantitative methods of forecasting.

Method: Mathematical

With the mathematical method, a formula or model is developed to predict the outcome of a variable or condition that may affect school performance.

Advantages
1. The mathematical method tends to be more objective than some other methods.
2. The method is accurate.

Disadvantages
1. Added expense of computer science may be necessary to arrive at an accurate prediction.
2. Insufficient data may adversely affect results.
3. Sometimes an expert may be needed to determine the best formula to use for arriving at a prediction.

Item

The assistant superintendent for business has been requested to arrive at a formula and to prepare a short-range planning assumption on what the cost of vandalism will be during the next school year.

The cost for vandalism for the preceding five years was:

Year	Cost
1	$ 780,000.
2	960,000.
3	875,000.
4	979,000.
5	1,001,000.

Formula: Mean Difference Method

Yn = Vandalism cost for the next school year

$$Yn = Yn - 1 + \frac{(Y2 - Y1) + (Y3 - Y2) + (Y4 - Y3)}{n - 1}$$

$$Yn = 1,001,000 + (960,000 - 780,000) + (875,000 - 960,000)$$
$$\frac{+ (979,000 - 875,000) + (1,001,000 - 979,000)}{5}$$

Yn = 1,001,000 + 44,300

Yn = 1,045,300

The answer was used as the basis for preparing the following planning assumption:

It is assumed for planning purposes that vandalism costs for the next school year will be $1,045,300.

Method: Trends and Cycles

The process of summarizing pertinent data from past trends and cycles by extracting information via graph, formula, or model, and making a prediction is the trends and cycles method.

Advantages
1. Similar situations can be used to make a prediction.
2. As the number of historical data increases so does the accuracy of the prediction.

Disadvantages
1. Future environmental changes may make the prediction invalid.
2. Historical data are important only if they are timely and accurate.
3. This method can be time-consuming, depending on the availability of data and human resources.

Item
The assistant superintendent of instruction has been requested by the superintendent of schools to predict the number of students *not* achieving on grade level in math in the eighth grade by the end of the next school year.

Using the following historical data, the following computation was made:

Year	Students not achieving on grade level in math	Tabulation
1	750	80
2	670	105
3	565	(195)
4	760	70
5	690	55
6	?	

Prediction for sixth year is 635.

Resultant planning assumption:

It is assumed for planning purposes that 635 eighth-graders will not achieve an eighth grade level in math.

QUANTITATIVE/QUALITATIVE METHODS OF FORECASTING

The following represents two quantitative/qualitative methods of making projections.

Method: Cohort Survival

The cohort survival method is used for forecasting enrollment in the school district. It is essentially a linear projection based on historical trend data. There are basically four steps to compute this projection:

Step I: Determine the number of live births in the school district for each year for the past ten years.

Step II: Using that birth information, indicate actual first-grade enrollment for the first five years.

Step III: Using the post-enrollment figures for the first five years, calculate the cohort survival ratio by dividing actual enrollments by resident live births.

Step IV: Complete the table of projected enrollment for all grades.

Advantages
1. The method is easy to calculate.
2. It can be easily accommodated by the computer.
3. Information is easily accessible.

Disadvantages
1. Because kindergarten enrollment fluctuates in most school districts, the first-grade enrollment should be used as a base to calculate future enrollment.
2. Forecasts may be more accurate if first-grade estimates are based on the number of four-year-olds counted in the school district census.
3. A "pure" situation hardly ever exists; therefore, many variables may influence future enrollments.
4. The method tends to be subjective.

Item
The superintendent of schools requested the assistant superintendent of administrative affairs to calculate first-grade enrollment for a five-year period. This information would subsequently be used to obtain a more accurate kindergarten enrollment for the same period. The assistant superintendent decided to use the cohort survival method to display the projections. The following chart and calculations resulted.

| | Births | First Grade Enrollment | | |
Calendar Year (1)	Number of Resident Live Births (2)	School Year (3)	Fall Enrollment (4)	Survival Ratio Col. 4/Col. 2
1970	200	1976–77	165	.825
1971	210	1977–78	169	.804
1972	238	1978–79	175	.735
1973	215	1979–80	171	.795
1974	207	1980–81	160	.773
1975	210	1981–82	165	.786

| | Births | First Grade Enrollment | | |
Calendar Year (1)	Number of Resident Live Births (2)	School Year (3)	Fall Enrollment (4)	Survival Ratio Col. 4/Col. 2
1976	202	1982–83	159	.786
1977	198	1983–84	146	.786
1978	194	1984–85	152	.786
1979	194	1985–86	152	.786
1980	190	1986–87	149	.786

Resultant planning assumption:

It is assumed for planning purposes that first-grade enrollment will be as follows for the next five years:

Year	Number
1982–83	165
1983–84	159
1985–86	146
1986–87	152
1988–89	152

Method: Amalgamated approach

The amalgamated approach uses a variety of methods to arrive at a single planning assumption. Each method is given a weight, and the resultant assumption is arrived at by a weighted average.

Advantage
1. This approach provides more accurate information than any single method.
2. It is useful in assessing uncertainty.
3. It provides a safeguard against cheating.
4. It reduces risk by increasing accuracy.

Disadvantages
1. Gains are no more likely on the long-range basis than on the short-range basis.
2. The approach provides only a modest improvement in accuracy.

Item
The board of education requested the superintendent of schools to predict the dropout rate of the high school in five years. To ensure greater accuracy, the amalgamated approach was used.

The results were:

Method	Weight	Prediction	Tabulated Results
Delphi	2	31 %	62
E-T-E	1	29 %	29
Mathematical	4	40 %	160
Trends and Cycles	3	38 %	114
Total	10		365

AMALGAMATED APPROACH RESULTS: 365 ÷ 10 = 36.5%

Resultant planning assumption:

It is assumed for planning purposes that the dropout rate in the high school will reach 36.5 percent in five years.

Method: Worksheet Approach

A worksheet is completed by a central planning unit administrator by identifying events or variables that may have a significant impact on the performance of the school district and listing them in order of importance. From these events and variables, planning assumptions are categorized, formulated, and continuously updated and tracked.

Advantages
1. A worksheet is useful for preparing planning assumptions for the budgetary process.
2. It can be used in association with many different methods.
3. It contains a system for keeping planning assumptions current.

Disadvantages
1. The method can be time-consuming, depending upon different methods used to arrive at planning assumptions.

Item
The superintendent has instructed the assistant superintendent of business to use the worksheet approach for drafting a list of planning assumptions for next year's school district budget. Refer to worksheet illustrated in Figure 5–1.

SOURCES FOR PLANNING ASSUMPTIONS

There are a number of areas that should be examined by the planning unit administrator before he or she prepares planning assumptions.

```
                WORKSHEET FOR FORMULATING PLANNING ASSUMPTIONS

    This worksheet has been prepared to enable the user
    expeditiously and systematically to develop planning assump-
    tions that should be used for planning and budgeting purposes.

    PREPARER  Dr. Ronald Boone            DATE  December 20, 19XX

    POSITION  Asst. Supt. for Business    SCHOOL  District-wide


    Step I.   State the primary reason for this worksheet and the
              period it covers:

                 __ Long-Range Planning  __ Short-Range Planning

                 _X_ Budgeting

                 _X_ One Year    __ Five Years    __ Ten Years

    Step II.  In the first column, designated "Describe Future
              Events or Variables," identify the items that are
              most likely to have a significant impact on the school
              or school district.  Complete this column before pro-
              ceeding to the next column.  In the second column,
              designated "Impact Probability," describe each of
              the items' impact probability as being very high (VH),
              high (H), low (L), or very low (VL).  Complete this
              column before proceeding to the next column.  In the
              third column, designated "Ranking Order," rank in
              order of importance all of these items defined as
              either VH or H.  Eliminate the others.
```

Describe Future Events or Variables	Impact Probability	Ranking Order
1. Inflation cost	VH	2
2. Declining enrollment (4200 to 4123)	L	7
3. Implementation of ZBB	VH	1
4. New unemployment insurance law	H	5
5. Cost-of-living index	VH	4
6. Across-the-board increase	H	3
7. Need for an additional principal	VL	8
8. Per-pupil allowance	H	6

Figure 5–1 *Worksheet for Formulating Planning Assumptions*

9. _____

10. _____

11. _____

12. _____

Step III. Group and designate those items indicated VH and H by major categories, and formulate planning assumptions in priority order.

MAJOR CATEGORY	PLANNING ASSUMPTIONS (It is assumed for planning purposes that...)
New Programs	ZBB will be the basis for planning the school district's budget.
Inflation	Equipment, materials, and supplies will be affected by inflation at a rate of 10%.
Across-the-board	Across-the-board increase will not exceed 6%.
Cost-of-living index	Cost-of-living index will not exceed 5%.
New Law	Unemployment insurance shall be computed at the rate of 7.8%.
Per-pupil allowance	The per-pupil allowance for supplies for elementary levels $4.00; middle levels is $4.25; and secondary levels is $7.00.

Figure 5–1 *Continued*

Step IV.   Discuss this worksheet with members of the central

           planning unit; modify, revise, delete, and add to it

           as necessary. Record any adjustments in the

           following:

           "Cost-of-living index will not exceed 6%." _____

           _____

           Modification is reached in December as a result of __

           using the Delphi Method for formulating planning ___

           assumptions. _____

           _____

           _____

           _____

Step V.   The cost-of-living index was actualized at 6.4%, ___

           an   increase of .4%. _____

           _____

           _____

           _____

           _____

Step VI.   Reduce maintenance supplies and materials accounts __

           to accommodate the increase in the cost-of-living __

           index. _____

           _____

           _____

Step VII. Complete a planning exception report and file it ___

           with the central planning unit. _____

           _____

           _____

Figure 5–1 *Continued*

Key Result Areas

Key result areas of central planning unit administrators can be effective indicators of where planning assumptions should be established. Job descriptions are an invaluable source of information.

Item
A key result area of the assistant superintendent for instruction revealed the following: "Implements a results-oriented curriculum."

Planning assumption:

It is assumed for planning purposes that the attainment of behavioral objectives shall be the index for judging students' success.

Current School Budget
The current school budget should be examined to develop appropriate planning assumptions, either to prepare next year's budget or to establish long- or short-range plans.

Item
Current school budget revealed that last year's overall budget increase was 8.4 percent.

Planning Assumption:
It is assumed for planning purposes that increases in the overall operating budget, including salaries, will not exceed 9.0 percent.

Established Priorities
A list of priorities, either for the current school year or for the succeeding year, is an invaluable source of major planning assumptions.

Item
The program priorities were ranked as follows:

1. Math.
2. Reading.
3. Bilingual education.
4. Science.
5. Sex education.

Planning Assumption:
It is assumed for planning purposes that instructional program improvement will be emphasized in math, reading, and bilingual education.

Needs Assessment Data
One of the best methods for determining planning assumptions is by reviewing information collected through the critical analysis and formulating planning "boundaries."

Item
Critical analysis data revealed the need to have a person to procure state and federal funds.

Planning Assumption:
It is assumed for planning purposes that the board of education will approve the hiring of a person to seek and obtain additional funds.

Legislation Requirements
Planning unit administrators must review new legislation to determine its impact on the school district. For example, federal and state affirmative-action opportunity legislation mandates that administrators use a program for selecting personnel that gives equal consideration to all ethnic groups.

Item
A new state law mandates that unemployment insurance be deducted from teachers' salaries.

Planning Assumption:
It is assumed for planning purposes that unemployment insurance be computed at the rate of 4.5 percent of gross salary.

Existing List of Planning Assumptions
No planning unit administrator should prepare planning assumptions without reviewing the existing list, which will be a reminder about current planning assumptions and enable the administrator to update those assumptions which are relevant to the upcoming school year.

Item
The current list of planning assumptions revealed the following: "No more than three reading programs are to be implemented on the primary and intermediate levels."

The Board of Education recognized through the testing program that one reading program was more effective by a large measure than the other two, and instructed the superintendent to eliminate the other two programs.

Planning Assumption
It is assumed for planning purposes that the Cureton Reading Program will be the sole reading program implemented in the school district on the elementary level.

USING PLANNING ASSUMPTIONS FOR CONTROL PURPOSES

Planning assumptions must be clearly stated and tracked continuously during the planning and execution periods to determine if they are valid. Figure 5–2 demonstrates how planning assumptions can be used for control. The predicted planning assumption gives a cost-of-living index of 7.2 percent. Although the objective of purchasing supplies and materials was initially irrelevant to this assumption, it became relevant when it was determined that cost-of-living index was understated by 1.3 percent. The supply and material account is usually the one to suffer when the salary account is understated and the predicted planning assumption must be corrected to conform to the actual figure. The corrected planning assumption is used as the basis for modifying all appropriate short-range objectives. The final step is to make adjustments in the worksheet and complete a Planning Exception Report.

Planning assumptions can act as an early warning system as indicated above, however, only if they have been clearly stated, recorded, and constantly monitored.

RECORDING PLANNING ASSUMPTIONS

When school environments were more stable or predictable, it was all right to generate single projections or planning assumptions to be used in the budgetary process in public education. However, rapidly changing times and conditions have produced a requirement for multiple projections. Several descriptions of the future provide more information for planning purposes.

The instrument used to record planning assumptions is a scenario. More specifically, a scenario is a description of a possible or probable future. The word is usually used in the plural; scenarios depict various possibilities for the future.

There are basically three types of scenarios:

1. Individual: This type of scenario usually depicts a single set of assumptions about a general subject or multiple subjects.
2. Multiple: This type of scenario describes ranges of the future or alternative future possibilities.

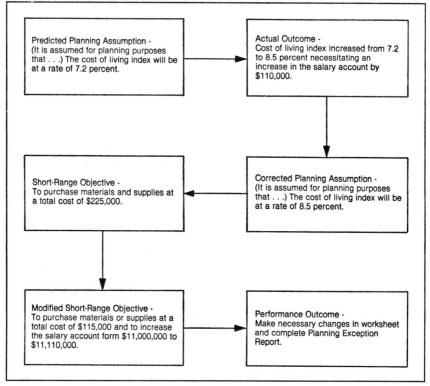

Figure 5–2 *The Sequence for Stating and Tracking Planning Assumptions*

3. Specialized: This scenario identifies a set of planning assumptions for a specialized subject area such as "legislation that might affect public education."

Scenarios are intended to:

• Increase planning unit administrators' awareness of the future to avoid surprises.
• Serve as a springboard for reverting to an alternate plan if the original plan becomes invalid.
• Be used by a team to study and comprehend the future to plan more effectively.

An example of a form used to record multiple planning assumptions is on page 336 of the Appendix. A single topic can be given one of three probabilities. By examining each probability, the planning unit administrator can decide whether he or she should make plans based upon the most probable, pessimistic, or optimistic forecast. It is possible for plans to be devised using the most probable forecast for one item and pessimistic forecast for another item. It depends entirely on the administrator's best judgment at a given point in time.

Scenarios can be developed for a host of subjects or themes; in fact, any subject that can have an impact on the school district can be used to develop a scenario. However, scenarios are usually used for specialized subjects, such as in the following cases:

1. The effects of the classification system of the state department of education on the school district.
2. The increasing rate of staff illness absenteeism.
3. The availability of needed staff members.
4. The effects of public education on the outcome of the governor's election.
5. The costs for duplicating documents in the school districts.
6. Social changes in the school district.

Scenarios can be constructed using any one of the following groups of probabilities:

- Most probable—Pessimistic—Optimistic
- Good—Bad
- 50 percent probability—70 percent probability—100 percent probability
- Best guess—Optimistic—Pessimistic
- Most likely—Higher—Lower

WHO SHOULD DEVELOP SCENARIOS

Development of scenarios is usually the responsibility of the central planning unit. However, the following methods can be used to prepare scenarios:

1. Special task force.
2. Environmental study team.
3. Team of experts or consultants in a specialized area.
4. An administrator who is assigned to interrogate knowledgeable persons for the purpose of developing scenarios.
5. Environmental observer or analyst.
6. Other side organizations.
7. Department for forecasting.
8. Research and evaluation division.
9. *Ad hoc* committee.

PREPARING SCENARIOS

The process for developing scenarios is similar to that for preparing planning assumptions; however, there are some essential differences. Basically, there are five steps involved:

1. Conduct the critical analysis as prescribed in this book.
2. Select critical indicators by analyzing what environmental factors will have a major impact on the school district and determine key indicators from these factors. A committee can be established to assist in evaluating the future of the school district.
3. Establish a base for each indicator. Analyze the reason for the past performance, and prepare the Delphi instrument to be used by the committee.
4. Activate the Delphi panel. Have the panel do the following:
   a. Assess past performance and trends.
   b. Assess the potential impact probability of trends on school districts.
   c. Project the future event.
   When this analytical process has been completed, prepare planning assumptions for each indicator based upon a documented and sound rationale.
5. Prepare the scenarios using three probabilities.

IMPORTANT POINTS TO CONSIDER WHEN PREPARING PLANNING ASSUMPTIONS

The following represent some crucial points to remember whenever planning assumptions are developed.

Planning assumptions:

1. Are dynamic variables and as such are subject to change.
2. Should be developed for long- and short-range plans.
3. Should be prepared by those at the central planning unit level.
4. Whenever possible, should be developed using the worksheet approach.
5. Should be disseminated and discussed with those responsible for planning.
6. Should be changed when conditions warrant and appropriate adjustments should be made in the plans.
7. Are required to be prepared prior to the preparation of the school budget.
8. Should be prepared with meticulous care by each planning unit administrator, with the help of supervisors, and then re-

vised, modified, and completed by central planning administrators and finally submitted for scrutiny and approval to the board of education.

9. Necessarily have some shortcomings, but the shortcomings are very slight compared with the advantages they offer.
10. Suppress and reduce hesitation, false steps, and unwarranted changes of action, and help to improve personnel performance.
11. Should be disseminated with care, particularly if they contain sensitive information regarding other persons and/or organizations.

SALIENT POINTS

When planning assumptions are prepared for the first time, they will require a great deal of hard work and a considerable amount of time. However, each repetition will make the task easier. Soon the formulation of planning assumptions will become habit-forming, reducing the amount of work and time involved. When this element of the strategic or operational planning process becomes a way of life in a school district, it will be received with increasing interest and usefulness because of the attention necessarily given to the planning for the future, the need to make a comparison between predicted and actual facts, and the quest for improving predictions about numerous events and variables that will have a significant impact on performance.

The more planning assumptions are used, the more interest is generated by planning unit administrators. This heightened interest is not due solely to the use of planning assumptions, but to an effective managerial system. A well-thought-out plan can rarely be achieved without a sound organizational framework, policies, procedures, coordination, and controls. Formulating and effectively using planning assumptions can exert a positive influence on the practice of school management either in planning or the budgeting process. Planning assumptions tend to be needed most during difficult moments. Although they cannot anticipate all the unexpected occurrences that may arise, they can be used as a red flag to trigger positive actions in order to concentrate maximum possible intellectual ability and resources on the negative event or variable and to correct unwarranted changes in the school-community environment.

APPLICATION STRATEGY 5

Interview a school superintendent to determine if there is a sensitive or critical issue or topic that, if predicted with some degree of accuracy, could aid the school district in planning. Gather as much information as possible about the subject through interviews, receiving internal documents, and performing additional research in the library, if necessary. Prepare a scenario using three probabilities: (1) most likely; (2) higher; and (3) lower. Review the completed product with the superintendent. Revisit the superintendent after an allowance has been made for the conditions to be realized. Determine the extent to which the scenario was on target.

6

SELECTING PROGRAM STRATEGIES

The previous chapters dealt with the concept and techniques of strategic planning. They provided excellent background, but will be of little value unless planning unit administrators learn systematically and comprehensively to think through the planning process, anticipating change and determining what alternative strategies are available to them for making sound decisions to fulfill the mission of the school district. When strategic planning is understood and applied effectively, planning unit administrators will be managing by strategies, a step beyond management by objectives.

This chapter has been written to provide a disciplined, sequential, and integrated approach to preparing and analyzing program strategies. A program strategy is defined to begin the chapter. The differences between strategies and tactics are explained. A brief discussion of the various approaches to planning strategy is undertaken. Also included are the types of program strategies. Considerable attention is given to the process of strategic thinking. Several approaches to making strategies are explained and classified. A form that facilitates this process is illustrated. The chapter ends by evaluating program strategies, and offers some concluding remarks on the causes of ineffectual strategies.

DEFINING STRATEGY

A strategy is a statement describing how a school organization intends to utilize its resources and skills to capitalize on its strengths, correct its weaknesses, and change threats into opportunities for the improvement of the overall educational process. A strategy is both an art and a science. As an *art*, it means that planning unit administrators must gather and evaluate information for making judgments. As a *science*, it means that a systematic process must be developed and employed for formalizing plans. In addition, a strategy involves weighting information, considering both the internal and external environments, to maximize resources for educational gains.

The process by which a strategy is formulated is strategic thinking. It is the most important aspect of the strategic planning process, and will require rigorous experimentation; questioning of old methods; exploring unfamiliar environments; confronting strengths, weaknesses, opportunities, and threats; encouraging change; and accepting uncertainties.

UNDERSTANDING THE DIFFERENCES BETWEEN STRATEGIES AND TACTICS

Strategies usually refers to long-range activities that attempt to realize a long-range goal. *Tactics* refers to the use of short-range activity to achieve a short-range objective. In general, a strategy describes the appropriate action to take to achieve a given end, and a tactic is performing the appropriate action.

UNDERSTANDING THE THREE APPROACHES TO FORMING STRATEGIES

There are basically three approaches to developing strategies. The particular approach to be used at a given time depends on the problems, strengths, and weaknesses of the school district and the extent to which the superintendent is willing to assume risk. The risk for implementing a proactive strategy is greater than for implementing either the reactive or emulative, and the risk for installing a reactive strategy is greater than for installing the emulative strategy.

Successful school districts are not reluctant to effect changes through proper strategy. The contemporary school district does not wait for things to happen. By assuming a proactive or emulative strategic policy, it makes things happen.

The proactive strategy approach is the process by which a school district is first to implement an innovation in order to improve performance results.

Item
A successful example of a proactive strategy approach was performed by the Philadelphia Public School District in the late 1960s,

when it implemented the "schools without walls" concept. This approach was initiated in an effort to make school more meaningful to students, and proved highly suffessful. Within a matter of years, school districts, colleges, and universities began to duplicate this concept.

The emulation strategy is the process by which a school district will utilize an existing innovation in order to improve performance results.

Item
When the Melborne (Florida) School District adopted the nongraded philosophy and implemented learning activity packages (LAP) to replace the standard basic textbooks, thousands of school districts throughout the United States became interested in LAPs and sent for and used, quite often unaltered, the same LAPs. This was a form of an emulation strategy approach used by these school districts.

The reactive strategy approach is the process by which a school district acts in response to some outside stimulus to improve performance results.

Item
An example of a reactive strategy approach occurred when the best-seller, *Crisis in American Education,* exposed the inhumanity that existed in many school districts across the nation and described the open education concept fostered in the schools in England. As a result, school districts by the hundreds began to investigate, develop, and adopt their own version of open education. Thus, the open education movement was put into motion with a reactive strategy approach that had an impact on American public education.

TYPES OF PLANNING STRATEGIES

There is no uniformity in the types of planning strategies used in the strategic thinking process. However, the major key result areas cited in chapter 4 reveal the following planning strategies:

- Financial strategies should include such areas as the sale or disposition of unusable buildings; acquiring local, state, and federal grants; school budget; expenditure on facilities; interest income investment; and financing special projects.
- Personnel strategies should involve union relations, perfor-

mance appraisal, training and development, recruitment and hiring of personnel, salary, and fringe benefits.

- Administrative strategies should embrace centralization and decentralization, job enrichment opportunities, organizational structure, administrative style, and organizational development.
- Student strategies should include such items as intellectual, physical, and social growth; school enrichment opportunities; college enrollments; and dropout rate.
- Innovative strategies might include such things as new instructional materials, new teaching techniques, grouping, creative staffing patterns, and unique instructional programs.
- Community strategies would include such items as public relations, marketing of services, position of school district on public policy issues (such as desegregation), and posture on community school concepts.
- Instructional program strategies might involve instructional services, program revisions and modification, program evaluation, and program obsolescence.

APPLYING THE STRATEGIC THINKING PROCESS

A number of approaches can be used to apply the strategic thinking process for formulating program strategies. Regardless of the technique, the process must link the critical analysis of intuition and analytical judgment considering all factors to arrive at the most appropriate program strategy.

The approaches that appear below should be considered when a decision is being made as to how administrators should formulate strategy during the planning process. At times, it may be more desirable to use two or more different approaches or a variation on them. For example, the planning unit administrator may favor the investigative approach for analyzing the competition and the planagement approach for critically reviewing the instructional program. The approach to be used with a particular variable or factor will depend on the judgment of the planning unit administrator or the dictates of the superintendent of schools.

.GUIDELINE APPROACH

The guideline approach for selecting program strategies is based on a carefully constructed instrument used to analyze several alternatives and make a quantitative and qualitative decision as to which one is the most appropriate to reach the related long-range goal as illustrated on page 302 of the Appendix. The following sections are included in the instrument:

1. List the *major key result area* that is going to be affected by this strategy.
2. Indicate the *long-range goal* for which program strategies will be formulated.
3. Indicate here whether the *strategy* will be the result of an existing innovation, a new innovation, or an improvement on an existing innovation.
4. *Analyze all of the possible strategies* that will help to achieve the long-range goal. This is the most time-consuming portion of the guide and the most important.

Use the following guide to complete the analytical section of the guide:

Alternative Strategies: Indicate all possible alternative strategies before proceeding with the other column. At times, it may be appropriate to request assistance from other staff members.

Cost: Project a cost for each strategy.

Maximizing Strength: Indicate (high, medium, or low) the extent to which a strength of the planning unit is being utilized.

Minimizing Weakness: Indicate (high, medium, or low) the extent to which a weakness of the school organization is being avoided.

Remedy Threat: Say (yes or no) whether a possible threat is being turned into an opportunity.

Stakeholder Expectation: Indicate (yes or no) whether an expectation of a stakeholder will be met by this particular strategy.

Respond to Competition: Indicate (yes or no) whether this particular strategy considers the competition.

Impact: Describe (high, medium, or low) the impact this particular strategy will have on the attainment of the long-range goal.

5. Describe clearly and completely the *most appropriate program strategy* that will achieve the long-range goal.
6. *Compare the long-range goal and program strategy.* Determine if the program strategy will truly achieve the long-range goal. If either is unacceptable, change the long-range goal, or formulate an additional strategy.
7. *Implement the strategy.*
   a. Indicate who is responsible for executing the various steps of the program strategy.
   b. Indicate when the program will be launched.

  c. Describe what support services will be required.
  d. Identify the key tasks that need to be performed for the strategy to be implemented.

PLANAGEMENT APPROACH

The planagement approach is a product of Robert M. Randolph.[1] Planagement is "a process that integrates the art and science of converting a concept into reality through the rise of a practical method."

Planagement, when applied to strategic thinking, is the determining of a program strategy by the collection and analysis of pertinent information about a situation and the making of a judgment as to what course of action should be taken to fulfill the mission of the school district.

Basically, the planagement approach has four elements:

1. Collect and analyze all appropriate facts about a given issue to define the situation or problem.
2. Apply analytical rigor, intuition, and judgment to formulate planning assumptions and to establish a base.
3. Make a decision as to what should be accomplished and by when by setting a long-range goal.
4. Develop the program strategy using item 3 as a base and indicate the general direction that will be used to reach the long-range goal.

The following example of a process for arriving at a program strategy uses the planagement approach as a guide.

1. *Key Result Area:* Financial resources.
2. *Present Situation:* A large number of young couples are leaving the community. The school budget is increasing at an average rate of 12 percent per year.
3. *Predicted Situation:* The taxpayers, many of whom will be senior citizens with no children in the schools, will eventually balk at the school taxes and reject the budget.
4. *Recommended Course of Action:* The school district will reduce the average increase in the school tax rate by at least 25 percent over the next two years.
5. *Recommended Program Strategy:* The strategic emphasis will be to implement zero-base budgeting over the next three years by ranking

---

[1] Robert M. Randolph, *Planagement—Moving Concept into Reality* (New York: AMACOM, 1975).

programs by priority and determining different levels of efforts of performing the same function, as well as different ways of funding the same function. We should be able to halt the spiraling tax rate and, in some instances, reduce certain objects of expenditure.

6. *Rejected Program Strategy and Basis for Rejection:*
   a. Install PPBS: too time-consuming and will not guarantee the budget increase will be halted.
   b. Reduce the number of elective courses from 104 to a reasonable level of 45: this may not in itself bring on a substantial reduction; problems with teacher union.
   c. Close down one elementary school: community problems are too great and enrollment figures do not substantiate the need.

SWOP APPROACH

The swop approach to formulating strategy is the process of identifying either strengths and weaknesses or problems and opportunities of a given condition to arrive at a long-range goal and program strategy. The program strategy should be designed to maximize strengths, avoid weaknesses, and turn problems into opportunities.

Key Result Area: Performance Evaluation and Training
Strengths/Opportunities:
- Teachers are highly receptive to attending in-service courses.
- School districts grant teachers in-service credits for engaging in selective training and development activities.
- An allocation is set aside in the budget to support in-service programs.
- Ninety percent of the staff have made use of the services of the Education Regional Services Center.
- Superintendent is a strong advocate of in-service education.

Weaknesses/Problems:
- Staff evaluation is not dovetailed to the training component.
- An insufficient appropriation is included in the budget for in-service education.
- School district failed to take full advantage of the Education Regional Services Center long-term agreement program.

Program Strategy:
Strategy to improve the training component of the school district will be based on: (1) extensive use of the long-term training agreement with the local Education Regional Services Center (needs to be decided by a committee of teachers, supervisors, and adminis-

trators); (2) an increase in the school budget for training and development amounting to no less than 3 percent of the total budget; and (3) releasing students from school one Friday per month to support in-service programs, as well as to conduct extensive training services with a stipend during the summer months in critical need areas and for certain teachers.

INVESTIGATIVE APPROACH

The investigative approach to formulating strategy is credited to William E. Rothschild[2] and is ideal for investigating either the resources of the school organization or of others. This approach involves three steps:

Investigate Past Results

This step may involve either an examination of the results of the school district, which in this case would mean reviewing items such as academic achievement results, cost to educate students, recipients of honors and awards, number of students entering college, and the like; or obtaining this same data on other organizations or agencies that may have an impact on the school district. Information on others may not be accessible to school personnel. If this is the case, administrators will have to do some digging for information about the past results of other entities affecting the school district. Basically, this step is an attempt to secure as much information as possible about the track record of either the school districts or others. A review of the following can be useful for obtaining past results of others:

1. Academic achievement profile.
2. Budget.
3. Newspapers.
4. Bulletins.
5. Newsletters.
6. Memos.
7. Plans.
8. Informal Discussion.
9. Interrogation Sessions.
10. Clandestine Sessions.

Reconstruct Successful Strategy

This step is based upon the author's success emulation theory: by obtaining as much information as possible about what made the orga-

[2] William E. Rothschild, *Putting It All Together: A Guide to Strategic Thinking* (New York: AMACOM, 1976).

nization successful in delivering services and/or products and by providing those services and/or products with appropriate modifications success is more or less guaranteed. To do this, the successful strategies must be reconstructed and studied. These strategies will include an examination of the investment in the overall organization, how well the organization is managed, and which operations made for success. These operations should cover the creative capacity of the organization, how the services and/or products are marketed, financial position of the organization, and the capabilities of the administrators.

The following represents an example of the reconstruction of a successful strategy of a private school, which was made so that a public school district could gain a competitive edge over the private school.

Competition: Nova Private School

Management Strategy: Highly structured educational programs offered by the school.

Finance Strategy: School budget is within plus or minus 10 percent of the budgets of all public schools within a 75-mile radius.

Creativity: The school has a modern building, offers the basic, as well as enrichment, subjects, uses a variety of educational technology, maintains a strict discipline code, and incorporates at least six unique school-wide programs per year, such as the young authors' conference and artists-in-residence.

Achievement: The school feeds into the Bishop (private) and Beta (public) high schools. About 90 percent of their students enter college after graduation. Their students rank in the eightieth percentile in math and the eighty-fourth percentile in reading on the Standard Achievement Test. A three-hour remedial program is offered to students after school, and late transportation is needed for students to make use of the program.

Market: A highly impressive orientation program is conducted for all parents of prospective students. A multicolor brochure on all facets of the school is available and disseminated to all real estate brokers within and without the community. It does not tolerate discipline problems, and students displaying serious disruptive behavior are quickly expelled. During parent-teacher meetings, which are held quarterly, 90 percent of the parents are in attendance.

Finance: The school spends $2,750 per student. It hires only teachers with Master's degrees. Financing of the school is through church contributions, which account for 35 percent of the total revenue, and tuition of $2,500 per student.

Administrator's Capabilities: The schoolmaster has ten years of experience. He received his B.A. from Stanford, his M.S. from Temple, and Ph.D. from Harvard. He is adored by parents, teachers, and students.

Assess Human and Nonhuman Resources

Assessing another organization's resources is a very difficult task. It may mean that some assumptions may have to be formulated, and a system will have to be established to monitor the assumptions to determine whether or not they are valid. Regardless of the approach used, the information obtained should be preserved after plans have been prepared, so that the plans may be updated annually or when conditions warrant.

Item
A clandestine activity is not an illegal activity. It means that an attempt is made by a person to obtain information about an organization by failing to disclose the full reasons for gathering the information. It does not mean telling lies, breaking and entering, or doing anything against the law. In one school district that was reconstructing the successful strategy of a private school, a parent actually attended an orientation session for parents. This same parent subsequently related to the planning committee that the highly professional and comprehensive manner in which the administrator conducted her presentation was extremely impressive, in fact, so impressive that it was a wonder that the public schools had any enrollment. In another school district, a group of parents contacted the parents sending their children to private schools and made telephone calls interrogating these parents as to what the private schools offered that the public schools did not. These comments were recorded, analyzed, and used for planning purposes.

RANKING ALTERNATIVE STRATEGIES

One useful method for ranking program strategies is to assign a weight from 1 to 5 to each of the columns under item 4. For example, project cost might be given 5 points, maximizing strength 4 points, minimizing weakness 5 points, and so on. When the analytical process has been completed, each horizontal column should be added for each program strategy, and the result should be inserted in the "Total" column. Ranking the strategies by the number of points received establishes priorities.

Even though program strategies may be ranked by quantitative value, the author seriously recommends that a qualitative decision be made considering all possible implications and ramifications for those program strategies that were ranked high, but were not selected. The most preferred program strategies may not be ranked the highest.

WHY SOME PROGRAM STRATEGIES FAIL

There are a host of reasons program strategies fail to produce the desired results. The following are some of the most salient.

Failing to Respond to Major Stakeholder Expectations

Perhaps one of the most serious flaws in conventional long-range planning in education is that administrators fail to consider seriously stakeholders' expectations when developing and implementing plans. How many times has the superintendent presented neatly packaged plans to the board of education for consideration only to be rejected because a powerful community group had other expectations? However, by identifying the major stakeholders in the community, analyzing their attitudes and expectations, and establishing goals and objectives to satisfy their needs, wasted time and personnel anguish can be avoided or at least minimized. School administrators must make every attempt to change a potential enemy into an ally. Even when a school building is going to be closed, the strategic-minded administrator can reduce the impact on the community by planning to meet trouble before trouble meets the school district.

Failing to Consider the Competition

A few years ago, competition was only a problem for urban school districts. The enrollment in private schools was rising at the expense of public schools. However today, even in the best suburban areas, private schools are competing with public schools and in many instances are winning the battle by offering additional educational programs and services, marketing their services effectively, and realizing the need to gain the competitive edge through a host of activities.

The serious planning unit administrator must improve the strategic thinking process and identify threats. The first step toward the solution of a problem is the recognition that one exists. At this point strategic plans can be developed to change threats into opportunities for growth and prosperity.

Failing to Identify Planning Assumptions

Very few school districts forecast or try to predict the future. As a result, most long-range plans are established as though the future were going to be like the present. If the future is not considered it is better not to plan than to plan, because the futility of the latter will only frustrate those who are making decisions.

Even when planning assumptions have been used, such as in the Washington, D.C., Public Schools, they tend to have been of the controlled type or aimed directly at the internal environment. It is more likely that change will occur externally than internally. If planning assumptions covering the external environment are not identified, the planning process will have a serious defect.

Failing to Profit From the Past

The "blame the kids" syndrome seems to affect tens of thousands of school administrators and teachers each year. Every year, the same ineffectual teachers continue to get the same poor results from students. Rather than critically analyze the reasons for their failures, they take the easy way out and blame the children for coming from poor families or impoverished communities. They fail to realize the changing times have produced different students. They fail to understand that although they may have been successful in the past with a predominantly white student body, they may not have the same success with a predominantly black or hispanic class. They fail to realize that during the 1960s, the life span of the education degree was approximately ten years. Today, the life span of that same degree is about five years. They fail to understand that, unless they stay abreast of changing techniques and methodologies in education, they will gradually become obsolete. They fail to understand all of these ramifications in public education because they have failed to profit from the past.

Planning for Too Much Too Soon

One of the prevailing initial problems in education, when a new program is being implemented, is that school administrators do too much too soon. Such is also true of the planning process. Strategic planning is too complex to be implemented over night. It will probably take a full five years before the process is fully implemented and accepted. Therefore, the wise planning unit administrator should install the concept piecemeal first, then with several more planning units, and finally district-wide. In this way, problems, which are bound to emerge at the onset, can be accommodated with less trouble than if they encompassed the entire school district. By implementing the process in this manner, the planning unit administrator can use trial-and-error to resolve problems. One school district began the long-range planning process by concentrating first on the personnel department, and after two years of experimenting with this area, expanded the program to include three other critical areas of the school district.

Mismatching Human Resources and Strategies

Another prevailing problem in public education is that teachers are being requested to introduce new programs and techniques without being properly trained. The improvement strategies are mismatched with the teachers because of improper training. Whenever a strategy is being considered, an analysis of the resources should be conducted to determine the extent to which training is needed for the strategy to succeed.

EVALUATING PROGRAM STRATEGIES

George A. Steiner has produced an analytical tool for evaluating strategies that consists of a number of thought-provoking questions. The questions, which are listed under Figure 6–1, have been modified to be pertinent to education.[3] In addition, two columns headed with "Yes" and "No" have been added so that the planner can keep a tally of the results when evaluating planning strategies. Some questions may not be appropriate with certain kinds of strategies. It therefore behooves the planner to give a weight to each question. An effective way to use the list is to review each negative response and make a judgment as to the seriousness of the omission.

SALIENT POINTS

The process for developing a program strategy can be summarized in the following steps:

1. Science: Collect the essential and critical facts about the school organization and analyze, synthesize, and evaluate them to arrive at an accurate assessment.
2. Art: Apply analytical rigor, intuition, and judgment to the facts to arrive at a base of facts and to formulate appropriate planning assumptions.
3. Decision: Identify what needs to be accomplished to fulfill the mission using items 1 and 2 above, by establishing long-range goals.
4. Strategy: Formulate and describe program strategies, and select the most appropriate one to attain the long-range goals.
5. Action Program and Budget: Develop an operational plan and budget to achieve the long-range goal.

[3] Reprinted with the permission of Macmillan Publishing Co., Inc. from *Strategic Planning—What Every Manager Must Know* by George A. Steiner. Copyright © 1979 by The Free Press, a Division of Macmillan Publishing Co., Inc.

Evaluating Program Strategies

Planning Unit: _____   Date:_____

Planning Unit Administrator: _____   Page _____ of _____

The following instrument has been devised using George A. Steiner's thirty-nine questions for evaluating program strategies. Read each question carefully and indicate the appropriate response. Some program strategies may only pertain to certain questions. The main thrust of this instrument is to raise the proper questions so that decisions can be made as to the strengths or weaknesses in program strategies.

A. Is the Strategy Consistent with the Environments?   YES   NO
  1. Is the strategy consistent with the environments of the school organization? ☐ ☐
  2. Is the strategy acceptable to the board of education? ☐ ☐
  3. Is there an honest and accurate appraisal of the competition? Is the competition being underestimated? ☐ ☐
  4. Is it possible that other federal government agencies will prevent the school organization from achieving the objectives sought by the strategy? ☐ ☐
  5. Is the strategy legal and in conformance with moral and ethical codes of conduct applicable to the school organization? ☐ ☐

B. Is the Strategy Consistent with Board Policies, Styles of Management, Philosophy, and Operating Procedures?
  6. Is the strategy identifiable and understood by all those in the school organization with a need to know? ☐ ☐
  7. Is the strategy consistent with the internal strengths, objectives, and policies of the school organization? ☐ ☐
  8. Is the strategy under evaluation divided into substrategies that interrelate properly? ☐ ☐
  9. Does the strategy under review conflict with other strategies in the school organization? ☐ ☐
  10. Does the strategy exploit strengths and avoid major weaknesses? ☐ ☐
  11. Is the organizational structure consistent with the strategy? ☐ ☐
  12. Is the strategy consistent with the values of the superintendent and other key people in the school organization? ☐ ☐

C. Is the Strategy Appropriate in Light of the Resources:

Finance
  13. Do you have sufficient funds or can you get them, to see the strategy through to successful implementation? ☐ ☐
  14. What will be the financial consequences associated with the allocation of funds to this strategy? What other projects may be denied funding? Are the financial substrategies associated with this funding acceptable? ☐ ☐

Physical Plant
  15. Is the strategy appropriate with respect to existing and prospective physical plants? ☐ ☐

Managerial Resources
  16. Are there identifiable available and committed administrators to implement the strategy? ☐ ☐

Figure 6–1 *Analytical Tips for Evaluating Strategies*

APPLICATION STRATEGY 6

Develop a form for facilitating and expediting the construction of program strategies. Make certain this form has all of the information essential to prepare a comprehensive program strategy. Before proceeding with this application strategy, the reader may wish to digest the following books or chapters: William E. Rothschild, *Putting It All Together—A*

D. Are the Risks in Pursuing the Strategy Acceptable?

	YES	NO
17. Are the superintendent and other administrators willing to bear specific risks, etc.?		
18. Does the strategy balance the acceptance of minimum risk with the maximum potential consistent with school organization resources?		
19. Do you have too much funds and human resources tied into this strategy?		

E. Does the Strategy Require the Production of Materials?

20. Is the school rushing an innovation?		
21. Does the strategy involve the production of a new product for a new program? If so, have you really assessed the requirements to implement successfully?		

F. Is the Timing of Proposed Implementation Correct?

22. Is the timing of implementation appropriate in light of what is known?		

G. Are There Other Important Considerations?

23. Overall, can the strategy be implemented in an efficient and effective fashion?		
24. Have you tried to identify the major forces inside and outside the organization that will be most influential in ensuring the success of the strategy and/or in raising problems of implementation? Have you given them the proper evaluation?		
25. Are the assumptions realistic upon which the strategy is based?		
26. Has the strategy been tested with appropriate criteria such as consistency with past, present, and prospective practices?		
27. Aside from the above questions, are there any others that are pertinent to an evaluation of this strategy?		

Figure 6-1 *(continued)*

Guide to Strategic Thinking (New York: American Management Association, 1979); George A. Steiner, *Strategic Planning—What Every Manager Must Know* (New York: The Free Press, 1979), pp. 175–197; and William C. Giegold, *"MBO—Volume I, Strategic Planning and the MBO Process* (New York: McGraw-Hill Book Co., 1978), pp. 117–136.

Next, prepare appropriate program strategies for each long-range goal developed in Application Strategy 5, using the form constructed above.

7

DEVELOPING OPERATIONAL PLANS

When all of the internal and external variables that may affect the school district have been critically examined, and when strategies have been formulated, the school district is ready to engage in operational planning. Operational planning is the process of reaching long-range goals through a succession of systematic plans devised and revised over a period of a year. These plans are the basis for activating and motivating human efforts to increase the probability that short-range thrusts will eventually reach the point where the educational goals and mission of the school district are realized.

The rationale for this chapter is to describe the process for developing operational plans. Preparing operational plans using the concept of management by objectives is discussed and defined, and its benefits are explained. The management-by-objective cycle is also briefly discussed, and some attention is given to maintaining valid operational plans. Several approaches or formats are presented for constructing operational plans. The reader is introduced to an organizational ailment, called the AT disease by this author and referred to by George Odiorne as the activity trap. The chapter closes by making a distinction between strategic and operational planning.

PREPARING OPERATIONAL PLANS USING MANAGEMENT BY OBJECTIVES

In strategic planning, management by strategy is the basis for implementing the long-range planning process. In operational planning, management by objectives is the most appropriate approach to installing the short-range planning process.

DEFINING MANAGEMENT BY OBJECTIVES

Management by objectives is a participatory process in which the planner and planning unit administrator agree on short-range objectives to reach long-range goals, performance standards to use as guidelines for assessing performance, and action plans to steer and direct human efforts to attain the short-range objectives.

BENEFITS OF MANAGEMENT BY OBJECTIVES

Management by objectives helps to eliminate many of the problems usually associated with managing human resources. The traditional definition of management was "to get things done through people." Now that management by strategies and objectives that stress participatory decision-making processes has emerged, it is more appropriate to redefine management as "getting things done with people." The term "with" is substituted for "through" because it more appropriately describes the process of team work as well as a democratic process. Both of these procedures denote team membership and working together for a common purpose.

Some specific benefits of management by objectives are:

1. Performance is measured in terms of concrete results rather than by personality.
2. It provides a means to monitor performance results and to take corrective action, if necessary.
3. It provides the means to carry out the strategies selected in the strategic planning process.
4. It is an excellent method to identify expectations of the planner and planning unit administrator.
5. It is a means to evaluate both the achievement of the short-range objective toward the attainment of long-range goals and the achievement of individual efforts.

IMPLEMENTING THE SYSTEM

Figure 7–1 identifies the operational planning process or the management by objective cycle. The cycle begins with the strategies selected during the strategic planning process. The strategies are used as guidelines for establishing short-range objectives to reach long-range goals. Each component of the cycle is fully explained in subsequent chapters of this book.

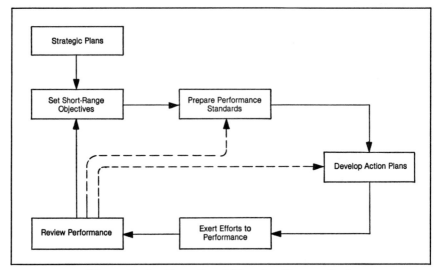

Figure 7–1 *Operational Planning Process Cycle*

1. Set short-range objectives. A sufficient number of short-range objectives are set to implement the selected strategies. All short-range objectives are developed in accordance with the instructions in this book.
2. Prepare performance standards. Once short-range objectives are set, some criteria must be developed in order to assess the degree to which short-range objectives are being achieved.
3. Develop action plans. Most planning unit administrators require that action plans be developed to achieve short-range objectives.
4. Exert performance. Once the first, second, and third phases of the cycle have been completed, efforts should be exerted to attain the short-range objectives.
5. Review performance. The planner and planning unit administrator should meet periodically to discuss progress toward short-range objectives. How frequently the parties should meet is predicated on the system itself, the needs, short-range objectives, and other factors dictated by the planning unit. If performance is found to be outside acceptable limits, the short-range objective, performance standards, and/or action plan should be analyzed to determine if changes are in order. The year-end results are the basis for reviewing long-range goals and re-evaluating the selected strategies. Appropriate adjustments are made as necessary to ensure the attainment of long-range goals.

MAINTAINING VALID OPERATIONAL PLANS

Operational plans are valid only if they meet the following conditions:

1. Plans must contain short-range objectives, performance standards, and activities designed to carry out the strategy arrived at through the strategic planning process.
2. Plans have been agreed to by the planning unit administrator and supervisor.
3. An agreement has been reached between the planning unit administrator and staff as to what the former can do, should do differently, or must stop doing to help the latter to achieve its goals.
4. An agreement has been reached with others outside the planning unit, holding them responsible for achieving specific activities denoted in the plan.
5. A quarterly progress review program has been developed and implemented.
6. Plans are used as the basis for applying appropriate motivational theories in order to obtain improved performance.
7. Plans are used to monitor and control performance so that if projected plans are not going to be achieved as expected, corrective actions can be determined, appropriately recorded, and taken.
8. Results of operational plans are used as the basis for updating strategic plans.
9. Plans are used to appraise individual performance results.

PREPARING OPERATIONAL PLANS

Operational plans identify the specifics of selected strategies. Although the instructions for arriving at strategies may be imprecise, the format makes the plans relatively easy to identify and to complete. Several different structural formats have been used to record operational plans; however, most of them require the following essential information:

- Description of major key result area.
- Description of program.
- Short-range objective.
- Performance standard.
- Plan of action.
- Assignment of responsibility.
- Cost.

Other items sometimes found in operational plans are:

- Cost/budget analysis.
- Coordination required from others.
- Priority of program.

The approach used to record the operational plan will depend on the expectations and needs of the school district. There are two approaches for preparing operational plans.

The Multiple Plan Approach

The multiple plan approach is the process of recording all short-range objectives with their accompanied performance standards and action plans within a single plan. One advantage of using this approach is that all of the planning unit's short-range plans are contained under a single cover. A disadvantage is that the plan may become too cumbersome, depending on the amount of paperwork generated.

The Single Plan Approach

The single plan approach is the process of recording short-range objectives with their accompanying performance standards and action plans for one major key result area under a single plan. Therefore, a plan may be prepared for programs and services, staff evaluation, organizational management, and the like. A distinct advantage of this approach is manageability. Separate plans for each major key result area are easy to keep track of because of the limitation of paper work for individual plans. Another advantage of the single plan approach is that individual plans can be sorted like decision packages in zero-base budgeting and ranked for decision-making purposes. The disadvantage of using this approach is that it may produce more paperwork than the multiple approach when all of the single plans have been consolidated. An example of the single plan approach is found on page 328 of the Appendix.

THE ACTIVITY TRAP

Although the main objective of operational plans is to guide and direct human efforts so that concrete results can be produced, in many instances this objective has not been realized. There is probably one reason for this, as described by George Odiorne:

> It is the abysmal situation people find themselves in when they start out for what once was an important and clear objective; then became

so enmeshed in the activity of getting there that they forgot where they were going . . . everyone got busy, engaging in activity designed to carry the organization toward its objectives. But once-clear objectives may evolve into something else. The objective moves, but the activity persists and becomes a false objective. This false objective becomes the extension for making decisions, and the decisions get progressively worse.[1]

The operational plan can help prevent the activity trap, referred to here as the AT disease, from infecting staff members: superintendents of schools, planning unit administrators, teachers, and others. Therefore, what is needed is a concentrated effort made by persons in high administrative positions to explain the disease's symptoms to the staff, and to take precautionary measures to immunize staff members against the AT disease by effectively developing, implementing, and evaluating operational plans to attain concrete results.

Item
The AT disease seems to manifest itself in sizable organizations, such as large school districts, state departments of education, higher educational institutions, and various governmental agencies. Smaller organizations, however, have been known to have contracted this job-related ailment. The degree of affliction tends to worsen as it travels up the organization level, that is, the infected persons in high positions have a tendency to spread the disease by employing AT victims or those who are likely to become victims. The disease tends to gravitate toward maintenance seekers, whose disposition, personality, and nonthreatening characters tend to perpetuate AT dilemmas. Those who are immune, the goal seekers and high achievers, are seldom hired, or if hired, soon become outcasts. The more competent and achievement-oriented a person is, the more he or she is seen as a threat to the manifestation of the disease and to the organization. As the organization gravitates toward a quarantine level of infestation, the pseudo-achievement-oriented persons succumb to the disease, while the authentic goal seekers are usually deposed from the organization.

The AT disease is reaching epidemic proportions, as evidenced by the yearly decrease in the nation's employee productivity rate. Unless responsible administrators and managers detect and implement creative remedies, the nation is doomed to become a second-class one, crippled by a disease just as devastating as cancer.

[1] From *MBO II: A System of Managerial Leadership for the 80's* by George S. Odiorne. Copyright © 1979 by Fearon-Pitman Publishers, Inc., 6 Davis Drive, Belmont, CA 94002. Reprinted by permission.

Odiorne identifies some side effects of the AT disease:

1. The victims diminish in capacity rather than grow.
2. The victims kill the motivation of employees.
3. The victims seldom face reality and will avoid it if they can.
4. The victims are comfortable living with ambiguity.
5. The victims usually resist information that might help to change a situation.
6. The victims fail to solve most problems and in some instances the problems become worse.[2]

The operational planning that results from the activity trap generally necessitates a great deal of paperwork. Those afflicted by the AT diseased victims are usually affected in the planning process as follows:

1. Forced to perform work on the planning process that is not actually required.
2. Required to produce plans that are seldom referred to.
3. Confronted with inconsistencies that usually lead to frustration and waste of valuable time.
4. Required to respond to problems in a reactive mode.
5. Confronted with top-of-the-head and seat-of-the-pants planning.
6. Required to plan, but the victims seldom do, at least effectively.

Item
Although 33 percent of the nation's state departments of education mandate long-range planning, less than half of them admitted engaging in the planning process for a period of more than one year.

7. Received very little competent technical support.
8. Received glowing reports of unsubstantial results of the planning process.

To a large extent, operational planning, using the management-by-objective approach, will either curtail the disease or prevent it from infecting others. The effect of the AT disease on the operational planning process will be diminished when the following results have been attained:

1. Emphasis is placed on producing results rather than on creating activities.

2. Communication is improved so that both supervisor and planning unit administrator are aware of what the other expects.
3. The parties feel free to make decisions and take necessary action to achieve short-range objectives.
4. There is frequent feedback so that progress toward the short-range objectives is always in focus.[3]

STRATEGIC PLANNING AND OPERATIONAL PLANNING

Some distinct differences between the strategic and operational planning processes are:

Strategic Planning	*Operational Planning*
1. Planning is for a period in excess of one year.	1. Planning is for a period within one year.
2. Planning is achieved through management by strategies.	2. Planning is achieved through management by objectives.
3. Planning tends to be more informal.	3. Planning tends to be more formal and systematic.
4. Planning is proactive, that is, plans are drawn to prevent conditions from having an adverse impact on the school district.	4. Planning is reactive, that is, plans are prepared to react to factors affecting the school district.
5. Budgeting aspect can be achieved through program planning and budgeting systems.	5. Budgeting aspect can be improved using zero-base budgeting.
6. Planning is more dynamic.	6. Planning is less dynamic.
7. Planning is an outgrowth of result-oriented movement.	7. Planning is an outgrowth of the human relation era.
8. Planning is intuitive, anticipatory, and systematic.	8. Planning is systematic.
9. Planning is more directly related to achievement of educational goals and mission.	9. Planning is more directly related to attainment of long-range goals.

[3] From *MBO II: A System of Managerial Leadership for the 80's* by George S. Odiorne. Copyright © 1979 by Fearon-Pitman Publishers, Inc., 6 Davis Drive, Belmont, CA 94002. Reprinted by permission.

RELATING INDIVIDUAL EFFORTS
TO OPERATIONAL PLAN

Some school districts may go beyond the development and implementation of operational plans to enhance their attainment. The institution of individual performance plans and professional improvement plans are two excellent ways to improve the performance of the school districts not only on an individual, but also on a school level.

Individual Performance Plan

For the individual performance plan, each staff member in the school district prepares a plan indicating key result areas, short-range objectives, and performance standards to outline individual efforts toward the objectives and standards of the operational plan. When all individual plans are realized, the operational plan should be achieved either on or above plan. The individual performance plan should be keyed to the job descriptions and job requirements of teachers and administrators. It should definitely include routine as well as creative short-range objectives and performance standards.

Professional Improvement Plan

In the professional improvement plan, each staff member who has prepared an individual performance plan develops a plan for improving his or her individual ability to perform his or her job better, citing short-range objectives and performance standards for an assortment of training and development activities. When this plan has been achieved either on or above plan, there will have been a change in the behavior and/or attitudes of the individual toward improving job effectiveness. Those superintendents who desire to use the individual performance plan and professional improvement plan should seriously consider consolidating these two plans to reduce the paperwork.

PAPERWORK REQUIREMENTS OF PLANNING

Quite often administrators and teachers complain about the paperwork associated with the planning process for two reasons: (1) they are not accustomed to the planning process; and (2) they do not understand how the paperwork relates to individual requirements.

Figure 7–2 demonstrates that the base for the paperwork requirements lies with the strategic plan. This is the data base from which plans are originated. It is chiefly a central administration responsibility; however, each building principal is also required to contribute to the strategic plan. Operational plans are the basis upon which each school

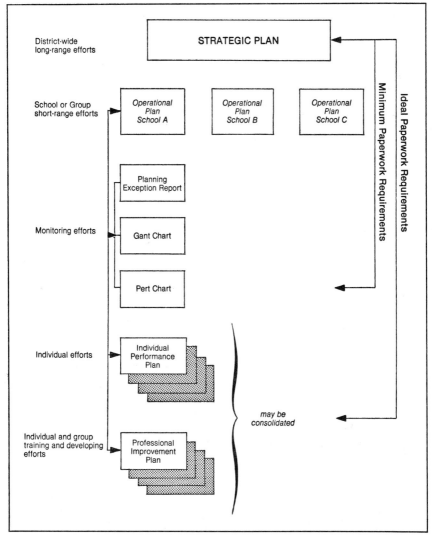

Figure 7–2 *Paperwork Requirements of the Planning Process*

acts to help realize the strategic plan on a year-by-year basis. Three monitoring techniques may help attain short-range objectives: (1) planning exception report; (2) Gant chart, and (3) Pert chart. Most planning unit coordinators are familiar with the latter two techniques. The former technique has been discussed elsewhere in this book.

Strategic plans, operational plans, and monitoring reporting procedures constitute the minimum paperwork requirements of a school district. A more desirable paperwork requirement would consist also of the individual performance plan and professional improvement plan, or a combination of both.

Tabulated on various levels, the paperwork required should be as follows:

School District Level	Plan	Paperwork Requirements (pages)	
		Minimum	Maximum
District-wide	Strategic	75	100
	Operational	All Schools	
School	Strategic	30	50
	Operational	Each Subunit	
	Individual/Professional	All Staff Members	
Individual	Individual/Professional	5	10

This also includes monitoring reports as warranted by plans.

SALIENT POINTS

The following represents some ways to make operational planning a creative and enjoyable process:

1. Have an "attack committee" interrogate the makers of the plan and make revisions accordingly.
2. Use only creative or innovative short-range objectives.
3. Prepare performance standards that are creative and innovative in nature.
4. Identify and achieve performance standards that challenge human efforts.
5. Refer to the operational plan at least twice monthly and detect at least one way to improve on the plan; then implement it.
6. Have an expert comment on the quality of the plan. Make revisions accordingly, and then carry out the changes.

APPLICATION STRATEGY 7

Collect a copy of the form used by several school districts for short-range planning. Identify the strengths and weaknesses of each. Using the strengths of each plan as a guide, construct a form for preparing operational plans. Identify three problem areas of a school district and construct an operational plan using the previously prepared forms. Present the completed plan to a knowledgeable person, and request an evaluation of quality and quantity of the short-range objectives, performance standards, and creativity of effort.

8

PREPARING SHORT-RANGE OBJECTIVES

Short-range objectives for planning unit administrators fulfill several important functions. First, when established correctly through proper interaction, they help provide the kind of involvement that gives ownership of plans and substance to the planning process. Second, they can be used as the basis for motivating human efforts to achieve a level of performance that may exceed the projected result. Third, they can be used to improve staff relationships as a result of the preparation and execution of activities. Fourth, they can be useful in appraising plans and closing performance gaps through proper training. Finally, if for no other reason, short-range objectives are the medium for achieving a common understanding among staff concerning the year-by-year attempts to achieve the long-range goals of the school district.

The rationale of this chapter is to elaborate on the use and benefits of short-range objectives. The short-range objective is defined, and criteria for the effective short-range objective are briefly covered to add meaning to the definition. The two approaches for writing short-range objectives are discussed to emphasize the cost factor, and some attention is given to the relationship between short-range objectives and long-range goals. This chapter also focuses on the influence of the central planning unit on objective setting in order to illustrate how the scope is narrowed through successive organizational levels of the school district. Also highlighted are reasons some short-range objectives fail and preparation of short-range objectives in subjective areas to disprove the myth that intangibles cannot be measured. The chapter concludes with comments regarding the judgment and evaluation of short-range objectives.

DEFINING SHORT-RANGE OBJECTIVES

A short-range objective is a statement of results that describes a specific plan to be achieved by either an individual or a group within a one-year period; usually it is designed to attain a long-range goal. The short-range objective must be oriented toward the mission of the school district and supported by staff commitment.

CRITERIA FOR EFFECTIVE SHORT-RANGE OBJECTIVES

The following represent essential criteria for correctly writing short-range objectives.

1. Formalized in writing. All short-range objectives should be specified in writing. When objectives are not written down, the parties involved may change their projected results to conform to actual results. Written objectives force participants to be more honest about success or failure. In addition, short-range objectives act as contractual obligations between two parties. Obviously, written contracts are more binding than verbal ones.

Item

There seems to be some conflict over the need to put all short-range objectives in writing. For example, would a superintendent set an objective to get rid of a poorly performing building principal? The answer to this query is no. However, "to get rid of the building principal" is not an objective; it is more like a task or activity. "To improve the organizational health of the school" would be one way to cite this situation as an appropriate objective. An objective is an end result, not an interim step or activity. Obviously, sensitive activities or tasks should never be stated in writing. Most publications would support the author on this recommendation.

2. Simply stated. Short-range objectives should be written in a concise manner and free of jargon to avoid confusing either party.
3. Standardized format. All short-range objectives should be written using either the improvement-action or prediction approach. If at all possible, intermingling these approaches should be avoided.

4. Understandable. Short-range objectives need not be understood by everybody, but by the parties who agreed to them.
5. Related to long-range goals. Short-range objectives can have a devastating effect on long-range goals; therefore, they should relate directly to the attainment of these goals in the long run.
6. High risk-oriented. Low risk-oriented short-range objectives do not stimulate and motivate human effort. Therefore, every attempt should be made to develop high risk-oriented short-range objectives in order to challenge the performer.
7. Realistic. Short-range objectives should be set with a realistic point of view. In an effort to maintain realism, they should be set neither too high or too low.
8. Related to planning assumptions. When possible, short-range objectives should relate to planning assumptions so that a realistic view of the future is projected for producing results.

APPROACHES TO WRITING SHORT-RANGE OBJECTIVES

There are two approaches for preparing short-range objectives, the improvement-action approach and the prediction approach. However, operational plan development often also calls for the computation of a cost factor, and therefore cost may be required for each short-range objective. A short-range objective using the improvement-action approach and an added cost factor is:

> To increase the number of primary students reading on grade level from 19 percent to 29 percent by June 30, 19xx (one year) at a cost not exceeding $290.00 per student.

A short-range objective using the prediction approach and an added cost factor is:

> By June 30, 19xx (one year), the number of intermediate students achieving on a grade level in math will increase from 35 percent to 45 percent at a cost not exceeding $350,000.

One effective way to depict long-range goals and short-range objectives is to display all long-range goals using the improvement-action approach and all supportive short-range objectives using the prediction approach. This practice will make it easy to differentiate between goals and objectives without referring to the time frame.

SHORT-RANGE OBJECTIVES AND LONG-RANGE GOALS

Figure 8–1 illustrates the relationship between a short-range objective and a long-range goal. The long-range goal covers a period of three years; however, it can be extended beyond this time allotment. The assessment of a short-range objective is conducted quarterly. In Figure 8–1, the first quarterly review revealed that performance was on target and should be continued as described by the original objective. The second review, however, revealed a need to modify the objective, as it was determined that the performance as outlined by the original objective would not achieve the projected results. The third performance review revealed that the objective was once again on target and that the performance, as identified in the modified objective, should continue. The final annual performance review revealed that the objective was achieved above plan. A modified short-range objective had become the base for performance achievement during the second year of the long-range goal.

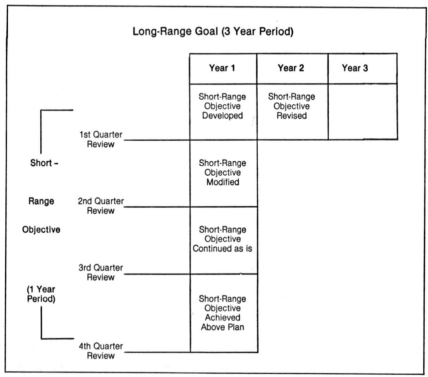

Figure 8–1 *The Relationship Between Long-Range Goals and Short-Range Objectives*

The explanation of the relationship between short-range objectives and long-range goals is further illustrated below. An examination of the critical analysis report and planning assumption was used as the basis for arriving at the following long-range goal, planning strategy, and short-range objective.

Long-Range Goal:

> To reduce staff illness absences from 11.5 to 4.0 percent by June 30, 19xx (three years).

Planning Strategy (abbreviated):

> A major strategic emphasis for the future will be to improve and utilize the leadership skills of planning unit administrators by requiring them to undergo appropriate training to learn desirable positive reinforcement techniques to be applied to the teaching staff in order to reduce absenteeism.

Short-Range Objective:

> To reduce staff illness absences from 11.5 to 8.5 percent by June 30, 19xx (one year).

First performance review results reveal that if performance continues as is, the objective will be achieved *on plan.*

Second performance review results reveal that the objective will be achieved *below plan.*

In reviewing the quarterly performance, the following items were critically examined by the planning unit administrator and a central planning unit administrator:

- Human efforts.
- Planning assumptions.
- Long-range goal.
- Short-range objective.
- Performance standards.
- Plan of action.
- Long-range strategies.
- Critical analysis report.
- Planning exception report.
- Planning controls.
- Budgets.

The results of the review reveal that human efforts were the major obstacles preventing the attainment of the objective; therefore, the original short-range objective was modified as follows:

> To reduce staff illness absences from 11.5 to 9 percent by June 30,
> 19xx (one year).

Third performance review results reveal that the objective will be achieved *on plan*.

Fourth performance review results reveal that the objective will be achieved *above plan* and reported as follows:

> Staff illness absences were reduced from 11.5 to 8.9 percent at a savings of $238,000, for the school year as attested by the business administrator's report attached to this report.

The short-range objective for the second year of the long-range goal is stated as follows:

> To reduce staff illness absences from 8.9 to 6 percent by June 30,
> 19xx (one year).

The short-range objective for the third year of the long-range goal is modified according to the performance results determined during the fourth quarterly review to reach the projected 4.0 percent in staff illness absences.

CENTRAL PLANNING UNIT AND SETTING SHORT-RANGE OBJECTIVES

Figure 8–2 is a flow chart that depicts the influence of the central planning unit's long-range goals and short-range objectives on other planning units of the school district. Each planning unit contributes to the overall long-range goal on a yearly basis. The reverse arrow indicates that the planning unit administrators and planning subunit supervisors have the opportunity and responsibility to shape and modify the short-range objectives of the central planning unit according to their individual needs and expectations. The arrows also depict the dynamics of the objective setting process, which consists of planning ideas (represented by the upward-moving arrows) and motivating human efforts toward meeting expected results (represented by the downward-moving arrows). The upward flow of ideas must be examined carefully to ensure that the main (central planning unit) short-range objectives will be attained.

Long-range goals and short-range objectives are developed for each formal planning unit. Only short-range objectives, either written or

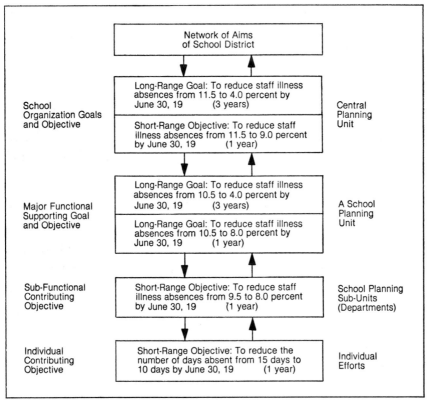

Figure 8–2 *The Scope of Short-Range Objective Setting Process*

verbal, are cited for the planning subunit and individual efforts. Long-range goals are required for only the formal planning units.

WHY SOME SHORT-RANGE OBJECTIVES FAIL

Short-range objectives have failed for a host of reasons.

Too Many Short-Range Objectives

In most instances, 80 percent or more of the long-range goals of a particular major key result area can be covered by no more than four or five major short-range objectives. If more are desired, they should be substituted as performance standards or replaced by activities.

Process-Oriented

Short-range objectives that are process-oriented are not objectives, but tasks or activities, and therefore may never help to realize the long-range goals of the school district. Every educator must recognize that the process is relatively unimportant if the end result has been achieved. Human efforts must focus on results.

Lack of Skill

There are a number of ways for preparing short-range objectives, but most of them advocate the use of: (1) the act or performance and (2) a time span. No short-range objective should ever be written without showing a "performance gap," a statement that indicates what is and what should be. However, this problem seems to prevail with most preparers of short-range objectives. Some may also include a cost. However, planning unit administrators still seem to have trouble preparing correctly written short-range objectives. During the first year of the planning process, it is acceptable that not all short-range objectives be correctly written; however, once the program is in its second or third year, all planning unit administrators and staff should have acquired expertise in preparing correctly written short-range objectives.

Related to Network of Aims

All short-range objectives should relate directly to the basic purposes, mission, and educational goals of the school district. If they do not, discard or rewrite them.

Lack of Controls

Controls are used solely to determine if the objective will be achieved. If proper controls have not been established, there will be no way in which to measure progress and thus take corrective action to achieve the desired results.

Lack of Commitment

Unless a staff member is committed to objective achievement, it is not worth the paper it is written on. Commitment will only result if: (1) the personal goals of the staff member are integrated with the goal of the organization and (2) the objective was developed by the staff member and negotiated and agreed on with the planning unit administrator.

Unrelated to Long-Range Goal

All short-range objectives should relate, whenever possible, to the long-range achievement efforts of the school district. In the final analysis, the attainment of long-range goals, achieved through the efforts of a succession of short-range objectives, will be responsible for the success or failure of the school district.

Punitive Measures

Short-range objectives, even if achieved below plan, should not be used as a punitive means by which to gain improved performance from educators. When they are regarded as a punitive measure rather than as a device to motivate and control performance, they are doomed to fail as a meaningful tool in the planning process.

Low-Risk Bearing

All short-range objectives should be written to challenge the efforts of their designers. When they are low-risk bearing, morale tends to suffer and interest in the planning process eventually diminishes.

PREPARING SHORT-RANGE OBJECTIVES IN SUBJECTIVE AREAS

For years a number of teachers and administrators have been proclaiming that objectives that measure certain intangible items, such as human characteristics or traits, cannot be adequately set. This was one of the reasons given by opponents of objectives for their disapproval of the use of short-range objectives. George S. Odiorne said that, "if it cannot be counted, measured or described, forget about it as an objective because the specific reason for setting it is not clear." There is a great deal of validity to this statement. Take, for example, the intangible word *love.* Although love may mean different things to different human beings, there are some common denominators (or performance standards) on which most people will agree. Such is true for all intangible short-range objectives. They are qualified to be adequately measured. Following is an illustration.

Intangible Short-Range Objective

10.1. To improve the communication network between the central and school planning units by June 30, 19xx (one year).

The word "improve" is an intangible term because it has different connotations for different people. However, by qualifying it with the following indicators or performance standards, the short-range objective can be measured.

This objective is satisfactorily achieved when . . .

10.1.1. A monthly planning newsletter is prepared and approved by the superintendent and disseminated to the staff by the first of each month.

10.1.2. Job enrichment, as prescribed by Dr. M. Scott Myers, is implemented by one school planning unit by June 30, 19xx.

10.1.3. A planning manual is developed and used as a guide for training teachers in the mechanics of planning, as approved by the planning coordinator, by October 31, 19xx.

10.1.4. An attitudinal correlated scale related to planning is prepared and distributed to the staff and the results reveal that the communication network between the central and school planning units has improved "significantly" by March 30, 19xx.

OMITTING PROCESS OBJECTIVES

Some school districts require school administrators to develop process objectives. A process objective is similar to a short-range objective; however, the process objective describes either an activity, a task, or a process, while a short-range objective describes the end result.

The following is an example of a process objective:

> Throughout the 19xx fiscal year, the building principal will conduct meetings (once a month) with building administrators and supervisors as documented in minutes of the meeting maintained on file.

Process objectives are unnecessary and should be avoided for the following reasons:

1. Other documents, such as the job description and an action plan specify process objectives.
2. They may involve the development of hundreds of statements, enlarging the amount of paperwork required in the planning process.
3. The end result is what counts, not the activity, providing the objective was attained without encroaching upon human rights.
4. The lack of sophistication in planning is evident because practical experience in effective planning would have revealed no need for process objectives.

If process objectives are required, try to convince the superintendent to opt for performance standards instead. The process objective indicated above has been transformed into a performance standard.

(Performance is satisfactory when . . .) the principal conducts monthly meetings with building administrators throughout the school year as evident by the minutes of the meeting.

The performance standard not only gives the desired result, but is less wordy.

JUDGING SHORT-RANGE OBJECTIVES

When short-range objectives have been set in the operational plan, they should be reviewed by all parties concerned to determine how well they meet the following criteria:

1. Are resources available to achieve the short-range objective? It is useless to establish an objective if cost will prohibit its achievement. The objective's scope may need to be reduced if sufficient resources are lacking.
2. Will the school organizational goals and personal goals be achieved through an integrated approach? One of the best approaches to integrating these goals is to allow staff members to set their own goals. This obviously will preclude the planning unit administrator's determining the short-range objectives for staff.

EVALUATING SHORT-RANGE OBJECTIVES

The effectiveness of a short-range objective is not based solely on whether it was achieved on or above plan, but also on the extent to which it contains the following characteristics.

Improvement on the Maintenance Performance Level

All operational plans should be developed with the single purpose of reaching various stages of the aspirational performance level for attaining long-range goals. No individual or group should be hired to maintain the *status quo*. School district improvement is the chief reason for setting and achieving short-range objectives.

Identification and Exploitation of Opportunities

Often unidentified or underutilized opportunities exist within a school district. Take, for example, a district that is experiencing declining enrollment because new homeowners are opting to place their children in private schools. The presence of 195 vacant lots slated for construction of new homes could be seen as an opportunity for administrators to form a liaison with real estate brokers to publicize the excellence of the school district and thus encourage new owners to enroll their children in public rather than private schools. Short-range objectives should not be set until all opportunities have been identified and exploited.

Overcoming Weaknesses and Problems

Short-range objectives should foster corrective action to eliminate weaknesses and problems. They should also be designed to overcome obstacles that hinder the achievement of long-range goals.

Minimization or Elimination of Threats

Another effective way to evaluate short-range objectives is to assess how well they prevented conditions that would hinder the achievement of long-range goals.

Maximization of Strengths

Short-range objectives should be developed to capitalize on the existing strengths of the school district. This, at times, is difficult to do in a district when the strength is the expertise of a particular person. Somehow people tend to place more respect on an outsider who is fully knowledgeable about a given topic than on an insider. The old adage that a king is king everywhere but in his castle tends to be true. At any rate, short-range objectives that correlate to the strengths of the school district are an excellent way to evaluate them.

A short-range objective that does not meet one or more of these characteristics should be reassessed and redesigned to include as many of the items as possible. Obviously the best short-range objective is the one that includes all of the characteristics mentioned above.

USING A FORM FOR ASSESSING OBJECTIVES AND STANDARDS

In addition to using the above criteria for evaluating short-range objectives, the author advocates the use of a form similar to Figure 8–3. This form is designed for planning unit administrators' use so that they can critically assess the extent to which individual as well as operational plans have met the variables identified on the form. Thus, the form is only as good as the selection of variables used to make the evaluation. The following illustrates the use of the form with an individual performance plan designed to assist in meeting the operational plan.

Short Range Objectives and Performance Standards
EVALUATION FORM

Name: __Mary White__   Date: __September 15, 19XX__

Position: __Teacher__   Reviewer: __Dr. John West__

SHORT RANGE OBJECTIVES								
1. Short range objective lacks a time span	10.1							
2. Short range objective is incorrectly stated								
3. Short range objective does not indicate a "gap"	10.1							
4. Short range objective is understated								
5. Short range objective is overstated								
6. Short range objective is not qualified								
7. Short range objective is not quantified								
8. Short range objective is not valid for plan								
9. Short range objective is not keyed to KRA								
10. Additional short range objective(s) are needed								
11. Short range objective is unclear								
12. Short range objective is incorrectly coded								
PERFORMANCE STANDARDS								
1. Performance standard is not quantified								
2. Performance standard is not qualified	1.1.1	1.1.2						
3. Performance standard lacks a time span	1.1.1							
4. Performance standard is understated								
5. Performance standard is overstated								
6. Additional performance standard is needed								
7. Performance standard is not valid for objective								
8. Performance standard is incomplete								
9. Performance standard lacks substance								
10. Performance standard is incorrectly stated	1.1.1	1.1.2						
11. Performance standard is unclear								
12. Performance standard is incorrectly coded	1.1.1	1.1.2						

Figure 8–3   *Form for Assessing Objectives and Standards*

Short Range Objective
10.1. To prepare a math curriculum using the behavioral objective approach.

A review of the form reveals that the evaluator cited the objective in items one and three. Therefore, the objective was found to be faulted because it did not contain a "performance gap" or a time span. The short-range objective was revised to include those items indicated on the evaluation form and the following resulted:

10.1. "To make a conversion from the skill to behavioral objective approach for teaching general eighth grade mathematics curriculum by June 30, 19xx."

Item
Some readers may say that the above short-range objective is not qualified, that is, there is no basis for evaluating the quality of the "behavioral objective eighth grade general mathematic curriculum." This is not true. Remember that the set of performance standards act as qualifiers. This is the paramount reason they should be written creatively and in quantitative, as well as qualitative, terms.

Performance Standard

The second half of the evaluation form is devoted to assessing performance standards. Two of the performance standards appearing in the individual performance plan are:

1.1.1. "Form a committee to help write the mathematics curriculum."
1.1.2. "Develop an outline for preparing the general mathematics curriculum text by June 30, 19xx."

A review of the evaluation form reveals that the evaluator cited the first performance standards in items two, three, ten, and twelve, and the second one on items two, ten, and twelve. The first performance standard was cited because it was incorrectly stated, not qualified, improperly coded, and lacked a time frame. The second performance standard was cited because it was incorrectly stated, not qualified, and improperly coded. The revised performance standards are:

10.1.1. A committee has been organized, consisting of three teachers, one from a high school, and the mathematics supervisor, for the purpose of preparing new eighth-grade mathematics curriculum, nominated by eighth-grade teachers, by November 1, 19xx.
10.1.2. An outline for preparing the text of the new eighth-grade general mathematics curriculum has been found acceptable by the assistant superintendent of curriculum and instruction by November 20, 19xx.

The revised performance standards are now recorded because they complete the statement "performance is satisfactory when . . .". They are now properly recoded because the goal is represented by the first two digits, the short-range is indicated by the third digit, and the performance standard by the fourth. Both performance standards have also been qualified. In the first standard, eighth-grade teachers are the qualifiers, and in the second standard, the assistant superintendent for curriculum and instruction is the qualifier. The first performance standard has also been modified to include a time span.

The evaluation instrument is an excellent method of assessing individual short-range objectives and performance standards. With frequent use, revisions, and modifications, most planning unit administrators will find it an invaluable source for improving the quality of both short-range objectives and performance standards whether they are recorded on the operational or individual performance plan.

SALIENT POINTS

Short-range objectives should be stated as results rather than activities to be performed. They should also be written to include the intended achievement and the anticipated time span for the accomplishment. Relative terms such as adequate, sufficient, and reasonable are poor qualifiers because they lead to numerous misunderstandings. If relative terms must be used, they should be qualified with performance standards.

APPLICATION STRATEGY 8

Improve on the instrument for evaluating short-range objectives and performance standards prepared in the preceding chapter, using the content of this chapter, as well as the recommendations given in: George L. Morrisey, *Management by Objectives and Results* (Reading, MA: Addison-Wesley Publishing Co., 1976) pp. 65–104.

Present the improved version of the evaluation instrument to a knowledgeable person for criticism and recommendations. Make revisions if they are warranted.

9

ESTABLISHING PERFORMANCE STANDARDS

Performance standards in public education are usually thought of in terms of student performance. A set of program objectives are developed to cover a particular area of instruction, and standards are annexed to these objectives as indicators for assessing progress. When all the standards have been attained, the program objectives have been accomplished. This basic technique is also used in the operational planning process. A number of short-range objectives are prepared and performance standards are indicated as criteria for measuring the achievement of each objective. When all performance standards have been met, the objective is supposed to have been achieved. The word *supposed* is highlighted, because standards do not guarantee that the objective will be achieved. However, when standards have been clearly identified, quantified, qualified, accepted, and written down, they provide a systematic and orderly basis for interaction, analysis, and a solid foundation for performance expectations. In so doing, they facilitate maximum individual achievement and self-realization, and enhance the probability that the objective will be achieved as planned.

This chapter explains the rationale for using performance standards in the operational planning process. At the onset, performance standards are defined, and examples are cited to demonstrate how performance standards help clarify short-range objectives. A step-by-step procedure is briefly discussed to show how they should be properly established and implemented. Examples are matched with the major key result areas for differentiation purposes. Some attention is also given to several approaches for arriving at performance standards. A few problems that seem to prevail among planners are discussed, as well as solutions, and reasons performance may deviate from preset standards are given. The chapter ends with the benefits of using performance standards as an integral component of the planning process.

DEFINING AND STATING PERFORMANCE STANDARDS

Performance standards, when related to the operational planning process, are statements of conditions that will exist when a short-range objective is satisfactorily achieved. These standards are the basis for evaluation of a completed objective, and should be realistic, feasible, specific, and of ample number to ensure its accomplishment. Short-range objectives can be achieved without realizing performance standards; however, such standards add substance and quality to an objective, as illustrated below.

A short-range objective without performance standards:

40.1. To convert from the line-item budget to program-oriented budget by June 30, 19xx.

The same short-range objective with performance standards:

40.1. To convert from the line-item budget to program-oriented budget by June 30, 19xx.
   40.1.1. All planning unit administrators have received one week of training in program-oriented budget by September 30, 19xx, and a survey indicates that a minimum of 80 percent of them are "highly satisfied" with the training.
   40.1.2. The prescribed program structure of the State Department of Education has been established by the school district and approved by the county superintendent by January 15, 19xx.
   40.1.3. The budget for all new programs has been developed into a program-oriented format by March 15, 19xx and approved by the superintendent of schools.

When performance standards are indicated with a short-range objective, they direct human effort. Without standards, any performance is acceptable as long as deadlines are met.

There are three important steps to consider when stating performance standards so that accurate measures of the results are obtained:

1. Begin by indicating all of the essential elements needed to achieve the objective.
2. State or describe each essential element by beginning with the words, "Performance (or this objective) is satisfactorily achieved when . . ."
3. Make certain each descriptive statement has been both quanti-

fied and qualified. This dual process is called strengthening performance standards. For example, it is insufficient merely to quantify the following standard:

The program-oriented budget process is fully implemented by October 31, 19xx.

The performance standard must also be qualified:

The program-oriented budget process *as prescribed by the State Department of Education* is fully implemented by October 31, 19xx.

A quantified performance standard is basically just an activity, or act, and does not provide a sound basis for measuring whether or not the objective has been achieved. Therefore, whenever possible, performance standards should be quantified as well as qualified.

The following represent indices for quantifying and qualifying performance standards:

Quantifying Indices
• Time line.
• Quantity.
• Weight.
• Frequency.
• Cost.

Qualifying Indices
• Person.
• Group or committee.
• Legislation or mandate.
• Report or some other document.
• Scale or some other form of measurement.
• Book or some other manuscript.
• Edict.
• Prescribed set of conditions.
• Policy and procedures.
• Regulations.
• Guidelines.
• Description.
• Formula.

SETTING PERFORMANCE STANDARDS

Assumption: Performance standards are administrative tools used to control the planning process and the achievement of short-range objectives. They should be viewed as signals that indicate when planning unit administrators should compare the situation with the objective and take the warranted corrective action.

As such, the following procedure is recommended to properly establish, implement, and fully utilize performance standards during the planning process:

1. The planning unit administrator and staff should agree on short-range objectives and the system of measurement and standards that will be explored to evaluate performance results. Obviously both objectives and standards should appear in writing and be included as an integral part of the operational plan.
2. Performance standards for a particular short-range objective should be complete and include the entire area being controlled.
3. The period covered by the standard should correspond to that of the objective being evaluated. Some activities are evaluated more frequently than others.
4. Short-range objectives and performance standards should be related to the most significant things being undertaken in any area of activity. One successful technique is to identify five or six of the most important things (objectives) to be accomplished, and list those things (performance standards) that will indicate whether these things are done well.
5. One of the most useful methods of control is that of time and time utilization. Performance standards should state the activities being completed and their duration.
6. Performance standards should be reviewed and revised when a method or activity has changed significantly. Performance standard costs should be consistent with the value of the short-range objective.
7. Even though the control period is shorter, it is often best to record information about an objective on a continuous basis. The frequency with which objectives and performance standards are compared varies depending upon the degree to which performance has been successful.
8. Performance standards should at all times be indices of the accomplishment of short-range objectives. However, they should be revised as quickly, as often, and as drastically as necessary to keep pace with changing times and conditions. Any proposed changes should be agreed on by the planning

unit administrator and the staff member(s) involved. This process will ensure understanding and correct standards.

9. Performance standards should be validated by using past experience and performance for preparing each statement. This substantially improves the probability that the objective will be reached.

SUGGESTIONS FOR PERFORMANCE STANDARDS

There are an indefinite number of measurable factors that can be used as performance standards. All individuals, in consultation with their planning unit administrator, must determine what standards will best serve their individual purposes. The following represent some performance standards for each of the major key result areas:

Major Key Result Area	Performance Standard
Student Learning and Growth	• Number of promotions.
	• Rate of absentees.
	• Number of students above grade level.
	• Students enrolled in college.
	• Dropout rate.
	• Reduction of failure.
	• Accident rate.
	• School year.
	• Number of books read.
	• Student attendance.
	• Materials consumption.
	• Vandalism.
Financial Resources	• Budget approval.
	• Proposals funded.
	• Dollars saved.
	• Interest received.
	• Reduced cost.
	• Budget finalized.
	• Cost per program.
	• Interest rate.
	• Census.
	• Compensation and fringe benefits.
Physical Resources	• Contraction completion date.
	• Number of units.
	• Cost per unit.
	• Dimensions.
	• Capacity.
	• Special construction requirements.

Major Key Result Area	*Performance Standard*
Innovation	• Cost per student.
	• Scheduled milestones.
	• Ideas generated.
	• Changes initiated.
	• Potential threats turned into opportunities.
	• New programs, methods, and techniques.
	• Cost reduction.
	• Successful pilot studies.
	• Cost savings.
Community Involvement	• Programs approved.
	• Number of activities involved.
	• Number of parent conferences.
	• Community meetings.
	• Number of complaints/praises.
Organizational Management	• Staff turnover.
	• Staff absentee rate.
	• Degree of acceptance.
	• Complaints/praises from staff.
	• Strikes and slowdowns.
Performance Evaluation and Training	• Staff with advanced degrees.
	• Years of experience.
	• Attendance at conferences, seminars, and the like.
	• Promotions.
	• Professional recognition.
	• Number and nature of training completed.
	• Staff skills, equipment utilization.
	• Problems overcome.
Instructional Programs and Services	• Number of programs.
	• Number of staff members.
	• Number of students per program.
	• Material consumption.
	• Education technology utilization.
	• Students served.
	• New students.
	• Request for services.
	• Course enrollment.

SOME APPROACHES TO PERFORMANCE STANDARDS

There are several approaches to developing performance standards. Usually they will involve an individual or staff member, the planning unit administrator, the individual and planning unit administrator together, a committee or other group, or the planning coordinator.

The Individual Approach

The person who prepared the short-range objective should be the first person to draft the performance standards. The rationale for this action is that no one knows more about the job than the person performing the job. In addition, when an individual has ownership of a standard, a greater value is placed on it and achievement is more likely.

The Joint Approach—Staff Member and Planning Unit Administrator

The ideal approach to setting performance standards is the joint approach, in which both the staff member and planning unit administrator participate in the process. There are several ways in which this can be done:

1. Performance standards are set by both parties through discussion.
2. A list of performance standards for each short-range objective is discussed by the parties concerned.
3. A list, prepared by the planning unit administrator, is subject to joint discussion and acceptance.
4. A list is prepared simultaneously, but independently, by both the staff member and planning unit administrator, discussed and mutually accepted.

Regardless of the approach used, the main point is to procure an exchange of ideas for the purpose of reaching agreement on standards.

The Group or Committee Approach

Although there are several ways to perform this approach, the usual method is to assemble a group of staff members in similar planning subunits (grade levels, departments, or teams) to identify appropriate performance standards for each short-range objective. The group then submits the drafted list to and discusses it with the planning unit administrator. Together they agree on changes and additions.

The Planning Coordinator Approach

There will always be the temptation to let the planning coordinator set performance standards because that person is usually most knowledgeable about the planning process. There is some validity in this approach; however, as previously stated in this book, the planning coordinator is not a planner, but the individual responsible for helping others to plan. The development, acceptance, and achievement of performance standards are too important to be determined by a single person, especially if that person is not going to be responsible or accountable for achieving them.

As a final word, performance standards are interim objectives set to achieve a short-range objective. Their effectiveness is enhanced when they have been jointly developed and accepted by the planning unit administrator and the individual staff member. The approach used to set standards should be based entirely on this posture.

PROBLEMS AND SOLUTIONS WHEN USING PERFORMANCE STANDARDS

Although most educators will maintain that performance standards are an invaluable aid in controlling performance results, some problems have been encountered during the implementation process as stated below:

Problem	*Solution*
Planning unit administrators and staff failed to establish realistic objectives and attainable performance standards.	Insist that planners look more critically at the reason(s) for the objectives and standards to analyze whether these objectives will help to realize the long-range goals, and if the performance standards will help achieve the short-range objectives. A workshop on developing more meaningful objectives and standards for school-related conditions should prove fruitful.
Standards have been developed as though they are activities in an action plan.	Most planners make the mistake of developing quantifiable standards only. The planning unit administrator should confer individually with staff members who

Problem	*Solution*
	are experiencing this problem to establish a process for devising qualitative standards. After some experience with this process, it should not take the planners much time to rewrite more meaningful performance standards.

ACCRUING BENEFITS OF PERFORMANCE STANDARDS

When performance standards are well entrenched in the planning process, certain benefits will be accrued, not only for the planner, but for the entire school organization. Some of these benefits are:

1. Performance standards enhance the probability that short-range objectives will be achieved.
2. Performance standards are an improvement over activities developed in an action plan. Each set of standards becomes an action plan as well as the basis for measuring the accomplishment of the short-range objective.
3. The relationship between the planning unit administrator and the individual is improved because each one knows what is expected from the other.
4. Self-appraisal is facilitated and motivation is improved.
5. When performance standards have been arrived at in a group setting, the staff begins to understand the relationship of goals to objectives and objectives to standards, with a positive effect on the entire school district.
6. Performance standards can act as a means of continuous and constant reassessment of objectives, methods, and results.
7. Performance standards can help locate problems that are hindering the achievement of an objective.

Performance standards can become the most viable forces in the operational planning process. When skillfully used as guides, motivators, and indices for measuring performance, they are invaluable. They should not be used for punitive purposes, but rather to help individuals achieve their personal goals as they work toward the school organization goals. Although standards should be used in a firm and consistent manner, allowances should be made if circumstances beyond human control prevent the achievement of particular criteria.

Planning unit administrators should rely on their own judgment when balancing performance standards with human consideration because they are solely responsible and accountable for both long-range and short-range performance results of their respective planning units.

REASONS PERFORMANCE MAY DEVIATE FROM STANDARDS

There are three basic reasons performance might deviate from the pre-set standards.

Uncertainties

Uncertainties are events that have a reasonable likelihood of occurring. They may be internal events, such as absenteeism, accidents, or strikes. External situations may involve meetings, legislative reviews, or routine correspondence.

Unusual Events

Unusual events are not likely to occur, but could and *would* adversely affect the school district's performance. These events might include the death of an administrator, a budget cut, a personnel freeze, or an epidemic.

Human Factors

One or more human factors may cause drastic performance deviation from preset standards. Human factors usually fall into two categories:

1. "Honest error," which may have occurred due to a variety of reasons even though the individual responsible is a capable and competent worker.
2. Incompetence, which resulted out of gross negligence, ignorance, or inability to perform.

Whenever there is a distinct deviation in performance, the reasons indicated above should be explored to determine if a single or multiple cause is responsible for the discrepancy. Appropriate steps should be taken to ensure that the objective will be obtained.[1]

[1] *See* George L. Morrisey, *Management by Objectives and Results* (Reading, Mass.: Addison-Wesley, 1976), pp. 156–158.

SALIENT POINTS

Two important points about performance standards should be highlighted. First, no more than five performance standards should be set for each objective. Those that are stated more precisely without becoming too detailed will be more useful. All available material, including past experience and current operating policies and procedures, should be used as resources. Second, performance standards should be used as a basis for preparing descriptive statements regarding short-range objective outcomes. A sentence or two, written in paragraph form, should state the degree to which each performance standard should be met. Then the short-range objective should be examined to determine if additional information is needed.

APPLICATION STRATEGY 9

Prepare a set of performance standards for each short-range objective developed in Application Strategy 8. List no more than five standards per objective. Evaluate each performance standard using the evaluation instrument indicated in the preceding chapter. Revise each standard if warranted.

10

DEVELOPING AN ACTION PLAN

Once the short-range objective has been set and performance standards have been devised, the next step in the operational planning process is to establish an action plan to reach the objectives. By way of analogy, consider the person who sets out to close a business deal. A number of activities are initiated to do this, which may involve driving to the airport, boarding the plane, arriving at the destination, meeting with the other parties, conversing over the deal, returning to the office, and so on. These actions are similar to the activities of an action plan initiated in order to achieve an objective, with the major difference being that the activities of an action plan are usually expressed in writing.

Developing an action plan may sound simple; in fact, the actual procedures for laying out an action plan are relatively easy. The degree of difficulty will depend largely on the complexity of the objective and the creativity and ingenuity of the planners.

This chapter explains some essential points about the process of developing an action plan. A definition of an action plan introduces the chapter. An example is given, and the value of an action plan is discussed. Some attention is also given to the procedural steps for producing an action plan as well as factors affecting its implementation. The chapter closes with some important considerations to be appraised during preparation of an action plan, and identification of some questions to be considered during its evaluation.

DEFINING AN ACTION PLAN

An action plan, sometimes referred to as programming an objective, is the process of describing the activities necessary to achieve an objective and matching them with a time frame and the person(s) responsible for their implementation. The cost of performing each activity has also recently been included in the action plan. While this plan does not guarantee that the objective will be achieved when all of the activities have been accomplished, it will greatly enhance the probability of its achievement, providing that all of the alternatives have been considered and the most appropriate one used as the basis for attaining the designated objective.

Item
This is one area in which the author disagrees with most of the literature on planning. He feels that the action plan is unnecessary if correctly stated performance standards have already been set. In effect, each standard can be viewed as an activity to help realize the objective. Having witnessed hundreds of action plans, he has concluded that: (1) they are a major contributor to the human outcry concerning the abundance of paperwork involved in the planning process; and (2) very few people refer to these plans after they have been prepared. Therefore, the author feels time spent on preparation of an action plan could be better utilized if devoted toward strengthening performance standards or achieving the objective as a whole.

The following is an example of a short-range objective and action plan:

Short-Range Objective

To revise the present high school graduation requirements to include those minimum items prescribed by law by June 30, 19xx.

Action Plan

Activity	Date	By Whom	Cost
1. Become familiar with the new state mandate governing high school graduation requirements.	8/1/19xx	Assistant Superintendent and Principal	
2. Request a minimum of twenty school districts across the nation to forward their high school graduation requirements to the principal's office.	8/15/19xx	Secretary to Assistant Superintendent	$ 5.75

Activity	Date	By Whom	Cost
3. Organize a committee representing each of the subject areas identified by the new mandate.	9/15/19xx	Principal and Assistant Superintendent	
4. Review all of the materials obtained in Activity 2.	9/30/19xx	Assistant Superintendent, Principal, and High School Graduation Committee	
5. Review present Board policy concerning high school graduation requirements as prescribed by new mandate and present to superintendent for approval; make necessary revisions and submit final copy to superintendent.	11/1/19xx	Assistant Superintendent, Principal, and High School Graduation Committee	
6. Seek approval of revised high school graduation requirements from Board of Education.	12/1/19xx	Superintendent	
7. Prepare a list of student competencies for each subject area required under the new mandate; submit to principal and superintendent for approval and make any revisions or modifications if necessary.	3/1/19xx	High School Graduation Committee	$550
8. Submit to the Board of Education student competencies for all required subject areas and changes, if necessary.	3/15/19xx	Superintendent	

Activity	Date	By Whom	Cost
9. Present a list of all student competencies required for each of the mandated subject areas to all teachers of ninth grade and above.	9/1/19xx	Subject Area Teachers	

Total $555.75

The literature gives several reasons an action plan is necessary to help attain a short-range objective.

To Help Determine the Most Appropriate Alternative for Achieving the Objective

George L. Morrisey recommends that an Alternative Evaluation Chart be devised spelling out the alternatives, contributions to the objective, cost, feasibility, and other items to be analyzed in order to determine the most appropriate alternative for developing the action plan. Another approach would be to use a brainstorming session to select the best alternative.[1]

To Provide a Time Frame for Achieving Individual Activities

Action plans could be used as a motivating factor because time limits do motivate action. The time frame is an invaluable catalyst for this purpose.

To Provide a Control Basis

By frequently referring to the action plan, the planning unit administrator and/or staff member(s) can determine if corrective action is necessary in order to achieve the objective either on or above plan.

To Communicate and Coordinate Activities with Others

At times, a particular action plan activity will require the efforts of an additional person from either inside or outside the planning unit. By soliciting agreement on a particular activity among all parties involved, the plan acts as an excellent communication and coordinating document.

---

[1] George L. Morrisey, *Management by Objectives and Results* (Reading, Mass.: Addison-Wesley, 1976), pp. 107–112.

To Determine Resources Needed to Achieve the Objective

A detailed development of an action plan will identify the resources essential to achieving the objective. These resources will usually include funds, human resources, equipment, and time.

To Determine the Viability of the Objective

A critical examination of the action plan can show whether or not the objective is viable. If the necessary resources are lacking due to insufficient funds or the absence of a particular expertise, most likely the objective will be unattainable. In this case, either the objective should be changed or another alternative selected.

PREPARING THE ACTION PLAN

The development of the action plan should include the following steps.

Examining the Short-Range Objective

Examine the objective to determine if it is clearly stated, specific, and measurable. If it proves not to be, the objective should be rewritten by the planning unit administrator to ensure there is no misunderstanding of its meaning or content.

Identifying and Selecting an Alternative

If a short-range objective is written in accordance with the acceptable format, alternative paths to the objective should be analyzed so that the most appropriate one can be selected. When considering alternatives, use a form, such as the one designated in Chapter 6, that provides a method for examining each alternative. Factors such as money, human resources, time requirements, demands made on others, and impact on staff and the objective should be considered.

Stating the Activity

After the most appropriate alternative has been selected, it becomes the basis for preparation of each activity used to reach the objective of the action plan. For maximum effectiveness, each activity should be:

- Stated using an action verb, expressed either quantitatively or qualitatively, and related to concrete results.

- Briefly and concisely written and limited to significant information.
- Tersely written so that long and detailed sentences are avoided.
- Devoid of repetition.

In an effort to limit the amount of paperwork that usually accompanies action plans, all future planning activities should not be confined to writing. When a proper communication network has been established in a planning unit, less paperwork will be required.

Indicating a Time Frame

A timetable should be projected for each activity of the action plan. The most appropriate way to design a timetable is to start at the end and work backward. The forward motion can also be utilized, particularly if a staff member has been given the green light to carry out a program. Regardless of the approach taken, the timetable must be realistic so that the probability of reaching the objective will be enhanced when all of the activities have been completed.

Fixing Responsibility

A person should be designated as the individual responsible for executing the activity. If a third party is involved, a verbal agreement should be sought and followed up with a letter or a reminder.

Determining Cost

Recently, budgeting for each action plan activity has become a consistently used practice. Basically, budgetary items are divided into two categories:

1. Human resources. Sometimes, these are expressed in personal costs, hours of labor needed to accomplish the activities, and cost to hire outside experts.
2. Nonhuman resources. These items include contracts, property, building, equipment, and the like. Nonhuman resources are usually expressed in dollars only.

Some planners include steps to validate, implement, and control action plans. Some consideration has already been given to implementing and controlling action plans. Updating action plans is not discussed here because very few, if any, planners have sufficient time to test activities.

FACTORS AFFECTING THE CONSTRUCTION OF AN
ACTION PLAN

The number of approaches to constructing an action plan is virtually limitless. The most appropriate approach at a given time is dependent upon many factors. The following are some action plan developmental approaches that have been used by educators in several school districts:

1. Sequential organization. There are certain educational activities that automatically fall in line sequentially. This normally occurs when each step is dependent on the successful completion of the preceding step.
2. Similar effort. Two or more steps requiring the same type of effort, such as attending a conference for the purpose of acquiring information necessary to implement an innovation, can be grouped together.
3. Terminal events or situations. Sometimes an action plan must relate to specific terminal events or situations connected with other objectives. This is particularly true when forming a personnel development objective to train or prepare teachers to implement a creative program through an innovative objective.
4. Technical development. Research and development efforts, such as constructing a curriculum guide to implement an innovative program, may have to be conducted in order to achieve the objective.
5. Individual or group orientation. Sometimes an action plan must relate to the potential or capability of an individual or group, and must be developed out of sequence to fit the timetable of this person or group.
6. Political consideration. The existence of political influences may have to be considered when developing an action plan for a particular objective.
7. Cost consideration. Cost is a factor that must be considered when developing an action plan for the attainment of an objective.[2]

IMPORTANT CONSIDERATIONS FOR DEVELOPING
AN ACTION PLAN

The process of developing an action plan to reach an objective must be approached in a systematic manner by careful examination of the scope and sequence of each activity. Failure to do so could result in a waste of

[2] George L. Morrisey, *Management by Objectives and Results* © 1970, Addison-Wesley Publishing Company, Inc., Reading, Massachusetts. Pp. 69–70. Reprinted with permission.

resources: human energy and money. The following questions should be analyzed in order to develop an action plan that will succeed in accomplishing the objective:

1. What vital steps are necessary to achieve the objective? A major activity of an action plan could conceivably be the accomplishment of an objective by another educator. "Assist the director of curriculum and instruction in compiling and editing the fourth-grade curriculum guide" could be a vital step in the plan of action, since the absence of such an activity could severely hinder the attainment of the objective.

2. What priorities should be assigned to each step of the action plan? In every action plan, some steps are more important than others. These more important steps must be given priority over the less important ones. As an example, training of personnel in a particular program should receive priority over the implementation of the program. Obviously, if the personnel are not trained to execute a certain program, it cannot be implemented successfully. Priorities must also be given to scheduling factors. This is the prime reason the activities of an action plan must be sequentially structured.

3. What minor subactivities are necessary to support major activities for accomplishing an objective? When the overall objective has been formulated, the major activities for achieving the objective must be broken down into minor or subactivities so that the first activities needed for attaining the objective are identified and clarified.

4. What method(s) or mean(s) should be employed to monitor the performance of person(s) or agency(ies) who have a share in the responsibility for accomplishing the objective? Objectives cannot be achieved by mere chance. Some method(s) or mean(s) of monitoring performance must be initiated so that progress toward objective attainment is checked periodically. "To submit to the reading supervisor the results of the monthly reading test that is administered to the fourth, fifth, and sixth grades" is an example of a method for monitoring the reading results of a school on a monthly basis.

EVALUATING THE ACTION PLAN

An action plan should be evaluated. This evaluation should be made separately by the planning unit administrator and a staff member. If either one has determined that the objective will not be achieved, a new activity(ies) or plan should be developed. The following questions will prove helpful in performing this task:

- Have all of the alternatives been identified and critically analyzed so that the most appropriate one has been selected to achieve the objective?
- Have the activities been correctly written and are all of them essential to help attain the objective?
- Have activities that involve a third party been accepted by that party?
- Has the time frame been properly evaluated and corrected, if necessary?
- Are the essential resources available to perform the activity?
- Are there too many or too few activities to achieve the objective?
- Has the action plan been received and accepted by the planning unit administrator?

SALIENT POINTS

Although this chapter mentioned some analytical questions that can be examined to evaluate an action plan, nothing was said about the various approaches that can be used to determine the validity and reliability of such a plan. Listed below are some of these approaches:

1. Individual evaluation. Either the planning unit administrator or a staff member can determine the value of the action plan; however, it would probably be better if an outsider were recruited to perform this kind of evaluation.
2. Team evaluation. All the members of the planning unit or sub-unit can be convened in a meeting for this purpose.
3. Planning coordinator's evaluation. Another useful method for evaluating an action plan is to have the planning unit coordinator assess and make recommendations for each activity in the plan.
4. Interrogation approach. A very effective approach to evaluate an action plan is to use a team of peers who will attack the plan, so that either the planning unit administrator or staff will be called upon to defend each step in the plan. This approach is also useful for examining short-range objectives and performance standards.
5. Committee evaluation. A conference of various respected individuals can be called to incorporate its ideas into the action plan.

Regardless of the approach used, the planning unit administrator must continuously examine action plans to prevent the waste of human effort on activities that will not achieve short-range objectives.

APPLICATION STRATEGY 10

Prepare action plans for all short-range objectives developed in Application Strategy 9. No action plan should exceed eight activities. Attach a cost to each action plan.

11

REPORTING OPERATIONAL
PERFORMANCE RESULTS

Every school district exists to fulfill one charge, either explicit or implied, and that is to improve student learning and growth. All planning accomplishments, from deciding on a mission statement to performing a short-range objective, are intended to produce results. Once these results have been realized, every attempt must be made to report performance in an appropriate manner. When this occurs, a systematic process is available to determine what obstacles, if any, prevented the attainment of projected results so that appropriate corrective actions can be taken.

The rationale for this chapter is twofold: (1) to identify a simple procedure for recording performance results and (2) to demonstrate techniques for analyzing certain performance outcomes.

DEFINING PERFORMANCE RESULTS

Performance results are the termination of planned human effort that has been exerted to reach either a short-range objective or a long-range goal. The term "planned" is emphasized because performance results are measured as "on plan," "below plan," and "above plan."[1]

On Plan Performance

Performance results are considered on plan when the performance has been achieved in accordance with a mutually acceptable level of performance as indicated and judged by performance standards, short-range objectives, or long-range goals.

[1] Lewis, *School Management by Objectives*, pp. 139–140.

Below Plan Performance

Performance results are considered below plan when performance has been achieved below a mutually acceptable level of performance as indicated and judged by either performance standards, short-range objectives, or long-range goals.

Above Plan Performance

Performance results are designated above plan when performance has been achieved above a mutually acceptable level of performance as indicated and judged by performance standards, short-range objectives, or long-range goals.

STEPS FOR RECORDING PERFORMANCE OUTCOME

When preparing the performance outcome section of the operational plan, the following steps should be taken:

1. Indicate whether the performance has been achieved on plan, below plan, or above plan.
2. Prepare a description of the performance outcome by referring to the objective itself and each performance standard. One or two sentences should be devoted to the outcome of each performance standard.
3. Indicate the reason(s) any objective was achieved below plan and say what corrective actions will be taken to attain the objective.
4. Indicate the reason(s) any objective was achieved above plan, and cite the instrument or evidence and where it can be located to substantiate objectives that were achieved on or above plan.

The following is an example of the way performance is recorded in the performance outcome section of the operational plan:

Short-Range Objective	Performance Standards	Performance Outcome
3.1 To implement long-range strategic planning throughout the school district by June 30, 19xx (second year of a three-year long-range goal).	3.11 All strategic and operational plans have been received and reviewed by the planning coordinator by Oct. 15, 19xx and he or she is satisfied with the results.	*Above Plan* The planning coordinator reviewed all plans on or before Oct. 15, 19xx and found them to be in excellent order. All plans were

Short-Range Objective	Performance Standards	Performance Outcome
	3.12 All strategic and operational plans have been reviewed and approved by the board of education by November 1, 19xx. 3.13 Year-end survey reveals that teachers and administrators are "highly" satisfied with the planning program as attested by the results of a five scale survey instrument. 3.14 A minimum of 80 percent of the operational plans have been achieved on or above plan by June 30, 19xx.	consequently approved by the superintendent and board of education. A survey was devised and administered to all teachers and administrators. The results indicated that the staff was highly enthusiastic about the program. Ninety-one percent of the objectives of the operational plans were achieved on or above plan. Because of the conscientious efforts of the planning coordinator, the planning program has been fully implemented within two years as opposed to the projected three.

THE REASONS FOR NOT ACHIEVING OBJECTIVES

There are a number of reasons that should be critically analyzed to determine why a short-range objective or a long-range goal was not achieved as planned. Following are the most important reasons results were not achieved as planned.[2]

Human Element

The most important reason for nonachievement of planned results, which embraces the human element, involves the planning unit administrator's performance, which is solely responsible for the achievement of his or her staff. Questions that should be considered when assessing

[2] Robert E. Lefton, V. R. Buzzotta, Manuel Sherberg, and Dean I. Karraker, *Effective Motivation through Performance Appraisal—Dimensional Appraisal Strategies* (New York: Wiley, 1977), pp. 314–327. Copyright © 1977 by Psychological Associates, Inc., St. Louis, Mo. Reprinted with permission.

the planning unit administrator's performance fall into five management areas: planning, organizing, leading, motivating, and controlling.

1. Planning—Did the planning unit administrator:
   a. give the staff inadequate or wrong information concerning a particular school situation?
   b. unintentionally mislead the staff so that the forecasting turned out wrong?
   c. recommend the wrong or inappropriate formula for arriving at a planning assumption?

   Setting Objectives—Did the planning unit administrator:
   a. set unrealistic goals and objectives?
   b. receive adequate support to achieve the goals and objectives? And did changes occur as indicated?
   c. evaluate the objectives using the instrument approach?

   Realizing Performance Standards—Did the planning unit administrator:
   a. develop performance standards that would, when executed properly, achieve the objective?
   b. prepare sufficient performance standards?
   c. evaluate the performance standards using the instrument approach? And did changes occur as indicated?

   Programming an Objective—Did the planning unit administrator:
   a. prepare adequate action plans to attain objectives?
   b. periodically review action plans?

   Time Management—Did the planning unit administrator:
   a. allow enough time to achieve obligations?
   b. approve unrealistic deadlines?
   c. overload staff with other assignments?

   Policies—Did the planning unit administrator:
   a. consider the fact that policies and procedures might interfere with achievement of the objective?
   b. let the staff pursue an objective that violated or infringed on policy?

2. Organizing Structuring—Did the planning unit administrator:
   a. impose the objective on staff or make them acquiesce to it even though they failed fully to understand or accept it?
   b. erroneously let the staff set their own objectives without supervisory involvement?

3. Leading—Did the planning unit administrator:
   a. make personal decisions that should have involved the staff?
   b. empower staff members to make necessary decisions on their own or treat them like puppets?

Management of Conflict—Did the planning unit administrator:

a. let disagreement with the staff get in the way of objective attainment?

b. explore conflicts and try to resolve them?

c. deny their existence, shrug them off, or joke about them, thus lessening their importance?

Communication—Did the planning unit administrator:

a. develop a climate in which he or she and the staff could exchange ideas freely and candidly?

b. talk with staff when requested?

Leadership Style—Did the planning unit administrator:

a. inhibit staff performance by arbitrary and autocratic practices?

Staffing—Did the planning unit administrator:

a. select personnel who lacked skills, know-how, experience, character, or drive as his or her back-up staff?

Initiative—Did the planning unit administrator:

a. procrastinate, thwart decisions, and sit on a fence when the staff needed firm, vigorous guidance?

Flexibility—Did the planning unit administrator:

a. provide the adaptable leadership when needed to pursue objectives in the face of changed conditions?

b. entertain new ideas and approaches, or turn thumbs down on any suggestions that were innovative or unusual?

4. Motivating

Gaining Commitment—Did the planning unit administrator:

a. involve staff members in setting the objectives and help them to understand their tangible needs prior to trying to link their objectives?

Inspiring—Did the planning unit administrator:

a. convey enthusiasm and encouragement to staff?

b. demonstrate a belief in the objective?

c. demonstrate that the objective was significant and urgent?

Feedback, Coaching, and Appraisal—Did the planning unit administrator:

a. give staff periodic analysis of its performance and the progress it was making toward the objective?

b. provide systematic insight into staff strengths and weaknesses?

c. help the staff to learn and improve as it progressed?

Development—Did the planning unit administrator:

a. give the staff a chance to acquire the necessary skills, know-how, and experience?

b. generate or stunt growth?

Climate—Did the planning unit administrator:

a. develop a serious, supportive, goal-directed climate that stressed high achievement and high morale?

b. develop a climate in which anything goes—in which one standard is as good as another?

5. Controlling

Performance Standards—Did the planning unit administrator:

a. establish clear-cut criteria by which performance could be evaluated?

b. understand the difference between effective and ineffective performance?

Performance Measures—Did the planning unit administrator:

a. schedule and conduct regular analyses of staff performance?

b. make sure the staff left these meetings with a clear understanding of its stance and what improved or altered performance was needed to reach its objective?

Involvement—Did the planning unit administrator:

a. involve the staff to the point where they felt ownership of the objective?

Effective Motivation Through Planning

The execution of well-developed plans is an effective way to motivate human behavior. Questions that should be considered when evaluating the planning unit administrator's performance fall into the following nine categories: budget, competition, legal, methods or systems design, compensation, materials, facilities, and back-up personnel.

1. Budget
   a. Did staff have the money needed to do the job?
2. Competition
   a. Did competition overwhelm the planning unit administrator with new or better products and/or services, a better public relations campaign?
3. Legal
   a. Did legal restrictions, threats of lawsuits, litigation, or injunctions hamper the planning unit administrator?
   b. Did state or federal regulatory agencies create. insurmountable problems?
4. Methods or Systems
   a. Was the planning unit administrator thwarted by unworkable methods or obsolete systems?

    b. Was the planning unit administrator slowed down by inefficient or overly complex procedures that could not be changed?

5. Design
   a. Was the planning unit administrator hamstrung by a faulty or inefficient product or service?
   b. Was the planning unit administrator given a second-rate product or service to use?

6. Compensation
   a. Was the planning unit administrator unable to hire the needed staff because of an inadequate compensation plan?

7. Materials
   a. Were the materials the planning unit administrator needed unavailable?
   b. Did the planning unit administrator encounter shortages that could not be overcome?
   c. Was the planning unit administrator prevented from getting materials by strikes, prohibitive prices, or the like?

8. Facilities
   a. Was the planning unit administrator required to work with outmoded or inefficient facilities, and, if so, did this affect performance?
   b. Was the equipment the planning unit administrator needed available when needed, and was it adequate?
   c. Did the planning unit administrator encounter frequent and damaging equipment problems?

9. Back-Up Personnel
   a. Did the planning unit administrator have qualified personnel to do the job?
   b. If not, was the planning unit administrator permitted to hire them?
   c. Was the planning unit administrator allowed to provide suitable training for staff?

Short-Range Objective or Long-Range Goal

There are a number of possible reasons an objective or goal was not achieved as planned. Chief among them are the following:

1. Unrealistic? Was the goal or objective:
   a. set too high or too low?
   b. wishful thinking?

2. Incomprehensible? Was the goal or objective:
   a. not understood by the staff?
   b. too windy?

3. Vague? Was the goal or objective:
   a. so general that any achievement would be considered meeting it?
4. Unfairly demanding? Was the goal or objective:
   a. too demanding?
   b. dependent on unethical or unscrupulous action?
   c. against the planning unit administrator's moral principles or sense of integrity?

School Environments

There are a number of reasons the school environments (internal and external) may have prevented the achievement of a goal or objective as planned. The chief reasons are:

1. Students
   a. Did too many students move into or out of the school district?
   b. Are too many students enrolling in private or commercial schools?
   c. Is there excessive truancy or lateness?
2. Staff
   a. Are there too many new teachers?
   b. Is the staff properly trained?
   c. Has the staff been adequately involved in the program or activity?
   d. Does the collective bargaining agreement prevent the staff from becoming meaningfully involved in the activity?
3. Labor Problems
   a. Did strikes, walkouts, or slowdowns hinder progress toward the goal or objective?
4. Competition
   a. Are private and commercial schools causing the school district's enrollment to decline?
   b. Has the competition been adequately analyzed?
   c. Are there plans available to compete with private and commercial schools?
5. Budget
   a. Were adequate funds available to support the activity or program?
6. Physical Resources
   a. Was the staff required to work with outdated or inefficient equipment. If so, did this affect progress toward the attainment of a goal and objective?
7. Materials
   a. Were adequate materials available to the staff to implement the activity or program?

b. Did a shortage of materials occur?

c. Did prices increase to the extent that all materials could not be purchased?

8. Legislation

a. Did a new law prevent the achievement of an activity or program?

b. Did state or federal regulatory agencies create problems?

9. Method or System

a. Did a method or system contain serious flaws that prevented the achievement of the goal and objective?

b. Did an outdated method or system delay progress toward a goal or objective?

10. Product

a. Did a faulty product prevent the achievement of the goal or objective?

b. Was the product outdated?

c. Was the product too expensive?

d. Was the product as useful as proclaimed?

11. Economic Conditions

a. Did a recession or inflation have an adverse effect on the goal or objective?

b. Were economic conditions properly forecast and used in the planning process?

12. Community

a. Did a community reaction have an adverse effect on the achievement of a goal or objective?

13. Stakeholders

a. Did a stakeholder have a negative impact on the attainment of a goal or objective?

b. Were stakeholders' attitudes and expectations considered in the planning process?

14. Planning Subunits

a. Did other subunits of a planning unit have a negative impact on the achievement of a goal or objective?

15. Other Items

a. Did other items have a negative impact on a goal or objective?

SALIENT POINTS

It is the responsibility of the planning unit administrator to record correctly and substantiate all performance achieved on plan and above plan for the planning unit. Each registered objective usually stands on its own, and the central planning unit administrator may or may not require proof of performance. Some school districts may require planning unit administrators to sign the operational plan attesting that it is a true statement of results. Some planning unit administrators may object to this practice. Regardless of whether or not the operational plan is signed by a planning unit or subunit, the person designated in charge can be held responsible and accountable for performance outcome.

APPLICATION STRATEGY 11

Develop a paper defining variations in performance results and presenting examples of each. Using this paper as a guide, complete the performance outcome section of the operational plan by:

1. Designing theoretical performance results using all variations.
2. Utilizing an assortment of items (documents, tools, and the like) to substantiate performances.
3. Revising or amending below plan performance results with corrective action statements.

12

PROBLEM-SOLVING PLANNING

There is probably no factor that weighs more on the success or failure of a school district than the identification and resolution of day-to-day problems that prevent or limit the effectiveness of school personnel. Strategic planning is necessary if a school district is to grow and prosper in the long run. Operational planning is required if an objective-by-objective approach is to realize long-range plans. These planning approaches, however, will not resolve day-to-day problems. Therefore, what is needed is a planning process that will put out brush fires before they get out of control.

This chapter highlights a new feature of the planning process—problem-solving planning. First, the concept is defined, and conditions that signal an existing problem are described. The advantages of problem-solving planning are mentioned briefly. A substantial portion of this chapter focuses on an understanding of the three essential phases of problem solving. The chapter ends with some comments related to an effective way to implement problem-solving planning by obtaining staff ownership of plans.

DEFINING A PROBLEM-SOLVING PLAN

A problem-solving plan is the systematic process for removing conditions, within a two-month period, which are seriously affecting personnel performance and are having an adverse impact on the school or school district. It involves jointly arriving at the definition of the problem and agreeing to the most feasible solution for removing the conditions that brought on the problem by committing resources for setting and implementing a short-range objective, performance standards, and an action plan. An example of a problem-solving plan is illustrated in Figure 12–1.

PROBLEM-SOLVING PLAN

Planning Unit_____   Date: _____

Planning Unit Administrator _____   Page_____of _____

Key Result Area _____

Citation of the Problem	
Date Problem Occurred	**Identify Unit/Project**
State Implications of the Problem	
Strategy Selected	
Strategies Dicarded	
Proposed Action (Objective)	

Figure 12–1 *Form for Preparing Problem-Solving Plans*

WHEN IS A SITUATION A PROBLEM?

A situation or event is a problem when it meets one or more of the
following conditions:

1. When a person's failure to perform a routine job has had seri-
    ous consequences on other staff members.

Proposed Action Plan			
Activity	Date	By Whom	Cost

Monitoring Performance Results

Controlling Activities	Review Dates	OP	BP	AP
1.		☐	☐	☐
2.		☐	☐	☐
3.		☐	☐	☐
4.		☐	☐	☐
5.		☐	☐	☐

Resources

Confirmation that problem has been solved:	To the best of my knowledge, the problem has been solved:
_____	_____
Signature	Signature
_____	_____
Position [Central Administrator only]	Position
_____	_____
Date	Date

Figure 12–1 *Continued*

2. When it creates a nuisance or interrupts the routine flow of the operation of a planning unit or subunit.
3. When a preset standard has not been met and performance has been adversely affected.
4. If an unusual number of staff members report it as a problem.
5. When the superintendent of schools officially announces that a problem exists.

6. When actual routine performance does not meet projected performance.
7. Whenever a crisis exists or is announced by someone in authority.

ADVANTAGES OF PREPARING PROBLEM-SOLVING PLANS

The following represent some of the benefits associated with the preparation and implementation of problem-solving plans:

1. When teams have been organized to identify and critically analyze and solve problems of the school district, the staff assumes ownership of plans and becomes more sensitive to circumstances preventing the solution to problems.
2. They foster analytical thinking and an objective approach to problem-solving.
3. They help solve little problems before they become big ones.
4. They have an immediate reward system because of the timely fashion in which plans are executed.
5. They provide opportunities for staff to determine problems in addition to arriving at an appropriate strategy for solving the problem.
6. The entire problem-solving planning process becomes an opportunity for staff to become mentally, emotionally, and physically involved in the job of problem-solving.
7. They establish a framework for in-depth analysis and systematic procedure for problem solving.
8. They give those involved, often the complainers, an opportunity to see many views of the situation, particularly when they have been given the responsibility of chairing a team for solving the problem.
9. They create a climate in which continuous and timely improvement is emphasized and attainable.

UNDERSTANDING THE THREE ESSENTIAL PHASES OF PROBLEM-SOLVING

Problem-solving planning is basically organized around three essential phases.

Analysis of the Problem

A complete analysis of the problem is broken down into four steps, which when followed will provide the educator with a practical and systematic process to problem-solving. Some of the steps involve an analytical study and completion of a specific step on the problem-solving plan, while other steps involve merely an investigation of facts.

Description of the Problem. The first step in problem analysis is outlining the problem that necessitates the corrective action. The outline should indicate current conditions (what is wrong) and the desired results (what is right). To determine whether a condition needs improvement, the educator, in most instances, must have three things:

1. Complete information as to a standard of performance in order to make a comparison.
2. Keen insight into what the actual level of performance in relation to established standards is.
3. Ability to extend the meaning of the problems by focusing on those hidden things that can later lead to difficulties.

Acquiring All the Facts. The second step in problem analysis is getting all of the facts. *All* must be stressed here because incomplete information or facts may not amplify the problem's significance or may lead to an erroneous conclusion concerning the problem. This step involves trying to determine all of the key factors surrounding the problematic condition. To some educators, this step may seem to be rather easy and somewhat academic; however, acquiring all of the facts will require a completely analytical and rigorous approach to deciphering information.

Determining the Causes. The third step to problem analysis involves an investigation of the causes and identification of the *real* problem. The particular event or occurrence that aroused an awareness of the problem may only be one element of the real problem. Unless the problem-solving plan deals with the real problem, the condition or situation may recur. The root of the problem must be determined for problem-solving planning to work effectively. The process of determining the causes must be approached with a great deal of caution. Whenever a problem occurs, there may be a tendency to rush into some type of corrective action. This is a foolish course to take, as most likely a rushed reaction will be an emotional rather than a rational one. A rational reaction will require deep thinking and insight. It will cause the educator to think about all of the possible determinants that have caused the problem and then, in light of the facts, to arrive at a decision.

Proposed Action. The fourth step in the problem analysis phase revolves around a proposed action to eliminate the problem. There are three reasons for this step:

1. It gives directions to the problem-solving plan by stating expected results.
2. It is a basis for generating additional information or facts.
3. It ensures objectivity in search of an alternative for eliminating the problem.

Developing and Selecting Strategies

Once the problem has been clearly defined, the next major step in problem solving involves the development and selection of alternative strategies for solving the problem, each one having its own advantages and disadvantages. The quality of the solution will be predicated to a large extent on whether or not some sound strategies have been developed in order to select the most feasible one. An insufficient choice of strategies will produce some significant implications to effective decision making. The most serious effect is that it will seriously restrict the strategic thinking process that is so vital to effective problem-solving planning.

There are basically two ways to develop alternative strategies for solving problems.

Use Results of Past Experience. The most widely used method for arriving at various strategies for problem solving is to profit from past experience. When confronted with a guess situation, the planning unit administrator compares it with similar experiences in which success has been realized. Adjustments may be made in the solution to accommodate the peculiarity of the given problem. The degree of experience with the problem will be the basis upon which alternative strategies will be developed and analyzed. However, because of the rapidly changing school environments, solutions used to solve yesterday's problem may not be successful today. Therefore, the planning unit administrator should also investigate the experiences of other administrators to arrive at other strategies, as stated below.

Use Results of Other Administrators. By coupling the administrator's experience with that of others who have found solutions to similar problems, the planning unit administrator can contribute greatly to the number and quality of alternative strategies generated to solve the problem. However, regardless of how well the marriage between the experience of the planning unit administrator and others is made, the dynamic nature of public education will demand a degree of ingenuity and creativity for problem solving.

The selection of an appropriate strategy to eliminate the problem will only take place if the following sequential steps are taken:

1. Identifying the advantages and disadvantages of each strategy considering the following factors:
   a. impact of the solution on the problem
   b. implications of the solution
   c. acceptability to staff
   d. unlikelihood of repetition
   e. costs
   f. specific benefits
   g. use of strengths
2. Assigning a weight to each strategy

Weight can be determined by assigning a value to each advantage and disadvantage cited in item 1 and by adding and subtracting to arrive at an objective weight. Each strategy should then be ranked according to the weight received.

The planning unit administrator should not be hasty and select the top-ranked strategy. It is at this time that rigorous analysis and intuition must be applied by comparing the first strategy with the following three or five methods. Only after this exercise has been completed should a selection be made.

When selecting the most appropriate strategy, the planning unit administrator should also identify all of the discarded options to demonstrate to the reviewer that all possible alternative strategies have been covered. Obviously, the planning unit administrator should be able to explain why the particular choice was made.

Sometimes a form or guide is used to analyze each strategy.

Implementing the Proposed Solution

Determining the most appropriate strategy to solve the problem is not enough. A plan of action must be developed to put life into the decision. Several activities must take place in order to do this.

1. Using the selective strategy as a base, prepare a short-range objective to solve the problem. The time span for the achievement of the objective should be set within sixty days.
2. Identify success indicators by describing performance standards for each short-range objective.
3. Prepare an action plan to delineate all of the activities, the dates, and persons responsible for their completion.
4. Indicate resources and a projected budget for each activity. Human and nonhuman resources should be identified as well as equipment, materials, and supplies.
5. Give the name and signature of the person responsible for solving the problem, as well as the name of the planning unit administrator who must verify that the problem is indeed solved.

Item

Problem-solving planning, when developed and executed appropriately, can be one of the most beneficial and enjoyable stages of the planning process. Some school districts have begun to implement a formal problem-solving planning process using the collective skills, experiences, and talents of their teachers, in order to alleviate conditions that are hampering the day-to-day operations of the school. Experience has demonstrated that problem-solving planning pays high dividends in terms of giving teachers the opportunity better to understand the factors that brought on the problem, why some problems cannot be solved easily, and what their options are to remove the problem. As a result, teachers' morale is improved because of the critical and participative roles they play in improving the organizational health of the school.

IMPLEMENTING PROBLEM-SOLVING PLANNING

In Chapter 15, job enrichment is introduced as an effective and contemporary concept for improving staff performance. This same process can be used in problem solving. The following steps have been found to be effective:

1. Request staff to generate descriptions of problems associated with routine operations of the school that can be resolved within a sixty-day period.
2. Analyze these problems and decipher which ones are critical (those that can be solved within sixty days), short-range, and long-range.
3. Prepare a list of critical problems under appropriate categories.
4. Organize the staff into four- to five-member problem-solving teams. Select the "chief complainer" on each team and designate that person as team leader responsible for the solution of the problem.
5. Distribute the list of problems among the team according to personalities and complainers. Try to equalize the distribution of problems, if there are many.
6. Have each team think through each problem and complete the problem-solving plan.
7. All problem-solving plans should be reviewed by either the planning unit administrator or the planning coordinator to determine if there are any gaps in the plans and to identify the person who is to testify that the problem has been solved.

This author has found that cancelling school for a day and involving the entire staff, in the manner described above, will pay high dividends in more than one way:

1. Staff members begin to work on problems as a team.
2. Morale is improved.
3. Some problems are solved, and the staff understands and, in many instances, accepts why others are not resolved.
4. Staff members begin to understand and appreciate the role of the planning unit administrator.
5. The untapped creative talents of the staff are utilized in solving the school's problems.

SALIENT POINTS

The form used to record the problem-solving plan should consist of some descriptive statements written on a sheet of paper or printed form. It is not the plan that is of paramount importance, however, but the process used to solve the problem. The form only provides direction and guidance, in order to facilitate and expedite the activities essential to solve the problem.

APPLICATION STRATEGY 12

Read the following or a similar book on quality circles: James Lewis, Jr., *Establishing Quality Circles in Profit and Nonprofit Organizations* (New York: The Institute for Advancing Education for Management, 1982), or Donald L. Dewar, *The Quality Circle Handbook* (Red Bluff, Calif.: Quality Circle Institute, 1980).

Armed with information on these two concepts, prepare a working paper for organizing and implementing a planning improvement circle for a school district. This working paper should include the following minimum elements:

1. Definition of planning improvement circle program (PIC).
2. Purposes.
3. Objectives.
4. Composition.
5. Duties of membership on PIC.
6. Techniques to solve problems.
7. How training will be instituted.

8. How meetings should be conducted.
9. The operations of PIC programs.
10. Key elements to a successful PIC program.
11. Problems likely to be encountered and tenable solutions.

Prepare a program to train a group of teachers who will successfully implement the PIC program.

13

UNDERSTANDING PLANNING CONTROLS

Establishing proper controls in the planning process is one of the most difficult tasks confronting school administrators. This may be one of the reasons proper control techniques have been lacking in many of the long-range planning models observed by this author. Nevertheless, unless controls are carefully developed and installed, the efforts of the planners may be to no avail. Controls are a warning system to alert those responsible for implementing plans to what is occurring and to what may occur if corrective action is not taken. To be effective, controls must directly relate to the standards, objectives, goals, and mission of the school district. Therefore, controls should be an integrated component of all long- and short-range plans.

The rationale of this chapter is to define planning controls, illustrate and explain the closed-loop planning control cycle, describe some of the advantages of planning controls, and exemplify types of planning controls. Some attention is given to management by exception as a planning control technique. The chapter concludes with causes of variations in standards and offers some final words concerning general characteristics of planning controls.

DEFINING PLANNING CONTROLS

The process of establishing controls in a planning unit, which involves the collection of essential information, reporting and analysis of useful data, and the taking of corrective action, is analogous to a thermostat. The thermostat is set at a certain desired temperature. The mechanism not only activates the equipment to produce the desired heat level, but also automatically reports the end result. In education, the corrective

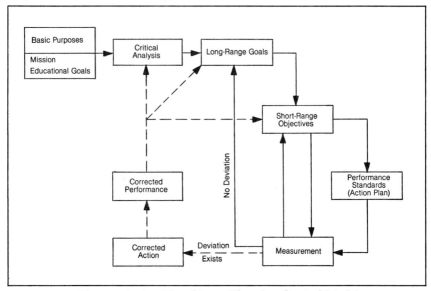

Figure 13–1 *Closed-Loop Planning Control Model*

action is not automatic. Because education is a dynamic process that interacts with internal and external variables, the control system must be adaptive and capable of reacting to changing times and conditions in order to be effective.

Planning controls can be defined as a systematic process for providing planning unit administrators with effective information about the status of plans in order to assist them to take corrective action to enhance the attainment of the school district's short-range objectives and long-range goals.

THE PLANNING CONTROL CYCLE

One of the most popular approaches to establishing planning controls involves the closed-loop model illustrated in Figure 13-1. This model begins with the establishment of long-range goals to fulfill the basic purposes, mission, and educational goals of the school district and complete its cycle with their attainment.

Critical Analysis

All corrections to plans should be recorded in the appropriate sections of the critical analysis. This critical analysis data base is only useful when it contains updated information. A planning exception report, which is explained later in this chapter, is used to record and correct performance and should be kept with the critical analysis even though changes were directed at long-range goals or short-range objectives.

The central model requires that standards of performance be developed in areas that affect the achievement of goals and objectives. Performance must be assessed to determine whether or not it has met the standard. If performance is achieved below plan or outside acceptable limits of variation of standard, corrective action must be taken in order to achieve the goals and objectives. As the closed-loop model is based upon a systematic process of controlling, each component in the model is an integral part of whole system, and the omission of any one item will jeopardize the effectiveness of the entire control cycle.

Long-Range Goals

The first phase of the control cycle is the development of long-range goals to achieve the basic purposes, mission, and educational goals of the school district. It is not enough merely to establish long-range goals. They must be clarified and disseminated to the persons who are going to be affected by them. When understood, long-range goals are common denominators for guiding human efforts in the school organization. Because of the time span allowed to achieve long-range goals, they seldom change, although deviations may occur in the plans. Usually corrective action must take place within a short time, and it rarely affects long-range goals. Changes in long-range goals are the result of a difficulty with the goals themselves. The planner will have the option of discarding the goal (only under extraordinary circumstances), revising the attainment date, or modifying the performance itself. Changes should be recorded on the planning exception report and transmitted to the appropriate planning unit administrator. Long-range goals act as standards for the basic purposes, mission, and educational goals, and therefore should be established with great deliberation.

Short-Range Objectives

The second phase of the control cycle is the preparation of short-range objectives. More often than not, deviations in plans will affect short-range objectives. When deviations do occur, the short-range objective should either be discarded, revised, or modified, or a completely new one may have to be developed. As with long-range goals, the vehicle used to register deviations in plans and the appropriate corrective action is the planning exception report. Short-range objectives act as standards for long-range goals; however, sometimes these short-range objectives are qualified with performance standards. When this is the case, the standards should be either revised or modified to accommodate deviations in the plans.

When deviations in plans occur, the planning unit administrator should carefully analyze the reasons for the change, review the essential information in the critical analysis report, and scrutinize the internal and external environments. When this task is accomplished, a decision should be made as to how much variation is allowable before the deviation is considered an abnormal situation. The establishment of upper and lower limits of deviation will prove helpful for guidance purposes. If, after careful scrutiny of all the facts, the planning unit administrator is not convinced that the short-range objective needs to be changed, a case should be made before the superintendent.

Performance

The third phase of the control cycle involves the assessment of performance to determine whether or not the appropriate standards have been met. Performance deviations will most likely be detected as illustrated in the following example:

Item	*Time*
Critical event or problem	Immediately
Program deviation	Immediately
Quarterly report (operational plan)	Every three months
Annual report (strategic plan)	Yearly

When performance is found to be within the allowable limits it is usually assumed that the system is okay. This may not be absolutely true, because short-range objectives or performance standards that seem adequate at one point in time may seem to be set too high or too low when analyzed at another point in time. This is the main reason a dynamic planning system is imperative if school organizations are to survive and prosper in these rapidly changing times.

Corrective Action

Proper controls have been established when the control system indicates that plans are not being achieved on schedule. The planning unit administrator should devise a continuous plan of action that will eliminate excessive variations from standards, even if it is merely directing close scrutiny of future performance results. Before a control system can be effective, someone must be given the responsibility for certain aspects of the system if deviations should occur. Only in this case will there be an accountability plan for taking corrective actions in a prompt and efficient manner.

SOME ADVANTAGES OF PLANNING CONTROLS

The establishment of planning controls is advantageous, as illustrated by the potential benefits listed below:

1. Means for correcting performance.
2. Means for alerting planners to deviations in plans and performance.
3. Means for ensuring the attainment of long-range goals and short-range objectives.
4. Means for taking appropriate follow-up action to assure that decisions have been implemented.
5. Means for providing the planning process with effective information to take corrective action to attain goals and objectives.
6. Means for assessing the internal and external environments to determine the degree to which plans or performance are within standards.

DEFINING MANAGEMENT BY EXCEPTION

One of the most powerful planning control concepts, which is relatively new in public education, is management by exception (MBX). Like any other concept, it must be applied correctly and consistently if the full benefits are to be realized.[1]

Management by exception is the process of establishing and using an information reporting system to detect unacceptable variations in plans or performance, to analyze these variations to determine the causes, and to take corrective action to achieve maximum results.

IMPLEMENTING MANAGEMENT BY EXCEPTION

The following represent the three essential phases for implementing management by exception.

Phase I—Installing an Information Reporting System

Step I—Collection of Essential and Critical Information. Essential and critical information about the school district must be collected and analyzed to act as a data base for decision-making purposes. Without this base, plans cannot be prepared adequately, and controls would be useless.

---

[1] George L. Morrisey, *Management by Objectives and Results*, pp. 144–169.

This information can be collected either manually or by computer. It is insufficient merely to collect information, as the data must relate directly to the fulfillment of the school district's mission. Periodically a data base check should be made to determine whether all of the collected information is necessary and adequate to help produce the desired effect. Once the data base has been established, the next step involves its use.

Step 2—Utilization of Data Base. The data base is used to establish long-range goals to achieve the school district's mission. Strategies are carefully considered and selected to attain short-range objectives. Performance standards are indices for measuring the objective attainment, and action plans are the basis for realizing performance standards. Each of these items represents a different type of standard which will be used by the management by exception as control points. The following are the essential documents that will contain these standards:

- Critical analysis report
  - Essential information
  - Critical data
- Strategic plans
  - Planning assumptions
  - Long-range goals
  - Strategies
  - Long-range budget
- Operational plans
  - Planning assumptions
  - Short-range objectives
  - Performance standards
  - Action plans
  - Short-range budget

When management by exception is properly implemented, and when deviations occur in either plans or performance, one or more of the following standards must be revised or modified to report the exception. To do this properly, a planning exception report must be made.

Step 3—Institution of Planning Exception Reporting. One major fault of long-range planning is that once plans are developed and approved, they often lose their vitality. Frequently they become "dead" plans, delegated to storage in a drawer to be seldom if ever referred to and inadequately used. One way this situation can be avoided is to insist that all exceptions in plans or performance be recorded on a planning exception report.

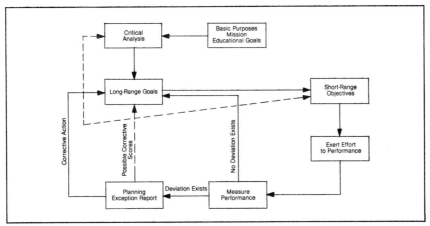

Figure 13–2 *Planning Exception Report: Safety Valve in the Control Model*

Figure 13–2 illustrates how to use the planning exception report in the closed-loop controlling model. Basically, the planning exception report form is used as a monitoring and feedback mechanism to communicate unacceptable variances in either plans or performance, so that timely corrective actions and adjustments can be made accordingly.[2] Note that all unacceptable deviations in plans and performance must be recorded on this form before any corrective action is taken. The purposes of this action are: (1) to make certain that all variances are in writing and used as the basis for revising and/or modifying appropriate plans and documents; (2) to give periodic injections of "life" to plans that hitherto may have been left unused; and (3) to maintain an accountability record.

ADVANTAGES OF THE PLANNING EXCEPTION REPORT

There are several reasons for using the planning exception report as an integral component of the management by objective concept. The following are some of the most important ones:

1. It is a means of communicating planning exceptions so that timely corrective actions can take place.
2. It can be used as a basis for determining if an administrator has been accountable in reporting the variances in either performance or plans in a timely fashion.

[2] Earl P. Strong and Robert D. Smith, *Management Controls Models* (New York: Holt, Rinehart & Winston, 1968), pp. 17–18.

3. It can act as a reminder to administrators continuously to monitor and evaluate performance to determine if expected results will occur.
4. It helps to motivate human effort to be responsive to ever-changing environments.
5. It acts as a safety valve in the closed-loop controlling model.
6. It can enable administrators to appraise their past decisions, plans, and performance in view of planning exceptions so that similar mistakes and/or poor judgments are not made.
7. It provides a system for identifying the problem and its causes.

THE PLANNING EXCEPTION REPORT ILLUSTRATED AND EXPLAINED

An example of a planning exception report is illustrated in Figure 13–3. As different school organizations may have different planning needs, the contents of this report may vary. The following represent some basic content for reporting planning exceptions.

Description includes general descriptive information pertaining to who prepared the report and the reasons for the required change in the plan or performance.

Reasons for the current or anticipated variance represent the nature and cause of the planning exception(s), which usually relate to information contained in the control analysis.

Corrective action to be taken represents the adjustments to be made and the results expected.

Impact of change—present or anticipated—represents implications of the exception to goal(s), objective(s), performance standard(s), or action plans.

Expected results before the change represent performance expectations prior to the exception and any appropriate comments related to any portion of the report.

When the planning exception report has been completed and all accompanying documents have been attached thereto, the full report should be forwarded to the appropriate planning unit administrator for approval. Once approval has been obtained, the report should be filed in its corresponding section of the plan.

Phase II—Identifying the Exception and Its Causes

Using a planning exception report helps identify the cause(s) of the unacceptable deviation in plan or performance in each section. In fact, the planning exception report cannot be adequately completed until the

Strategic Planning Process

Planning Unit: _____   Date: _____

Planning Unit Administrator: _____   Position: _____

Planning Component: _Planning Exception Report_   Page _____ of _____

Change Requirement: ☐ Planning Assumption   ☐ Long Range Goal   ☐ Short Range Objective
                       ☐ Performance Standard   ☐ Action Plan   ☐ Budget

1. Reason(s) for the present or anticipated variance:

2. Impact of change (present or anticipated):

3. Corrective action to be taken:

4. Impact of change on goal(s) and/or objective(s):

5. Expected results before the change: ☐ On plan   ☐ Above plan   ☐ Below plan
   Comments:

Approved by: _____   Submitted by: _____

Position: _____   Position: _____

Figure 13–3 *Planning Exception Report*

exact problem and its cause(s) are determined. All plans are developed
to fulfill goals and objectives related to the major key results areas.
Therefore, these same areas can be helpful in identifying diagnostic
tools and exception analysis for identifying exceptions and their causes.
Table 13–1 is useful for this purpose.

Table 13-1 Diagnostic Tools and Education Analysis

Major Key Result Area	Diagnostic Tool	Exception Analysis
Financial Resources	1. Budget and financial reports	1. Over-expenditure, misappropriation of funds; inefficient performance; budget inadequacy 2. Understatement of program costs
Performance Evaluation and Training	1. Operational plan 2. Individual Performance Plan 3. Personnel records	1. Failure to attain objectives and/or performance standards; and ineffective performance 2. Failure to meet objectives and/or performances; poor performance 3. Excessive absenteeism; reprimands
Physical Resources	1. Master Building Plan 2. Strategic and operational plans	1. Defects in building construction 2. Breakdown of equipment; failing to meet projected goals and objectives 3. Accidents due to construction
Student Learning and Growth	1. Academic achievement tests 2. Student cummulative records	1. Underachievement in students' academic, emotional, social and physical growth 2. Physical defects; social problems; excessive absenteeism
Organizational Management	1. Strategic, operational, and problem-solving plans 2. Surveys 3. Personnel and other records	1. Overall poor performance; failing to meet expected goals and objectives; unresolved problems 2. Unhealthy school 3. High teacher absenteeism; high turnover
Innovation	1. Strategic and operational plans 2. Individual Performance Plan 3. Academic achievement test	1. Failing to meet projected goals and objectives; understated budget allocations 2. Failing to meet objective; poor performance 3. Failing to meet achievement capabilities
Community Involvement and Relations	1. Operational plans	1. Failing to meet objectives; performance standards; and/or action plan; community complaints; budget defeats
Instructional Programs and Services	1. Program offerings 2. Program-oriented budget	1. Low enrollment; high absentee rate; insufficient or excessive program offerings 2. High program and services cost; net cost efficiency

Diagnostic tools that can be used to detect a financial resource problem are the budget and ratio analysis. In examining the budget, exception can be denoted because of the overexpenditure or misappropriation of funds, inefficient performance and an inadequate budget. The following represents how standards can be monitored:

Diagnostic Tool	Exception	Controlling Basis Document
Budget	Overexpenditure or misappropriation of funds	Monthly Final Reports Audit Reports
	Inefficient performance	Verbal indication that objectives won't be achieved "on" or "above" plan
	Inadequate Budget	Verbal indication

One approach planning unit administrators may wish to use for controlling human efforts in the school district prior to finalizing plans is identification of all possible exceptions in strategic and operational plans and designation of the means by which they may be detected. The means can be written or verbally stated, and standards should be devised for each one. In this way, the school district has a complete map for controlling all essential activities for its growth and prosperity.

Phase III—Taking Corrective Action

As in Phase II, the planning exception report should not be completed until this phase has been satisfactorily accomplished. If the planning process is to remain viable, corrective actions must be taken to eliminate exceptions. These actions can take several forms, as indicated by the following.

Adjust Appropriate Planning Assumption. Many activities of the planning process have been prepared assuming certain conditions will result if the projected condition is significantly below plan. If this is the case, the assumption should be altered appropriately. At times, additional assumptions must be added or the existing premise eliminated.

Revise or Modify Short-Range Objectives. Exceptions in either plans or performance may have occurred because the objective was either unrealistic or unchallenging. If this is the case, the objective should either be revised or modified. If the objective was understated, it should be revised upward; on the other hand, if the objective was overstated, it should be revised downward. Over- or understating an objective can have a serious effect on the morale of staff and consequently on performance. Objectives are designed to stimulate improved performance. If they fail to meet this criterion, they are useless.

Also included with short-range objectives are performance standards and sometimes an action plan. An exception may require not only revision or modification of the short-range objective, but of associated components as well. Performance standards that are used to determine satisfactory achievement of short-range objectives may need to be revised upward or downward depending on the objective and the exception. New standards may need to be added or old ones may be eliminated. Activities in the action plan may also necessitate modifications or revisions, and one or more may need to be added or eliminated. The top-down approach should be used to initiate a change in a short-range objective. First, determine how the short-range objective should be changed by relating it to the long-range goal. If the existing short-range objective is sufficient to attain the long-range goal, then the performance standard may need to be examined for possible revision or modification. This procedure should also be used with the action plan. At times an additional short-range objective must be added to help achieve the long-range goal. At other times, although on rare occasions, the short-range objective and accompanying components should be entirely eliminated from the plan.

Revise Operational Policies and Procedures. If these items have been found to be satisfactory, and variations still exist in either plans or performance, operational policies should be examined. This may indicate that more instructional time is needed for reading rather than for math or vice-versa, or that teams should be organized to maximize the efforts of the teaching staff. Not all operational policy changes will help to eliminate the exception, but when the planning assumption has hit the mark and objectives, standards, and activities are satisfactory, the exception can sometimes be eliminated through revision of operational policies and procedures.

Modify Personnel Practices and Policies. When all of the above items have been found to be satisfactory, the exception may need to be eliminated by changing staffing patterns or applying proper motivational techniques to improve performance. Plans cannot be performed properly if the staff works in an unhealthy school environment. Some techniques designed to improve the health of a school environment are:

- Open the lines of communication with staff. This can be achieved by instituting an open door policy, disseminating an inhouse newsletter, occasionally lunching with staff, becoming a classroom assistant to the teacher, and the like.
- Practice the concept of "every teacher a manager." Teachers' responsibility now is restricted to teaching. By practicing job enrichment in education, the administrator begins to share some administrative responsibilities, such as planning and controlling. Job enrichment includes teachers as an essential component of the planning process, thereby motivating their behavior and involving them in the whole process of education. Job enrichment is discussed at length in another chapter of this book.
- Disseminate and clarify the school district's long-range goals to the staff. A meeting specifically conducted for this purpose is an excellent way to do this.
- Involve the staff in problem-solving planning. Through this process, they will gain an improved understanding of the operations of the school district and as a consequence the health of the school will begin to improve.

IDENTIFYING PLANNING CONTROLS

There are numerous other controls that can be used in the planning process, some of which are more applicable to given situations than others. The effective use of planning controls is predicated on the time and effort required to employ them and the planning unit administrator's ingenuity in making use of them. The following represent other general forms of planning controls.

Visual Aids. Pert and Gant charts are two excellent examples of using visual aids as controls. Other examples may be line graphs, milestone charts, and bar charts with a variation of color codes.

Computer Printouts. Printouts are excellent controls for budgetary purposes. This technique of controls is also applicable to maintaining performance records of personnel, keeping tabs on inventory, and storing critical plans, such as projections or financial data.

Written Reports. Some standard controls involving written reports are the quarterly and annual performance reports.

Staff Meetings. Periodic verbal reports on performance and plans can easily be attained at regularly scheduled staff meetings. A few spoken words can save a great deal of paperwork and time, and can be more expeditiously acted upon if time is of critical importance.

CAUSES OF VARIATIONS IN STANDARDS

A deviation in a standard is any significant divergence from plans or performance that will require corrective action to regain the desired level.

Variations in standards fall into four categories.

1. Unexpected events may have an adverse effect on the school district. Among them are:
   • Death of a superintendent of schools.
   • Wildcat strike.
   • Personnel freeze.
   • Across-the-board decrease in the budget.
2. Human performance may adversely affect either plans or performance that is within the control of the person or his or her supervisor. Some examples are:
   • Lack of skill or knowledge.
   • Misinterpretation of instruction.
   • Gross negligence.
   • Inability to perform.
   • Willful misperformance.
3. Uncertainties are difficult to predict because of the high probability of fluctuation. Some examples are:
   • Teacher/student absentee rate.
   • Student accidents.
   • Loss of school aid.
   • Legislation changes.
4. Work stoppages are delays in the normal school day that are beyond the control of the planning unit administrator. Among them are:
   • Computer breakdown.
   • Excessive absentee rate of secretaries.
   • Fire.
   • Act of God.

GENERAL CHARACTERISTICS OF PLANNING CONTROLS

Earl P. Strong and Robert D. Smith identify the following general principles that should apply to all planning controls.[2]

[2] Earl P. Strong and Robert D. Smith, *Management Controls Models* (New York: Holt, Rinehart & Winston, 1968), pp. 17–18.

Flexibility. Planning controls should allow adaptation to individual situations and changes in the internal and external environments. If, for example, salaries have been projected assuming a 5½ percent increase in the cost of living index, and the actual increase is 6¾ percent, other budgetary items must be altered to compensate for this salary increase.

Consistency. Planning controls must be consistent with the mission and educational goals of the school district.

Clarity. Planning controls must be written and communicated to all personnel who are going to be directly affected by them.

Immediate Feedback. Performance or program deviations should be reported as soon as possible on the planning exception report form.

Discretionary Corrective Action. Corrective action should be taken only when necessary, and any decisions should be firm and reasonable.

Pervasiveness. Planning controls should exist on all levels of the school organization.

SALIENT POINTS

The most important steps in the comprehensive planning process are the implementation and use of planning controls. If they are not used, many plans may not be realized because of the ever changing internal and external environments of the school district necessitating changes in use of resources, methods, programs, and the like. If, on the other hand, planning controls are improperly implemented, not only will on and above plans' performances be seriously affected, but staff morale will be threatened. Good planning controls will mean a good chance that plans will be carried out and that the school district will ultimately grow and prosper.

APPLICATION STRATEGY 13

Prepare a model for monitoring the strategic and operational planning program developed in Application Strategy 1. Develop the short-range planning monitoring model first by dovetailing this model with a long-range planning monitoring model. Establish a complete monitoring schedule to cover a period that is at least as long as the longest long-range goal.

14

IMPROVING THE PLANNING PROCESS USING A COORDINATOR

Each year the job of operating school districts is becoming more difficult and complex. Changing times and conditions have brought new demands on administrators and teachers. Institutions of higher education, in many instances, have not helped the situation. They either have ignored the rapidly changing environment or have done relatively little to update the training needs of educators. As a result, school districts that are contemplating the implementation of strategic and operational planning must take other means to provide the necessary knowledge and training to install the planning program effectively. One method would be to establish a position of planning coordinator or director who will orchestrate all of the activities associated with the program. It is possible to implement planning without such a position; however, without the training and technical assistance of an expert, it will take longer to implement the system on a district-wide level, be difficult to provide highly qualified plans, take too much time to initiate the program's operation, and not allow the chief school officer the necessary time to devote to other aspects of operating the school district.

The rationale for this chapter is to discuss the role of the planning coordinator in order to focus on the multifaceted role of the person who occupies this position. A brief discussion highlights the qualifications of the planning coordinator to demonstrate the uniqueness of this assignment. Some comments are made as to whom the planning ocordinator should report. The chapter ends with some pros and cons for hiring an insider versus an outsider for this position.

THE ROLE OF THE PLANNING COORDINATOR

The planning coordinator or director neither directs nor plans, but orchestrates or acts as a sort of catalyst and general prodder to ensure the successful development, implementation, and evaluation of the strategic and operational planning processes. Given this charge, this person performs the following functions.[1]

Assists the Superintendent in Launching and Implementing the Planning Program

The planning coordinator helps the chief school officer establish the school district's network of aims and prepares a timetable to install the planning program, and all policies, procedures, and guidelines (via a manual) to ensure its success. In addition, the planning coordinator assists the staff in conducting a critical analysis and developing strategic and operational plans, and ascertains that proper controls have been developed and periodically reported on. The planning coordinator also plans, develops, and maintains a resource area for storing forms, materials, and books that will be of assistance to the staff.

Meets with Individuals, Small Groups, Departments, and Planning Units to Explain and Delineate the Program

The planning program cannot succeed without the complete understanding and cooperation of the faculty members. Therefore, it is imperative that the planning coordinator establish seminars with administrators and faculty members to orient them to the full scope, methods, and objectives of the planning system. Once the program has been set in motion, the planning coordinator should constantly advise and coordinate the efforts and activities of all groups involved.

Helps the Planning Unit Administrators Analyze Problem Areas for Developing Plans

The planning coordinator should carefully analyze all variances in outcome on plans at all levels and should look for relationships between "delays," "amendments," and "below plan results" to determine the extent to which they might reflect larger problems. The planning coordinator should also aid in developing improvement suggestions for individual planning unit administrators as well as for planning units.

---

[1] From the book, *School Management by Objectives* by Dr. James Lewis, Jr., © 1974 by Parker Publishing Company, Inc. Published by Parker Publishing Company, Inc., West Nyack, New York 10994.

Assists the Planning Unit Administrators in Identifying Problems that Emerge as a Result of the Plans

The planning coordinator should set up procedures for systematically reviewing the plans, determining which are above, on or below plan. In performing this duty visibility is important; that is, the planning coordinator must visit, confer frequently with staff, and in general make sure the plans are a working reality and not just "paper plans." It is possible that outcomes that are above (or even on) plan are the result of objectives that were set too low; in such cases the planning coordinator should re-evaluate these objectives.

Objectives that are below plan must be recognized and followed up on by the planning coordinator. In this case, the planning coordinator should meet with the involved staff member(s) and assist them in either revising, modifying, deleting, or adding new strategies, goals, or objectives. Correcting below plan outcomes must be one of the highest priority items.

The planning coordinator should also be alert to emerging patterns in particular areas if improvement is to be effected. From this vantage point, problems should be pinpointed that are perhaps too close to planning unit administrators to be identified by them.

Conducts Analysis of Training Needs and Initiates Training Programs

The planning coordinator must be able to assess the need for a training development program, create such a program, and be involved in its administration and total evaluation.

Since the planning coordinator's task is to improve the performance of planning unit administrators, decisions must be made as to where improvement is needed, how much should be provided, and what individuals are involved. Once this has been accomplished, the planning coordinator, assisted by the personnel administrator, should establish the training program or programs necessary to meet the needs of the staff. The planning coordinator's next step is to handle the task of bringing about the improvement itself. A training development program must be conducted to help others teach it, or advise on the program's approaches and developments. Finally, to be most effective in bringing about the desired change, the action or activities of the planning unit administrators should be checked after the training development program has been concluded. This check would enable the planning coordinator to determine whether the program was successful or if additional training is necessary.

Has Responsibility for Monitoring the Planning Program to Prevent Problems and to Correct Them

The planning coordinator must monitor planning unit plans to guard against confused strategies, imprecise statements of goals, inordinate degrees of attention and energy being expended upon trivial problems, inadequate controls, failures to raise the levels of performance expectations from year to year, unrealistic statements of objectives, and conflict between the objectives of the planning units and long-range goals of the school district.

Item
A commissioner of education attempted to implement a mandated long-range planning system state-wide without the use of a state coordinator. His excuse for not appointing a person to this position was, "I don't want a long-range planning czar." During the first year of the program, scores of questions poured into the county superintendent's office and the state department of education. Different staff members gave different interpretations to similar questions and problems. It wasn't long before administrators and teachers were complaining that the state department of education didn't have its act together. Fortunately, the commissioner acted in time to "put out the fire" that may have had serious adverse consequences for the planning program.

Assists in Conducting the Critical Analysis

Ever since the Sputnik crisis of the 1950s, public education has been faced with persistent calls for "progress." However, to move forward and progress, a school system must first be well aware of its current standing. In other words, if it does not know where it is, it will not know where it wants to go in the future. In order to assess the current situation, school districts need evaluative data. Unfortunately, most school personnel (from top level administrators to individual classroom teachers) are not trained to recognize relevant data or systematically to gather it for analysis. The planning coordinator would help train personnel in data collection and analysis so this information can be used effectively.

Counsels Planning Unit Administrators

The planning coordinator *must be the ultimate authority* in the functioning of the planning program and must be readily available to counsel, coach, and make decisions when difficulties arise. This person should be centrally located, yet free to meet in problem-solving situations in an attempt to bring group efforts together to improve plans.

Item

Some school superintendents may reject the statement the planning coordinator is the ultimate authority on long-range planning in the school district. If the coordinator is very competent and knowledgeable about the job of strategic and operational planning, then that person should be the "ultimate authority" on the subject. This statement does not preclude the chief school officer from vetoing or modifying either a decision or action taken by the planning coordinator. It is usually impossible for the superintendent to be the ultimate authority, because of a lack of time to do justice to the area; after all, one of the reasons for appointing a planning coordinator is to retain a person who would eventually become an expert or an authority on planning. It is high time that educators are given recognition when it is deserved.

Assists the Staff in Strategic Thinking

The planning coordinator should take steps to improve or stimulate strategic thinking by defining or redefining the network of aims, establishing strategic guidelines, or raising strategic questions, requiring central and school planning units to submit and obtain approval on strategic statements before developing operational plans, having school planning units explore strategic issues and queries developed by central plan unit, and employing strategically oriented planning concepts developed by other organizations.

QUALIFYING FOR THE POSITION OF
PLANNING COORDINATOR

Implementing strategic and operational planning is no ordinary job. One of the main reasons long-range planning has not been as effective in education as it has been in business and industry is that many superintendents and commissioners of public education have attempted to install planning without delegating one person with "full" authority to orchestrate the activities of the program, or the person selected to coordinate the program has not been competent enough to carry out such a difficult chore. The job of planning coordinator will require an extraordinary individual with a great deal of drive, motivation, creativity, insight, empathy, and human understanding. The following is a brief description of the special qualifications for the position of planning coordinator.

Academic Preparation

In addition to having either a B.S. or B.A. degree, the planning coordinator should possess an M.A. or M.S. degree in education with emphasis in elementary and secondary education, an M.B.A. degree in organizational analysis or development, and an Ed.D. or Ph.D. in educational planning.

Experience

The planning coordinator should have a minimum of five years of teaching experience in elementary and secondary education. A minimum of five years of experience in supervision and administration on the central administration level is also desirable. Experience in business or industry, particularly in planning, is highly desirable.

Special Features

The person chosen for the position should be well trained and extremely knowledgeable about strategic and operational planning: its techniques, implementation, and pitfalls. Although a school district might designate someone within the administrative team to oversee the program, the position must be an independent one; that is, the planning coordinator must have no responsibilities or duties other than overseeing and implementing the program. This person must have a free rein, be accountable solely to the superintendent, and be accessible at all times to personnel in the district. The planning coordinator cannot serve on a part-time basis, as there must be a trained authority constantly available for troubleshooting, analysis, diagnosis, and counseling, if the planning program is to succeed. Obviously, the individual filling this position cannot have shared responsibilities or obligations.

Important Job Skills

The planning coordinator must possess a number of important job skills to initiate, implement, and evaluate the planning program. Some of these skills are:

1. *Organization and efficiency:* The planning coordinator must have the ability to coordinate and supervise programs, establish a comprehensive operational structure to successfully implement the program, and be able to manage and oversee all programs to ensure their efficient operation.
2. *Ability to work with basic understandings:* The planning coordinator must be able to recognize basic conceptual problems

successfully to manipulate the programs to augment the plan's operational productivity and must have the ability to foresee and understand all problems that could arise during the implementation of the planning processes.

3. *Understanding of the operation of the school system:* It is essential that the planning coordinator be cognizant of the many and complex roles of the personnel involved in the school district's operation in order to relate successfully to the administrators and faculty members and their obligations and duties in the planning program.

4. *Ability to work with people:* The planning coordinator must be able to communicate and work with people in order to generate enthusiasm for the plan in the community as well as within the school district. This person must be aware of the social composition and community problems in order to implement a productive program within the limits of the social environment.

5. *Troubleshooting:* One function of the planning coordinator is to be aware of all snags that may develop. In essence, this person must be a troubleshooter and should either prevent problems from arising or find solutions as soon as possible after problems have developed.

6. *Conceptual skills:* The planning coordinator must maintain a "larger" view of the district's goal, in order to help those of shorter or narrower vision understand the implications of the broader view on their individual tasks.

7. *Professional knowledge and skills:* It is the planning coordinator's duty to utilize years of experience in school operation and teaching methods when making decisions, solving problems, and resolving issues that have arisen during the program. The "crisis in education" is due, in part, to the fact that educators are not making proper use of professional know-how in meeting present-day problems.

8. *Community consultant:* The planning coordinator must work not only within the school system but also within the community as a whole. This can be accomplished by consulting with key community individuals and by releasing publications that inform the public of the purpose, methods, and goals of the program.

9. *Marketing and selling skills:* The planning coordinator must be able to develop an effective marketing strategy to convince the public and district employees of the needs and benefits of the program, and must also possess the required verbal skills to speak intelligently about the program in order to maintain support once it has been obtained.

10. *Supportive ability:* The planning coordinator must continue to look for opportunities to provide staff support whether morale concerning the program is low or not, must consistently support the superintendent, regardless of personal beliefs; and must understand the extension of the superintendent's relationship in all planning matters.[2]

TO WHOM SHOULD THE PLANNING COORDINATOR REPORT?

The person who occupies the planning coordinator position must have the full support of the superintendent. It is primarily because of this relationship that the planning coordinator should report directly to the superintendent. However, there are several other reasons for taking this position:

1. The main function of the planning coordinator is to act as an extension of the chief school officer and to perform the planning duties of the superintendent if the latter had more time in the day.
2. The planning coordinator should be instantly available to the superintendent to investigate alternative approaches to problems and to submit recommendations.
3. The personal goals of the planning coordinator become more intertwined with those of the superintendent than with those of an assistant superintendent or principal.
4. Staff members will recognize the importance of the planning process by observing this reporting relationship.

Some planning unit administrators feel, however, that the planning coordinator should not report to the superintendent for the following reasons:

1. It will be difficult for the planning coordinator to dissociate from the superintendent. Because of this problem, the person occupying this position may fail to achieve an effective relationship with other school administrators.
2. The planning coordinator should be able to espouse the beliefs and ideas of others in the school district, for the purpose of transmitting this information to the superintendent. If the plan-

---

[2] From the book, *School Management by Objectives* by Dr. James Lewis, Jr., © 1974 by Parker Publishing Company, Inc. Published by Parker Publishing Company, Inc., West Nyack, New York 10994.

ning coordinator does not maintain a detached relationship with the chief school officer, the other planning unit administrators may hesitate to be open and honest when indicating their true feelings and ideas.

In any event, the planning coordinator must project influence on the superintendent in order effectively to implement the planning system. The planning coordinator should, as in strategic planning, capitalize on opportunities, accept challenges as necessary to perform a total function, avoid or improve on weaknesses, and consider both the internal and external environments to facilitate the fulfillment of responsibilities.

USING AN INSIDER OR OUTSIDER TO FILL THE POSITION OF COORDINATOR

There are some advantages to hiring either an insider or outsider to occupy the planning coordinator position. The following represent some of the salient reasons.

Advantages of an Insider
- It is easier for an insider to learn the mechanics of planning because of the respect and cooperation with administrators and teachers, which have already been gained.
- An insider is fully aware of "sensitive" points and issues of the school district.
- An insider has well-established relationships with planning unit administrators, which are essential for effective results.
- An insider is already familiar with human and nonhuman resources and therefore will save time in the execution of plans.
- Planning unit administrators are more inclined to share sensitive information with a person who is already known to them.

Advantages of an Outsider
- An outsider will bring new ideas to the school district.
- An outsider does not owe allegiance to anyone but the superintendent.
- An outsider may be more experienced and versed with multiple approaches to planning.

TRAINING: THE PRIMARY FUNCTION OF THE PLANNING COORDINATOR

The training of educators in the intricacies of planning is the primary responsibility of the planning coordinator. The subject or course materials for the training should be selected only after an assessment of the particular needs of individual planning units is made. The author seriously doubts whether external training courses would be of much help when installing strategic and operational planning for the first time. At any rate internal orientation mini-courses should be conducted to move the training program forward.

A comprehensive training program designed to provide knowledge and practical application of that knowledge, for installing strategic and operational plans, would resemble the following:

I. First Day
   1. Introducing strategic planning
      a. Performing strategic planning
      b. Identifying its essential features
      c. Understanding the differences between strategic and long-range planning
      d. Delineating the benefits of strategic planning
      e. Stating problems associated with strategic planning
      f. Identifying the steps for installing strategic planning

II. Second Day
   1. Conducting a critical analysis
      a. Including essential information
      b. Identifying critical information
      c. Collecting, recording, analyzing, and evaluating the information data base
      d. Written exercise: prepare a critical analysis
   2. Preparing or revising the network of aims in public education
      a. Developing the mission statement
      b. Preparing the basic purposes
      c. Establishing educational goals
      d. Written exercise: establish a network of aims in public education
   3. Establishing planning assumptions
      a. Identifying the types of planning assumptions
      b. Understanding the areas for developing planning assumptions
      c. Written exercise: develop planning assumptions for the critical analysis completed on the first day

III. Third and Fourth Days
   1. Developing long-range goals
      a. Defining long-range goals
      b. Understanding the levels of performance
      c. Citing the techniques for writing long-range goals

      d. Identifying major key results analysis

      e. Written exercise: prepare long-range goals using major key results analysis and the critical analysis

IV. Fifth Day

   1. Applying the strategic thinking process

      a. Managing by strategies

      b. Selecting and weighing alternative strategies

      c. Using a guide for strategizing

      d. Written exercise: develop strategies for each long-range goal prepared during the third and fourth days

V. Sixth Day

   1. Introducing operational planning

      a. Defining operational planning

      b. Identifying its essential features

      c. Understanding the difference between strategic and operational planning

      d. Delineating the benefits of operational planning

      e. Identifying the steps for implementing operational planning

   2. Establishing short-range objectives

      a. Defining short-range objectives

      b. Citing the techniques for writing short-range objectives

      c. Understanding the relationship of short-range objectives to long-range goals

      d. Identifying the criteria for preparing correctly written short-range objectives

      e. Written exercise: establish short-range objectives for the long-range goals and strategies developed previously

VI. Seventh Day

   1. Preparing performance standards

      a. Defining performance standards

      b. Citing the techniques for writing performance standards

      c. Identifying various kinds of performance standards

      d. Written exercise: establish performance standards for each short-range objective

   2. Establishing an action plan

      a. Defining an action plan

      b. Citing the techniques for preparing an action plan

      c. Understanding the benefits of an action plan

      d. Written exercise: prepare an action plan for each short-range objective

VII. Eighth Day
1. Reporting performance results
   a. Recording results
   b. Using the critical incident method for analyzing results
   c. Written exercise: assume performance has been exerted for each objective and record result statements using all types
2. Controlling and monitoring results
   a. Understanding the closed-loop critical model
   b. Developing the Gant chart
   c. Preparing Pert
   d. Completing a Planning Exception Report Form
   e. Written exercise: prepare controls for implementing strategic and operational planning using both methods

SALIENT POINTS

The planning coordinator must possess personal traits of tactfulness, diplomacy, attentiveness, intelligence, and perspective, in order to gain the respect and support of planning unit administrators. In addition, a supportive, rather than a critical or threatening posture, must be maintained at all times. To this end, the planning coordinator should help planning unit administrators look good and avoid problems. This does not mean that the former should refrain from disagreeing with the latter when such action is proper.

The planning coordinator should be a "political animal" as well as a "student of politics." As planning involves a political process, the planning coordinator must constantly be negotiating with individuals and groups, and must also be highly sensitive to planning unit administrators and their personal qualities and idiosyncracies in order to assist in reaching agreement on ideas and activities.

On the other hand, the planning coordinator must not recant a position, or fail to take a hard stand when necessary, even though resistance is met from one or more of the planning unit administrators. To do otherwise would lessen the coordinator's power in the planning process.

As a student of politics, the planning coordinator must fully understand the factions and power structure within the school district and community and must not become caught up in any of these factions. In essence, the planning coordinator represents the superintendent of schools, and as such, must exemplify the epitome of educational leadership and supervision.

APPLICATION STRATEGY 14

Before attempting to complete the activity described below, read Max S. Wortman, Jr., and Joann Specking, *Defining the Manager's Job* (New York: American Management Association, 1975).

Develop a prescriptive job description for the position of planning coordinator. Once this task is completed, evaluate and compare it with three similar job descriptions written by local school districts and three more from business and industry. Make the necessary additions, modifications, and revisions to enhance its scope and sequence. Finally, prepare a complete operational plan for the planning coordinator. This plan should be able to accommodate the schedule for implementing strategic planning developed in Application Strategy 1.

15

EFFECTING THE PLANNING PROCESS

The most important factor determining the success or failure of the planning process is how well the program has been implemented. Implementation will involve the establishment of a planning staff to prepare, carry out, and evaluate its effectiveness. For some school districts this will involve reorganizing the research and evaluation department into a planning department. For others it will mean hiring a planning staff, or possibly assigning the planning job on a part-time basis to an administrator. Regardless of the approach used to initiate planning, additional funds will be required. Some school districts may be reluctant to support such a move. In the long run, any funds expended on behalf of the planning process will be more than paid back. School administrators should not be penny-wise and nickel-foolish. When there is good planning there is good management; the two cannot be separated. In addition, the best made plans cannot succeed unless there has been adequate staff involvement. In this chapter, a new concept is introduced which, if implemented properly, will draw maximum and meaningful involvement from the staff.

This chapter has been designed to improve the planning unit administrator's ability to implement the planning process. Although the substantive part deals with using job enrichment as a tool to involve staff in the planning process, the initial section gives some attention to the planning staff and using planning consultants.

GETTING THE PLANNING JOB DONE

The superintendent must consider three questions before a planning process is implemented in a school district: How large should the planning staff be? How can consultants be utilized? And what is the most effective way to involve the staff in the process? Some recommendations follow that should prove of some value to most chief school administrators installing strategic long-range planning for the first time.

Establishing a Planning Staff

The size of the planning staff should be sufficient to perform the comprehensive planning process. However, there are a number of factors that should be considered before a final decision is made.

Size of the School District. The following should prove helpful.

Number of Students	Number of Planning Staff
1,000–5,000	1
5,001–20,000	2
20,001–50,000	3
50,001–100,000	4
100,001 and more	6

Following is a description of some of the positions that may be found in a contemporary school district planning department.

- *Assistant Superintendent for Strategic Planning.* Provides guidance and counsel to the superintendent and other members of the school district in the formulation and maintenance of a long-range strategic model that is the major vehicle for long-range planning.
- *Planning Assistant.* Assists the assistant superintendent for strategic planning in all matters pertaining to strategic and operational planning.
- *Public Affairs Administrator.* Provides the superintendent and assistant superintendent for strategic planning with information and assistance in reviewing legislation, influencing same, and maintaining contact with local, state, and national legislators and agencies.
- *Director of Information Systems.* Coordinates the management information system in all matters pertaining to the collection, compilation, evaluation, and dissemination of information to enable planning units to engage in strategic and operational planning.
- *Information Systems Assistant.* Assists the director of information systems in all matters pertaining to the formulation of data systems, collections, compilations, analysis, and dissemination of pertinent information to assist the school district to plan more effectively.

- *Director of Research and Evaluation.* Provides research on all matters pertaining to the planning process, including instructional program effectiveness, personnel effectiveness, and the like.
- *Research and Evaluation Assistant.* Assists the director of research and evaluation in all matters pertaining to research and evaluation.
- *Director of Environmental Data.* Provides analytical data pertaining to the microenvironment and macroenvironment of the school district in order to enhance the viability of plans.
- *Environmental Data Assistant.* Assists the director of environmental data in all matters pertaining to the microenvironment and macroenvironment of the school district.
- *Director of Forecasting and Trends.* Makes analytical projections and studies trends that may affect the school district and formulates planning assumptions and scenarios.

Number of Planning Units. Obviously in a larger school district, there will be a greater number of planning units, necessitating more planning staff members.

Extent to which Planning Units Have Their Own Staff for Planning. In most instances, units will not have their own staffs. However, many school districts have a research, evaluation, and development department. Many of the personnel in this department could be easily transferred to one or more planning positions mentioned earlier.

Extent to which Outside Planning Consultants Are Retained to Play a Vital Part in the Planning Process. In some school districts, outside consultants can be used to supplement a limited planning department if they are retained on a recurrent basis.

Item
In 1982, New Jersey State Department of Education, under the leadership of Commissioner Saul Cooperman, became the first department of education in the nation to implement the strategic planning process. A strategic planning unit was established as an out growth of an organizational study conducted by AT&T and Rutgers University. The strategic planning design is based after AT&T's organizational performance model.

PLANNING STAFFS IN LARGE PLANNING UNITS

The student population of many urban schools exceeds that of small school districts. This will demand that a part-time planning coordinator be assigned to each school or planning unit exceeding 2,000 students. In most cases budgetary limitations will prevent this. Therefore, an assistant principal should be given this charge.

The part-time planning coordinator:

- Should receive a job description that is agreed to by the planning coordinator.
- Should receive an initial five days of training conducted by the planning department. Periodically, other training workshops in planning should be offered on a needs basis.
- Should receive a copy of and training on the Planning Manual.
- Is expected to organize school committees to provide opportunities for the staff to become actively involved in the planning process using the job enrichment process covered in a subsequent portion of this chapter.

SELECTING A PLANNING CONSULTANT

When consultants are used in a school district to aid the planning process they are usually used in one of three ways:

1. They are retained on a one-time basis to guide the introduction of the planning process. This may mean conducting a presentation before board members, training school administrators, or helping the school district to solve a planning problem.
2. They are employed recurrently throughout the school year to give instruction in planning techniques, methods, and procedures to selected groups of staff members.
3. They are hired to evaluate the planning process and to make recommendations about areas needing improvement.

When carefully selected, planning consultants can be invaluable to the school district, particularly to the superintendent of schools, planning coordinators, and planning unit administrators.

Following are recommendations to be considered when retaining a consultant to assist in the planning process:

- Because of gaps in many of the public education planning systems, the consultant selected should have had some experience in profit and nonprofit organizations.
- There should be a good fit between the consultant's approach to planning and the training, experience, and abilities of the planning unit administrator.

- Before hiring a consultant for any length of time, it might be better to retain his or her services for a short duration. This will enable the school district to assess the consultant's planning ability before making any decisions regarding long-term arrangements.
- A good relationship should exist between the members of the consulting firm and school planners. Consultants who will talk down to staff members should not be hired.
- The superintendent of schools and planning coordinator should have easy access to the consultant in order to respond to the school district's immediate planning problems.
- Before hiring a consultant, determine how much of the superintendent's and planning coordinator's time will be required. If the consultant is going to use too much of the superintendent's time, do not hire the person.
- There should be an accommodating planning philosophy and practicality between the consultant and planners of the school district.

No consultant who attempts to mold a school district to a preconceived planning approach should ever be hired. The ideal consultant is one who will try to adapt an approach to the interests and needs of the school district.

THE TRADITIONAL FUNCTION OF SCHOOL ADMINISTRATORS

The traditional role of school administrators is thought of in terms of planning, organizing, leading, and controlling as illustrated in Figure 15–1. On the other hand, the traditional role of teachers is confined to teaching. As a result of these role differentiations, coupled with new variables such as changing perceptions of teachers and the increased role of technological, social, and economical changes, a serious dichotomy exists between school administrators and teachers. Teachers, who once thought of themselves as the oppressed, are disregarding guidelines or finding new ways of circumventing them. Attempts on the part of administrators to suppress nonconformity evoke more reactive behavior.

Many administrators are only beginning to realize the potential of their teachers' unused or misdirected talents. Thus, the challenge of contemporary administration is to channel teachers' talents and energy into constructive school-oriented activities.

Therefore what is needed is a new school organizational structure

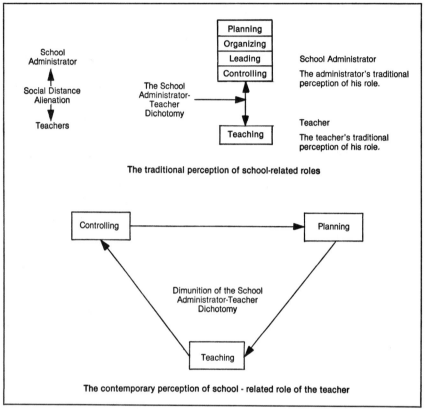

Figure 15–1 *The Traditional and Contemporary Roles of School Administrators and Teachers*

that will provide opportunities to utilize fully teachers' talents, skills, and ideas through a participatory involvement process. In such an organizational structure, school administrators will share their responsibility and, yes, some of their power, with educators.

This thought is not founded without solid motivational theories.

THE THEORIES BEHIND JOB ENRICHMENT

The motivational theories of Abraham Maslow, David McClelland, Chris Agryris, Frederick Herzberg, and M. Scott Myers support the concept of job enrichment for implementing the planning process. These theories are discussed briefly below in order to show how they apply.

Abraham Maslow's "hierarchy of needs" is one general theory of motivation that has gained wide acceptance among planners. The main point of this theory is that motivation is an internal process, and once a need has been satisfied it no longer serves as a motivator of behavior. He maintains that humans have five basic needs: physiological, security, social, esteem, and self-actualization. The first four are deficit needs, while the last one only results after the others have been satisfied.

The theories of David McClelland of Harvard are probably more directly related to the planning process because they are achievement-oriented. He postulates that a high achiever possesses certain characteristics, such as: a preference for situations in which he or she can take personal responsibility for judging solutions to problems; a preference for high risk situations in which he or she can set and achieve goals; a strong need to receive feedback on performance; and a disregard for personal likes or dislikes as long as the person or means can obtain the goal. McClelland's research substantiates the theory that the achievement itself is more important than money to a high achiever.

The research of Chris Agryris, who is currently serving in the Schools of Education and Business at Harvard University, indicates that the rigid bureaucratic structure of most large organizations forces employees into roles that prevent them from realizing their potential. This theory directly correlates with job enrichment because of its organizational focus. As a result of a confining organizational structure, the organization gravitates toward an unhealthy state. A healthy organization is one in which an open line of communication exists, along with a number of factors that foster trust among staff members.

Perhaps the theory that most directly relates to the job enrichment concept is Frederick Herzberg's contention concerning factors that lead to job satisfaction and dissatisfaction. He maintains that job dissatisfaction stems from hygenic or maintenance factors, such as policies and procedures, administration, supervision, interpersonal relations, salary, and working conditions. Job satisfaction, which he calls motivation factors, includes achievement, recognition, the job itself, responsibility, and promotion. The theory holds that job dissatisfaction should be avoided so that employees will be motivated to perform. This thesis is closely aligned with Agryris's.

M. Scott Myers, who is currently doing private consulting, developed the plan-teach-control concept. His research indicates that "satisfiers" and "dissatisfiers" are not always as discrete as Herzberg claims. He found that meaningful work motivates while meaningless work demotivates. Although Myers agrees that job content and self-reliance are essential for real motivation, he also stresses the influence of interpersonal competence, helpful systems, meaningful goals, and the opportunity for self-actualization. Myers stresses the importance of staff participation and the interpersonal relationships between the working parties.

MAKING SCHOOL MORE MEANINGFUL FOR TEACHERS

In order to make school more meaningful and challenging for teachers, their role should not be restricted to teaching. If the planning process is to be effectively implemented, teachers should be involved in planning and controlling as well as teaching, as illustrated in Figure 15–2.

The plan phase includes the planning and organizing functions of the school, problem-solving goal setting, and use of human resources, material, and systems. Planning is an essential ingredient that gives the job meaning by aligning it with goals. The teaching phase is the implementation of the plan that ideally involves the coordinated expenditure of physical and mental effort and utilization of aptitudes and special skills. Control includes measurement, evaluation, and correcting the feedback process for assessing achievements against goals. Feedback, even to a greater extent than planning, gives the job meaning, and its absence is a common cause of job dissatisfaction. The control phase is the basis for recycling planning, performing, and controlling.

When all of these phases have been properly implemented, the planning process provides an opportunity for teachers to unleash all of their untapped talents for the overall benefit of the school district.

USING JOB ENRICHMENT TO EFFECTUATE THE PLANNING PROCESS

A number of school districts that have installed long-range planning have resorted to organizing task forces or special committees to facilitate this process. Although the degree of success with this technique varied

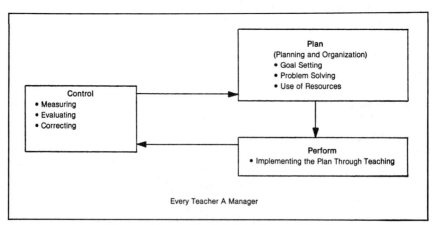

Figure 15–2 *The Job Enrichment Model*

with the individual school districts, each set out in its own way to involve staff, and quite often parents, in the planning process in an effort to lower resistance to change. Much of what was accomplished in these group settings was by trial and error. In an effort to elevate the effectiveness of staff involvement in the planning process a new organizational concept, job enrichment, is introduced. This concept is new to public education, but has been successfully used in business and industry. Job enrichment, which is referred to by this author as "every teacher a manager," will require planning unit administrators to think differently about the role of teachers. Regarding teachers as managers must be understood not as an act of good human relations, nor as a means of exploiting teachers, but rather as a sound practice that benefits both the school district and staff. The forward-looking planning unit administrator who implements this concept will realize he or she is not managing a technique or a program but a way of life that finds expression in all levels of the school organization. Through this way of life, administrators and educators become more knowledgeable and competent as they jointly engage in an effective planning program.[1]

DEFINING JOB ENRICHMENT

Job enrichment is the delegation of administrative responsibilities that have usually been reserved for school administrators. The traditional role of administrators is to plan, organize, lead, and control the performance of teachers, while the traditional role of teachers is to teach. Job enrichment implies that when teachers assume some of the planning responsibility and control over their jobs, they will be more responsive to educational change and improvement. Job enrichment also implies that although the content of the teachers' job changes, they will plan and control their own job or performance. The level of difficulty or complexity of the teaching job changes, as well as the number and variety of responsibilities. Thus with increased involvement, responsibilities also increase.

Specifically, job enrichment attempts to provide teachers with meaningful work in school or planning units by:

1. Organizing a phase of work in the school so that they can identify and strive toward a series of interrelated activities that will provide tangible results.
2. Providing the teachers with as many decision-making opportunities as possible concerning how they will perform and manage their job.

[1] M. Scott Myers, *Every Employee a Manager* (New York: McGraw-Hill, 1970).

3. Providing direct and immediate feedback through the job itself so that they will be able to assess their own performance.

Inherent in the job enrichment concept is a set of assumptions and expectations of teachers and the school organization that tend to have a positive effect on the planning process:

1. Most teachers want to participate in a meaningful way in the achievement of goals and objectives of the school district.
2. The majority of teachers are capable of performing better than they are currently doing.
3. Planning unit administrators' basic responsibility is to create conditions within the planning unit that allow teachers to contribute their talents and skills in a variety of ways toward accomplishing the school district's mission.
4. As teachers broaden their skills, new opportunities should be afforded them, particularly those that give them control over their performance.
5. When teachers are involved in a planning process that allows them better to utilize their capabilities, they are more prone to exercise self-direction and to improve their efforts toward the attainment of goals and objectives.

THE OBJECTIVES OF JOB ENRICHMENT

Job enrichment for teachers, which covers the plan-teach-control cycles advocated by Myers, is intended to enable teachers to perform as administrators. This is particularly true when it is related to the planning process, because there must be a total and collective assault on the goals and objectives of the school district if the mission is to be realized. Specific objectives of the job enrichment concept are: [2]

1. To provide an opportunity for teachers to make use of their capabilities and creative and imaginative skills, and to improve the job they are doing.
2. To enrich teachers' jobs by giving them managerial control over their areas of responsibility.
3. To unleash ideas and know-how of teachers to bring improvement to the school situation.
4. To effect cost savings through improvements made on the job by individual teachers.
5. To create an atmosphere and frame of mind that challenges

[2] *Ibid.*, p. 89.

current methods of operation and is conducive to constant change for improvement.

6. To create an atmosphere conducive to open communication and mutual trust among teachers at varying levels within the school organization.
7. To create teams that provide optimum opportunity for teachers to participate in and work together on planning, controlling, teaching, criticizing, and improving their performance.
8. To offer teachers a variety of opportunities to become actively involved in various phases of the strategic and operational planning process.
9. To create challenging situations in which teachers are equal partners in any gain experienced by the school district.
10. To improve the decision-making capabilities of the school district by sharing the responsibility among school administrators and educators.

SOME ASSUMPTIONS ABOUT JOB ENRICHMENT

Introducing job enrichment into the planning process works best when planning unit administrators understand and believe the following assumptions about teachers:[3]

1. Teachers don't resist change, they resist being changed.
2. Every job in a school situation can be improved.
3. Every teacher has the ability to improve performance.
4. Teachers like to improve their performance and to derive satisfaction from school.
5. Teachers like to participate in groups or on teams.
6. Improvements are best made by those who perform the job.
7. Teachers should be provided with the basic skills for school improvement through training.
8. The role of the planning unit administrator is one of advisor, consultant, and conductor.
9. The role of teachers is manager of their own area of responsibility.

These assumptions are supported by many motivational theories. Planning unit administrators who can use these assumptions to formulate and practice an appropriate leadership style will most likely be more effective than those who do not.

[3] *Ibid.*, pp. 89–90.

To realize fully the benefits of the job enrichment concept in the planning process, the planning coordinator must have some additional characteristics to those mentioned in Chapter 14.

1. Possess a firm belief that most teachers want to perform well if the school is organizationally structured in a way that will allow them to do so.
2. Appear to be credible in the eyes of teachers and capable of convincing co-workers of suggestions that should be tried. The planning coordinator's experience and relationship with staff should engender trust and respect.
3. Possess experience in group dynamics and effective communication skills to be used during group situations and meetings.
4. Know how to teach planning unit administrators to develop achievement-oriented activities, to assist them to re-design organization control systems, and to develop teamwork between planning units and among planning subunits.

The planning coordinator must be prepared to function as a consultant to planning unit administrators regarding the feasibility and appropriateness of certain school-related activities in the job enrichment concept. Of critical importance will be the behavior of the planning coordinator toward planning unit administrators and their staff.

GUIDELINES FOR USING JOB ENRICHMENT IN THE PLANNING PROCESS

Job enrichment calls for modifications within the existing school organization. These modifications will involve not only restructuring the planning unit, but also changes in roles, perceptions, and relationships.

One of the most prevalent problems confronting teachers and school administrators is that they are often afraid to trust each other. Thawing-out time will be needed so that attitudes may change because of the behavioral change of administrators resulting from the job enrichment concept. Another problem that often confronts administrators is their reluctance to take risks or give up close supervision in order to permit teachers to manage certain aspects of their jobs themselves. In fact, the greatest problem confronting planning unit administrators will not be how plans are arrived at or prepared, but the changing of their attitudes as well as behavior.

Job enrichment will not be effective in the planning process if school administrators and teachers fail to learn to adjust to, accept, and seek change.

Some guidelines follow for implementing the planning process using the job enrichment process:

1. Have the superintendent of schools address the entire staff to discuss the new role of teachers and give them a brief introduction to the school district's planning efforts.

Item
Prior to this presentation, the superintendent should have convened an informal meeting with the union representative to discuss the ensuing year's plan. It might be advantageous to meet over lunch or dinner, in order to update the official on the progress of the planning efforts. In addition, this is an excellent manner in which to get the union's impression on some of the problems so that appropriate steps can be taken.

2. Upon returning to the planning unit, the planning unit administrator should more fully discuss aspects of the planning process and elaborate on how it will be organized. Some administrators have found it fitting not to mention job enrichment as the program being implemented to establish the planning process.
3. Have the planning coordinator conduct two or three workshops on the planning process. Retain consultants if funds have been allocated for this purpose. Planning manuals should be distributed to staff members.
4. Divide the critical analysis phase of the planning process into subdivisions for teaming purposes:
   a. Essential information team
   b. Critical information team
   c. Stakeholder assessment team
   d. Competition assessment team
   e. Forecasting and trends team
   Appoint a chairperson to head each team and convene a meeting with the chairpeople, giving written instructions and objectives for each team to complete its particular component of the critical analysis phase.
5. The planning unit administrator and planning coordinator should review all plans and make suggestions for revisions, modifications, and changes. The revised draft of the initial analysis is forwarded to each staff member.
6. Planning unit administrators convene meetings with their staff and criticize the results of the planning activities thus far. Changes are made accordingly.
7. Teams are organized around major key result areas. Each team, using critical analysis, identifies no more than five long-range goals.

A variety of techniques are used to arrive at these goals. A meeting is held with the entire staff, and the chairperson of each team makes a brief presentation on the long-range goal. Changes are made as recommended by a consensus vote. The final list is approved by the planning unit administrator and sent to the superintendent for input. Recommendations are made and sent back to the planning units and acted upon.

8. Each team working with its long-range goals is allowed one day off from school to convene a strategic thinking session to identify, analyze, and select strategies for reaching long-range goals. Planning limitations, such as available resources, funds, and the like, are presented to each team prior to their strategic thinking sessions.

9. Strategies are discussed with planning unit administrators and changes are made by agreement. The final list is sent to the central planning unit for recommendations. Changes are then discussed and acted upon.

10. All of the materials that have been prepared up to this point are used as a basis for preparing operational plans. Each plan is discussed with the entire staff. Changes are made by consensus and joint agreement. A copy of the operational plan is forwarded to the central planning unit for further recommendations. Changes are discussed with the staff and made accordingly.

11. After the operational plans have been analyzed, each chairperson designates someone to monitor certain portions of the plan. If it appears that an objective is below plan, planning exception reports are filed immediately with the planning unit administrator so that corrective action can be taken promptly.

The extent to which the guidelines are implemented will depend on the sophistication of the planning unit administrator, the readiness of teachers, and the overall health of the school organization. In some school districts, it may be more appropriate to carry out a small portion of these guidelines, while in others the entire package can be installed. At any rate, the planning unit administrator should objectively evaluate the degree to which job enrichment should be established in the planning unit and proceed carefully to ensure positive results.

SALIENT POINTS

Job enrichment means sharing responsibilities and controls over teachers' jobs that were formerly reserved for school administrators. These additions are sometimes called vertical job loading. They tend to enrich teachers' jobs by increasing their autonomy. There are several methods by which this can be accomplished in the planning process:

- Reducing external controls or giving teachers the opportunity to monitor and correct their own performance.
- Giving teachers more challenging technical tasks, such as predicting educational trends in five years.
- Granting teachers new authority, such as preparing the lunch schedule for staff or establishing quality circles.
- Providing more responsibility for time management by letting staff members, as a team, prepare the instructional schedule.
- Giving teachers greater control over budget and other nonfinancing matters by training them in zero-base budgeting and letting them identify decision packages.
- Adding more managerial functions, such as leading the staff to implement an innovative program.
- Providing more authority to identify problems and to render decisions in times of crisis by instituting problem-solving planning as discussed in Chapter 12.

Before these methods are instituted, it may be best to acquire the sanction of the teachers' association or union. Because teachers are given additional responsibility through job enrichment, the recognized collective bargaining association may wish to use this concept as a bargaining point for higher salary or additional benefits. Unfortunately, in some school districts job enrichment may be impossible to implement due to union problems. If this is the case, the program should be implemented on an informal basis without much fanfare. Robert Anderson, co-founder of nongraded education, said, "A little bit of honey is better than none." Such is true for job enrichment when used in the planning process.

APPLICATION STRATEGY 15

Read the following book in order to better understand the concept of job enrichment: M. Scott Myers, *Every Employee a Manager* Second Edition (New York: McGraw-Hill Book Co., 1981), pp. 37–176.

Once fortified with this concept, prepare a policy and procedure statement for using the job enrichment concept for implementing the planning process effectively. Develop an operational plan for blending job enrichment with strategic and operational planning. Include in the performance standards and/or action plan, training activities for equipping teachers to carry out both concepts proficiently.

16

GUIDING HUMAN EFFORTS USING A PLANNING MANUAL

One of the most effective ways to introduce the planning process is to prepare a planning manual and disseminate it to appropriate staff members. The planning needs and approaches of planning unit administrators will vary with experience, administrative style, and individual needs. The planning manual is not intended to structure planning into a systematized process. Its primary function is to identify certain minimum requirements that must be met, and a specific time schedule and procedural steps that must be observed in order to implement a stable planning process.

At the onset of this chapter, the planning manual is defined and the criteria for producing it are briefly discussed. Some consideration is also given to the function of the planning manual as well as several sources that can be used to produce it. Because many long-range plans tend to be voluminous, some suggestions are offered to reduce the size of plans. The chapter ends with a comprehensive description of desirable contents for a planning manual.

DEFINING THE PLANNING MANUAL

The planning manual is a set of rules, guidelines, and illustrative reports and forms presented in a terse and concise manner in order to facilitate and expedite the strategic and operational planning processes.

FUNCTIONS OF A PLANNING MANUAL

One of the most effective ways to help guide human efforts during the planning process is to produce and use a planning manual. A manual does not guarantee that the planning process will be effectively implemented; however, it will help expedite the execution of activities associated with planning. The planning manual can stimulate and motivate people, particularly if they read it from cover to cover.

A planning manual also offers other benefits, discussed below.

Provides Training Guidelines

If the planning program is to be effective, planning unit administrators and staff must receive continuous training. One training session will not be sufficient to keep the planning process alive. In fact, it will take from three to five years of training before planning unit administrators are adequately trained in the mechanics of planning. By using a manual as a guide to keep pace with changing times and conditions in the school district, some success is bound to be realized. The training manual is the medium that helps foster living plans.

Stimulates Action

One of the goals of the planning manual should be to stimulate action on the part of planning unit administrators. As a stimulus, the manual will give a degree of security to its users by identifying the sequential development of plans, delineating school district's planning requirements, and providing illustrative examples of forms, reports, and the like.

Helps to Consolidate Planning Efforts

In a large school district the consolidation of all of the planning units' plans is a horrendous task. The ease with which these plans are assembled is determined primarily by the forms in which they are presented to the central planning unit. Very little difficulty in consolidating plans occurs when a planning manual has been prepared displaying illustrative reports, forms, and the like.

Serves as a Communication Tool

The planning coordinator should update the planning manual by inserting what activities were achieved on and above plan. This information is a stimulus for continued progress. However, positive information should not be the only data included in the manual. Information pertaining to potential threats, new problems, and avoided opportunities should also be clarified. Regardless of whether the information is positive or negative, the manual serves a vital communication function between central and school planning units and helps to enhance the whole planning process.

Explains Planning Concepts

The planning manual is the bible of the strategic and operational planning processes. As such, it should contain a message from the superintendent, terminology, time schedules for planning, concepts, practices, procedures, past performance results, basic purposes, mission, educational goals, critical analysis, long-range goals, planning assumptions, strategies, short-range objectives, performance standards, action plans, budget, and illustrative forms for the completion of the planning processes. The main purpose of the manual is to make it easier for those with the responsibility to plan to carry out their task.

Sets Standards for Evaluating Plans

The quality and usefulness of the planning manual are primarily based on how well the plans were conceived. A poorly developed manual will lead to ineffective plans. A planning manual that promotes explicit directions, easily understandable content, and sufficient illustrative forms and reports should augment well-thought-out and prepared plans.

Gives Leverage to Planning Coordinator

Because the planning coordinator has prepared the planning manual and knows its contents better than anyone else, it provides leverage with the administrators in the planning units. Acting as an extension of the superintendent, the planning coordinator is responsible for the success or failure of the planning processes. Therefore, the planning coordinator should have the responsibility for using the planning manual in a flexible manner depending on the needs and wants of the individual planning units.

CRITERIA FOR AN EFFECTIVE PLANNING MANUAL

The planning coordinator is responsible for producing an effective planning manual. In order to perform this job well, he or she should make certain that the manual is developed and used in consideration with the following criteria: [1]

---

[1] Reprinted, by permission of the publisher, from *Corporate Planning: Techniques & Applications,* © 1979 by AMACOM, a division of American Management Associations, pp. 251–253. All rights reserved.

Flexibility

The planning manual should be flexible to accommodate changing times and conditions in the internal as well as external school environment. After the planning processes have had an opportunity to thaw out, the program will no doubt change. With change, fewer forms will be required, human efforts will be better utilized, and the quality of the planning process will be improved largely due to a dynamic system which is adaptable to needs and desires. Flexibility is enhanced when the content is contained in a loose-leaf folder in which changes and revisions can be easily inserted.

Sequential Development

The flow of activities associated with the planning process will be predicated on how well the guidelines have been presented in a sequential format. This helps bring clarity to the concept and provides the planners with the necessary continuity for successfully implementing the planning program. In addition, a sequentially developed format helps planning unit administrators conceptualize strategic planning, a process that many will find difficult to do at the onset.

Explicit Composition

The manual's directions should be tersely written and void of jargon and grandiose terms. The planning process itself will be difficult to understand and implement during the first year without an added obstacle of undecipherable instructions. A manual that is difficult to read and comprehend will result in poor morale, frustration, and a host of other problems.

Communication with Planning Unit Administrators

Production of a manual will not be sufficient, as its contents must be communicated to co-workers. This may be accomplished through several mini-workshop sessions to be followed by dialogue sessions that will enable the planners to assess how well or poorly they are doing with their own planning units.

Periodic Updates

The planning manual must be updated periodically with current information about the internal and external environments. These updates should occur on a quarterly basis, but at least semiannually. Some planning assumptions, objectives, performance standards, and activities may have to be modified or revised as a result of changing circumstances.

DEVELOPING THE PLANNING MANUAL

As previously stated, it usually takes several planning cycles to properly tailor-make a planning process to meet the individual needs of a school district. Even after a trial run, mistakes and gaps may occur that will not become evident until the entire planning cycle has been implemented.

There are several sources that can be used to help produce a planning manual.

Planning Manuals of Other School Districts

The best tool to utilize when formulating a planning manual is a similar guidebook produced by another school district. However, as long-range strategic planning remains in an infancy stage within the educational field, these manuals may be difficult to obtain. The next best substitute is a planning manual from the business and industry sector. However, these too may be difficult to acquire since many firms consider their planning documents to be confidential. The substance of these materials, whether from another school district or an industrial organization, should be used only as a guide in order to avoid major gaps in the planning process.

Workshops

One effective way to become armed with the essentials of planning and subsequent development of a manual is to attend workshops and other training activities. One course in strategic or operational planning will not suffice, and several training activities should be attended before the first training cycle is over.

Planning Books and Articles

Planning literature, such as professional books and articles, can be an invaluable asset when combined with one or more of the previously mentioned sources for formulating a planning manual. Of particular importance are illustrated articles.

DEALING WITH THE SIZE OF PLANS

One of the most prevalent problems confronting school districts when engaging in long-range planning for the first time is the amount of paperwork generated by the process. Some plans have consisted of 300 to 400 pages. Very few school administrators are willing to take time out of their busy schedule to read such a lengthy document. One of the chief complaints of school administrators when long-range planning was first mandated by the state of New Jersey was the horrendous paperwork required for the process. Even when the paperwork is not too excessive, some administrators, who may be uninterested in the process, may use it as an excuse for avoiding proper planning.

The superintendent of schools is primarily responsible for the amount of paperwork associated with a long-range planning program. One of the most effective ways to keep paperwork to a minimum is to produce and utilize a planning manual.

Some of the techniques that can be used to limit the size of plans in a planning manual are:

1. Place a limit on each element of the plan.
2. Detail page size, spacing, margins, and number of paragraphs.
3. Specify a format that circumscribes the amount of data that can be offered.
4. Limit the text of each planning unit to a specified number of pages.
5. Restrict the number of long-range goals, short-range objectives, strategies, and so on.
6. Decrease the number of exhibits, graphs, or tables.
7. Request plans for half of the planning units one year and the other half the succeeding year.
8. Update the previous year's plans.
9. Include only changes that will have a significant impact on the school district.

Although the following planning manual outline may seem comprehensive, its size is controlled by a number of carefully constructed forms that will call for inclusion of only significant information about the school district. This will help to limit the size of the plans.

THE PLANNING MANUAL

I. Glossary of terms

II. Message from superintendent of schools on the importance of planning and expectations for the year

III. Time schedule for implementing the planning process.

IV. Critical analysis of school district
  A. Network of aims
    1. Basic purposes
    2. Mission
    3. Philosophy
    4. Educational goals
  B. Past performance results
    1. Briefly describe performance results achieved by all planning units. Cite performance results as follows and explain fully any significant deviation from the plan.
      a. On plan
      b. Above plan
      c. Below plan
    2. Tersely describe how each planning unit as a whole is progressing toward the long-range goals of the school district.

  C. Essential Information
  Cite significant facts about the school district and community. Make certain the following are included:
    1. Population, age, and sex
    2. Race
    3. Occupations and professions
    4. Family income
    5. Foster children
    6. Welfare children
    7. Description and age of school facilities
    8. Description of school organization and chart

  D. Critical information
    1. Assess the internal environment of the planning unit's human, physical, financial, and other resources using the major key result areas as guidelines.
  E. Assess the external environment
  List all of the competitors that are having an impact on the school district. This should include an analysis of the competition with respect to:
    1. Exploration of past results
    2. Reconstruction of past strategy
    3. Evaluation of competitors' resources

  V. Planning assumption

        A. Continue the process of analyzing the external environment by describing present conditions and major changes expected to occur within the school district in the next three to five years that will have a significant impact on planning units and the school organization as a whole. Planning assumptions should cover the following areas:

            1. Society
            2. Government or legislature
            3. Economy
            4. Commerce
            5. International relations

  VI. Long-range goals

        A. All long-range goals should be designed to move toward the school district's mission. The primary tools for setting long-range goals should be the major key result areas and the critical analysis. However, other methods can be used for this purpose:

            1. Trends
            2. Negotiation
            3. Edicts from the superintendent

  VII. Programs or long-range strategies

        A. Select strategies that will identify how long-range goals will be achieved. The foundation for strategies should focus on maximizing strengths, minimizing weaknesses, and changing potential threats into opportunities. This will require intuition, rigorous analysis, experimentation, questioning of old methods, exploring unfamiliar environments, facing up to threats and opportunities, and acceptance of uncertainties. Strategies should cover the major key result areas.

  VIII. Short-range objectives

        A. Short-range objectives should be set to achieve the long-range goals of the school district by using the strategies as a base. They should be specific, timely, result-oriented, and written in a precise language.

IX. Performance standards

   A. Set performance standards as the basis for evaluating and determining if an objective has been achieved.

X. Action plans

   A. Action plans should be developed to achieve short-range objectives. Using action verbs, they should describe the activity, person(s) responsible for achieving the activity, the date, and cost.

SALIENT POINTS

Guidelines are an abbreviated version of a manual. They are usually disseminated in memo form and cover areas, such as the current achievement level of the school district, expectations of the staff, planning assumptions, priorities, and constraints, which should be seriously considered in the preparation of plans. Some planning unit administrators may wish to use guidelines only as a prelude to the planning manual, and as the process is successfully tried out on a small scale, a manual will evolve through trial and error.

APPLICATION STRATEGY 16

Identify the subjects to be covered in a planning manual. Using this information as a table of contents, prepare a planning manual to help implement the long-range strategic and short-range operational planning processes.

17

EVALUATING PLANNING EFFECTIVENESS

The superintendent of schools is under continuous pressure to improve the school district's performance. Many different methods can be used to assess this performance by various groups within the school community such as students, parents, taxpayers, board members, state department of education personnel, and the federal government. In business, the bottom line is profit or loss, whereas in education, the bottom line is an increase or decrease in student learning and growth. However, tax savings, quality of personnel, programs and services provided, administrative effectiveness, percentage of college entry students, and a host of other indices can also be used to evaluate planning effectiveness. Thus, school districts must periodically assess their performance on various levels and compare the actual results with projected standards. When plans, regardless of how poorly they were conceived, do not produce the desired results, planning unit administrators must improve performance through better administration of resources. As results are not likely to be better than the planning process and the execution of plans, attention must be given to the evaluation of the planning process in order to improve the system and thereby enhance the total operation of the school district.

This chapter examines a variety of ways to determine the effectiveness of the planning process. First, the human problem related to planning is discussed to identify symptoms sometimes associated with the process. Considerable attention is then given to a system for gauging the effectiveness of the planning process. George A. Steiner's pitfalls of strategic planning are covered as are several approaches to measuring planning effectiveness. The chapter terminates with a focus on why some planning systems fail.

HUMAN PROBLEMS ASSOCIATED WITH PLANNING

Even though planning facilitates and expedites the decision-making process, produces better informed and trained administrators, and improves the morale and effectiveness of the staff on the whole, the most prevalent problem associated with developing strategic and operational plans remains human-related. School administrators, like other human beings, resist being changed. Whenever an innovation is introduced into a school organization, new demands are made on administrators, new methods and techniques have to be mastered, and new challenges and opportunities necessitating a different approach that may disrupt the comfortable way of doing things will emerge. These chores, when added to the day-to-day operations of the school, may cause the administrator's anger over the prospect of change.

A major problem that occurs when the planning process is first installed in the school district is the administrator's reluctance to devote sufficient time to the process and resentment at having to do so. Following are several reasons for this behavior:

1. Administrators' performance is evaluated on immediate accomplishments rather than what they are prepared to do in three or five years.
2. Their day-to-day responsibilities receive primary consideration, while everything else becomes of secondary importance.
3. Planning is often seen as an academic exercise because plans are often unused or severely modified by either the supervisor or unforeseen circumstances.
4. Planning constitutes a threat because it explores gaps, inefficiency, poor performance, and the like.
5. Planning generates too much paperwork, taking valuable time away from the day-to-day operations of the school.

Another human-related problem in the planning process is the impact of change in terms of creative and intellectual demands. This is primarily because the planning process will require a great deal of analysis, synthesis, and evaluation, which do not come easily to untrained minds. Planning unit administrators will need to be meticulously trained to improve these thought processes. Some reasons for this behavior are:

1. The planning quotient (P.Q.) of planning unit administrators is not at an acceptable level.
2. Many school administrators find intuitive thinking and rigorous analysis too difficult to master, and all viable alternatives sometimes are not intellectually realized.

3. There is insufficient imagination and insight among planning unit administrators.
4. Few planning unit administrators are able to make the required intellectual abstractions involved in devising adequate goals, strategies, and objectives.

GAUGING THE EFFECTIVENESS OF THE PLANNING SYSTEM

Someone once said that, "Long-range planning is more than the organization and analysis of information: it is a decision-making process." As such, can the effectiveness of a planning system be measured? Are there positive and tangible results that can be traced to planning? In short, does planning make a difference? To respond to this question, Figure 17–1 depicts indirect and direct effects of planning on the planning units within the school district, and its effect on student achievement.

An effective planning process should accomplish four things:

1. Improve decision-making ability of planning unit administrators.
2. Enhance planning unit administrators' ability to function.
3. Affect all major key result areas of the school district positively.
4. Increase student learning and growth.

Improving Decision-Making Ability of Planning Unit Administrators

If the planning system fails to improve the planning unit administrators' ability to make sound decisions to move the school district forward, the system is probably in need of a serious overhaul. The decision-making quality of the planning system is the driving force that gives substance to all of the major key result areas and effects improvement in the overall education process. The indicators listed below represent successful criteria for judging whether the planning system produced improved decision making. Does the planning system

1. Reduce the likelihood of costly mistakes?
2. Explore weaknesses in assumptions and force appropriate action?
3. Reduce the number of crises in planning units?
4. Increase interaction among planning unit administrators at all levels?
5. Produce a framework for resolving current questions?

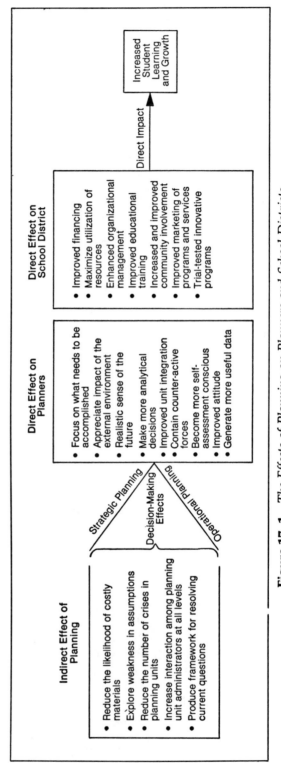

Figure 17-1 *The Effects of Planning on Planners and School Districts.*

How well or poorly planning unit administrators make decisions will most likely be based upon their individual PQ's. Therefore, it is extremely important that a great deal of consideration and resources, if necessary, be given to this aspect of implementing the planning process. At present, no study exists that measures the positive effect of planning on the public education field. However, there are at least three major studies on business and industry that maintain that planning does make a difference in the quality of decision-making abilities of managers, as well as in productivity.

Enhance Planning Unit Administrator's Ability to Function

When planning unit administrators become fortified with training and knowledge about the planning process, their decision-making ability should significantly improve. Another positive effect of planning is that planning units operate better. This is chiefly because planning administrators are able to function better as they begin to:

1. Focus their attention on what needs to be accomplished and the obstacles preventing progress.
2. Appreciate the significance of internal and external environmental forces that may have an impact on the school district.
3. Look at where the school district or planning unit is today and where it might be in the future in a rational, analytical, and systematic way.
4. Make analytical decisions concerning general administrative questions.
5. Pull together as a team through improved coordination and integration.
6. Contain counterproductive forces by reducing the number of crises and preventing complacency.
7. Self-assess their performance as to where they are in the planning process with predetermined time schedules and procedures.
8. Develop an improved attitude about their jobs because of the training and experience received in the pursuit of plans.
9. Generate more useful information through plans and data collection.

Produce a Positive Effect on All Major Key Result Areas of the School District

An effective planning system will increase planning unit administrators' decision-making ability and enhance their capacity to function. The interaction of these two attributes should help produce viable long-range goals, sound program strategies, attainable short-range objectives, valid performance standards, and reliable action plans to effect increased student learning and growth. To perform this task, the major key result areas should be effected as follows:

1. Financial resources are being used in the most cost efficient and effective manner.
2. All physical resources are being utilized to their maximum capability. Waste is kept to a minimum, and a thorough study is made before investing more money in resources.
3. School organization is being operated in a democratic manner. Teachers are treated as managers, too. Administrators exhibit a democratic style of leadership.
4. An objective approach is implemented to evaluate the staff. Staff members and planning unit administrator agree to the objectives, and the process contains provision for self-evaluation, as well as evaluation by the planning unit administrator. The training program is tied to staff evaluation, and strengths and weaknesses are treated.
5. The community is actively involved in the school system, and whenever possible, its members participate in setting standards for the school district.
6. Marketing of the school district's programs and services is thoroughly planned to keep the community informed.
7. Innovative programs are being implemented continuously to strive for improvement. Programs are only installed after an effective trial test.
8. Attempts are consistently made to improve programs and services to maximize financial resources.

Increase Student Learning and Growth

All of the activities of the previous stages have been accomplished to lead to increased student learning and growth, which is the bottom line in public education. First, the planning process enabled planners to make improved decisions, and, second, it enabled them to function more effectively so that appropriate long-range goals, strategies, and short-range objectives could be analytically arrived at to bring about the desired results.

Any evaluation system that is designed to judge the effectiveness of the planning process should assess the sequential stages that lead to improved academic achievement. A gap or deficiency in any one of these stages will prevent the process from attaining the end result.

WHY PLANNING HAS FAILED

Each year more and more educators are beginning to believe in the merits of effective planning. However, as in many other fields, planners can talk a good game, but when it means putting the planning game into motion, the results fall short of what is desired. Talk to most administrators and teachers who have been involved in long-range planning and the discussion will usually revolve around how the system failed, how it has generated a huge amount of paperwork, and how the system is producing an adverse impact on other aspects of the school district. One thing is certain, the school district that experiences the most difficulty in installing the planning process is the one that needs planning the most. An effective school district is one that is performing most of the activities associated with planning, and, therefore, the transition from informal to formal planning can be made without too much difficulty. The following represent some of the common reasons planning has failed to produce a positive effect in many school districts. Some solutions are also suggested. Depending on the uniqueness of individual school districts, the solutions may have to be altered to fit the situation.

Problem	*Solution*
1. The planning process is not really woven into the fabric of school administration.	1. Select a person to become the planning coordinator who will report directly to the superintendent of schools. Have that person assess the strengths and weaknesses of the existing program. Request a written plan that will improve on the former and eliminate the latter. If the planning process contains too many major gaps, it may be more feasible to abandon the present program and start anew; however, make sure that procedures are methodically and deliberately taken to avoid making the same mistakes as in the past.
2. Many school administrators are not comfortable with	2. School administrators are not committed to the planning

Problem	*Solution*
planning, thus they don't want to be involved in the process; therefore, it is not used as an administrative tool.	process probably because the superintendent has not shown much enthusiasm for the program. Commitment tends to be contagious, but only if the chief school administrator is committed. Commitment comes through proper and adequate knowledge and training. Outside users of planning should be invited into the school district to discuss particulars about their programs. Attendance at seminars, workshops, conferences, and the like, on long-range planning is also helpful. Once all administrators have become fortified with sufficient knowledge about the planning process, an attempt should be made to implement the program on a small basis first, and then enlarge it as they become more comfortable with the process as an effective administrative tool.
3. Objective statements are written for program strategies.	3. The most difficult concept to master in long-range planning is the preparation of strategies. Each strategy should contain certain criteria. Check to determine if the statement identifies how the planning unit intends to set priorities among its resources, concentrates its management thrust, and specifies the ways it will use its strengths and correct its limitations to

Problem	*Solution*
	pursue the opportunities and avoid potential threats. If the strategy statement does not contain these essential ingredients, discard it and start anew.
4. Although the planning process has been implemented with some success, the superintendent is not satisfied with the results.	4. If a planning coordinator has not been appointed, the chief school administrator should appoint one at once. If a planning coordinator is available, it may prove timely to hire a consultant on a *per diem* basis either for a week or periodically throughout the school year, to assist the staff to improve the program. An outsider can more easily identify problems within the planning process, because that person is much more removed from the situation than the insider. However, as long-range planning in public education is in its embryonic state, competent planning consultants may be hard to come by.
5. Board members are looking for some immediate results from the planning process.	5. Convince the board that the planning process is an administrative tool and as such, it is not directly responsible for producing improvement in student achievement. It is, however, an analytical device to be used to enable human beings to function and thus improve the overall educational process. Also inform them that significant student learning and growth will not take place overnight, but will

Problem	*Solution*
	surely occur if the planning process is being implemented in an effective manner. Relate to the board that it took scores of years for the school district to retrogress to the present level, and time is needed for planning and implementing plans in order to rid it of the problems that are responsible for its decline in achievement.
6. Planning administrators are complaining about the paperwork required for the planning process.	6. Place a limit on the cost element of the plan, and on the plan as a whole. Institute planning for special projects only, such as a reading program, computer application plans, and the like.
7. Even though all the forms have been properly filled out and a district-wide strategic plan has been consolidated, key issues and threats have not been confronted.	7. This problem is not easily resolved. It is one of the most challenging tasks of the planning process. Use exemplary statements of strategies to illustrate the type of thinking required. Continuous training in strategic thinking will also be required.

PITFALLS TO AVOID

Several years ago, George A. Steiner sent a questionnaire concerning planning pitfalls to more than five hundred companies. Response was received from approximately a third of those surveyed. Until long-range strategic planning in public education has had an opportunity to germinate, and surveys of this nature are conducted throughout the country's public school systems, Steiner's survey results can provide adequate information to school organizations concerning planning pitfalls. The following represents several of these stumbling blocks, which have been adapted to apply to public education:[1]

[1] Reprinted with the permission of Macmillan Publishing Co., Inc. from *Strategic Planning—What Every Manager Must Know* by George A. Steiner. Copyright © 1979 by The Free Press, a Division of Macmillan Publishing Co., Inc.

I. Pitfalls in Getting Started
1. Central administrators assume that they can delegate the planning function to a planner.
2. Planning is rejected because there has been success without it.
3. Formal planning is rejected because the system failed in the past to foresee a critical problem and did not result in substantive decisions that satisfied the central planning unit.
4. It is assumed that the present body of knowledge about planning is insufficient to guide fruitful comprehensive planning.
5. It is assumed that a planning unit cannot develop effective long-range planning in a way appropriate to its resources and needs.
6. It is assumed that comprehensive planning can be introduced into a planning unit and miraculous results will appear overnight.
7. It is believed that a successful comprehensive plan can be moved from one planning unit to another without change and with equal success.
8. It is assumed that a formal system can be introduced into a planning unit without a careful and perhaps agonizing reappraisal of current practices and decision-making processes.
9. The power structure of the planning unit is ignored during the organization process.
10. There is failure to develop a clear understanding of the long-range planning procedure before the process is actually undertaken.
11. There is failure to create a congenial climate that is not resistant to planning within the planning unit.
12. The individual designated as the planning coordinator is not on a high enough level within the organizational hierarchy to be effective.
13. There is failure to ascertain that the planning staff possesses the necessary qualities of leadership, technical expertise, and personality to discharge properly its responsibilities in making the planning system effective.

II. Pitfalls Related to a Misunderstanding of the Nature of Strategic Planning
14. It is forgotten that planning is a political, social, and organizational, as well as a rational process.
15. It is assumed that comprehensive planning is something separate from the entire administration process.
16. There is failure to make certain that central and school planning unit administrators understand the nature of long-range planning and what it will accomplish for them and the school district.

17. There is failure to udnerstand that systematic formal planning and intuitive (opportunistic) planning are complementary.
18. It is assumed that plans can be made by central planning administrators for school planning unit administrators to implement.
19. The fact that planning is and should be a learning process is ignored.
20. It is assumed that planning is easy.
21. It is assumed that planning is hard.
22. It is assumed that long-range planning can bring a school district out of a current crisis.
23. There is failure to see that comprehensive planning is an integrated administrative system.

III. Pitfalls in Doing Strategic Planning
  A. Administrative Involvement
    24. Central planning unit administrators become so engrossed in current problems that they spend insufficient time on long-range planning, and the process becomes discredited among other planning unit administrators and staff.
    25. Long-range planning becomes unpopular because central planning unit administrators spend too much time on long-range problems at the expense of short-range ones.
    26. There is failure to involve all administrators in the planning process.
    27. There is too much centralization of the long-range planning within the central planning unit so that school planning units feel little responsibility for developing effective plans.
  B. The Process of Planning
    28. There is failure to develop long-range goals suitable as a basis for formulating long-range plans.
    29. It is assumed that equal weight should be given to all elements of planning (that is, that the same emphasis should be placed on strategic as on operational planning, or that the same emphasis should be accorded to major functional plans).
    30. Too much formality is injected into the system so that it lacks flexibility, looseness, and simplicity, and thus restrains creativity.
    31. There is failure to make realistic plans due to overoptimism or overcautiousness.
    32. The process is extrapolated rather than rethought; that is, if plans are made for 1985 through 1990, adding 1991 in the 1986 cycle rather than redoing all plans from 1986 to 1991.

33. There is a development of such a reverence for numbers that irreverence for intuition and value judgments predominates the thinking process involved in planning.
34. Precision of numbers is sought throughout the planning horizon.
35. It is assumed that older methods should be discarded in favor of newer techniques.
36. It is assumed that new quantitative techniques are not as useful as qualitative ones.
37. Long-range planning is implemented periodically, but forgotten in the interim cycles.

C. Creditability of Results
38. There is a failure to develop planning capabilities in major operating units.
39. There is failure among the central planning unit administrators to give school planning units sufficient information and guidance.
40. Too much is attempted to be accomplished in too short a time.
41. There is failure to secure that a minimum of systems and information makes the process and its results creditable and useful.

IV. Pitfalls in Using Strategic Plans
42. The central planning unit administrators fail to review with the school planning unit administrators the long-range plans that they have developed.
43. It is forgotten that the fundamental purpose of the exercise is to make better current decisions.
44. It is assumed that plans once made are blueprints and should be followed rigorously until changed in the next planning cycle.
45. The central planning unit administrators consistently reject the formal planning mechanism by making intuitive decisions that conflict with the formal plans.
46. It is assumed that because plans must result in current decisions it is the short run that counts, and planning efforts, as well as evaluations, should concentrate on the short run.
47. There is failure to use plans as standards for measuring planning unit administrator's performance.
48. It is forgotten to apply a cost-benefit analysis to the system to make sure advantages are greater than costs.
49. There is failure to encourage planning unit administrators to do good long-range planning by basing reward solely on short-range performance measures.

50. There is failure to exploit the fact that formal planning is an administration process that can be used to improve administrative capabilities throughout a planning unit.

Mr. Steiner admits that the list of pitfalls is incomplete because it does not include the entire management process. He maintains that the list only includes the most important pitfalls concerning understanding the planning process prior to commencement, and implementing and using it once plans have been formulated. He further maintains that the pitfalls do not relate to other factors, such as analyzing the wrong subject, conducting the wrong type of analysis, and arriving at incorrect conclusions based on available data.

MEASURING PLANNING EFFECTIVENESS

As previously stated, strategic planning in public education is in the embryonic stage, and, therefore, very little has been done to measure the effectiveness of the planning system. However, following are some techniques or approaches that can be applied to determine how well the program has been implemented.

Construct a Questionnaire

A questionnaire is an excellent way to determine the value of the planning program. It can be prepared by determining what areas should be evaluated, and developing questions by subsuming indicators under each area, as illustrated in Figure 17–2. This questionnaire has been divided into four parts. Part A revolves around a commitment to planning. Without this attitudinal assessment, it would be difficult to determine the success or failure of the planning process. Part B has been included because insufficient consideration has been given to this phase of the planning process in public education and may be one of the most salient reasons some planning systems fail. Part C has been included primarily to assess the breadth and depth of the planning process. A large number of planning systems take on a static quality by not relating properly to outside factors and forces interacting with the school district. Part D is obviously included to judge the effects of the planning process on the staff and students in the school district as a whole.

More insight into the planning process can be gained if the questionnaire is discussed among planning unit administrators rather than merely distributed to them to react on their own. However, if time is a critical factor, it may be more appropriate to have the planning administrators complete the survey independently.

Planning Questionnaire

Name: _____ Position: _____

Planning Unit: _____ Date:_____

Directions:
This questionnaire is intended to give you an opportunity to express your views on the planning process. Information gathered from this questionnaire will be used to improve the planning program through a variety of activities. We, therefore request that your response reflects careful thought and that you feel free to make any comments in the blank spaces provided.

A. Commitment to the Planning Program is Evolving

	Strongly Disagree	Disagree	Undecided	Agree	Strongly Agree
1. The superintendent of schools has demonstrated commitment to the planning process through words, actions, resources and deeds.	☐	☐	☐	☐	☐
2. The commitment of the chief school administrator is rubbing off on planning unit administrators.	☐	☐	☐	☐	☐
3. A comprehensive resource library on planning has been established in a central location in the school district.	☐	☐	☐	☐	☐
4. The superintendent has received training in strategic and operational planning.	☐	☐	☐	☐	☐
5. A planning plan has been prepared and implemented to provide continuous training and development activities in training to planning unit administrators and staff.	☐	☐	☐	☐	☐
6. The board of education has been throughly informed of the planning program and has voted to implement it.	☐	☐	☐	☐	☐
7. A long-range budget has been allocated for the planning process.	☐	☐	☐	☐	☐
8. A process has been installed to nurture the planning process.	☐	☐	☐	☐	☐
9. A planning coordinator has been appointed to orchestrate the activities associated with the planning process.	☐	☐	☐	☐	☐

Remarks: _____

_____

_____

_____

_____

_____

_____

Figure 17–2 *Planning Questionnaire*

B. Training Program Is Implemented on a Continuous Basis

	Strongly Disagree	Disagree	Undecided	Agree	Strongly Agree
10. A planning Guidelines or Manual has been prepared to assist staff to implement various phases of the planning process.	□	□	□	□	□
11. A per diem consultant has been retained to assist the staff to implement the planning process on a need basis.	□	□	□	□	□
12. Training in planning is based upon an analytical study of needs.	□	□	□	□	□

Remarks: _____

_____

_____

_____

_____

_____

_____

C. Planning Program Is Implemented

	Strongly Disagree	Disagree	Undecided	Agree	Strongly Agree
13. The network of aims has been developed and clarified to the staff.	□	□	□	□	□
14. A comprehensive planning system has been developed and implemented.	□	□	□	□	□
15. The critical analysis involves the collection of essential and pertinent information and critical data about the school district.	□	□	□	□	□
16. Past performance results have also been included in the critical analysis.	□	□	□	□	□
17. The core of the critical analysis should involve development of strengths, minimize weaknesses, avoid problems, make the most of opportunities, and anticipate threats.	□	□	□	□	□
18. The critical analysis also contains information on the attitudes and expectations of stakeholders and analysis of competition.	□	□	□	□	□
19. Adequate long-range plans have been set to achieve the mission of the school district.	□	□	□	□	□
20. Strategies have been properly recorded for realizing each long-range goal.	□	□	□	□	□
21. Short-range objectives have been prepared in accordance with strategies and have been evaluated to make maximum use of strengths, minimize or eliminate weaknesses and exploit opportunities.	□	□	□	□	□
22. There are neither too many or too few short-range objectives to meet the long-range goals.	□	□	□	□	□

Figure 17–2 *Continued*

C. Planning Program is Implemented (continued)

	Strongly Disagree	Disagree	Undecided	Agree	Strongly Agree
23. Performance standards or other indicators of success have been devised to determine if short-range objectives have been achieved.	□	□	□	□	□
24. An action plan has been included with the short-range planning process.	□	□	□	□	□
25. A short-range budget has been included with the short-range planning process.	□	□	□	□	□

Remarks: _____

_____

_____

_____

_____

_____

_____

_____

D. Assessing the Planning Program for Effectiveness

	Strongly Disagree	Disagree	Undecided	Agree	Strongly Agree
26. Proper controls have been established to monitor performance.	□	□	□	□	□
27. A variety of techniques and methods have been used to evaluate the effectiveness of the planning program.	□	□	□	□	□
28. A formal evaluation program has been established to assess the effectiveness of the planning process.	□	□	□	□	□

Remarks: _____

_____

_____

_____

_____

_____

_____

Figure 17–2 *Continued*

E. Positive Effects of the Planning Process

	Strongly Disagree	Disagree	Undecided	Agree	Strongly Agree
29. Planning unit administrators are able to make better decisions.	☐	☐	☐	☐	☐
30. Attitudes and morale of planning unit administrators have improved.	☐	☐	☐	☐	☐
31. Crises are anticipated and planned for before they get out of control.	☐	☐	☐	☐	☐
32. New and innovative ideas are given an opportunity to be tried through the planning process.	☐	☐	☐	☐	☐
33. Planning unit administrators possess more useful information about their individual planning units and the school district as a whole.	☐	☐	☐	☐	☐
34. Improvement in the major key result areas has been noted.	☐	☐	☐	☐	☐
35. Planning unit administrators believe that the planning process has made a difference in the effectiveness of staff and students.	☐	☐	☐	☐	☐

Remarks: _____

_____

_____

_____

_____

_____

_____

_____

_____

_____

Figure 17–2 *Continued*

ASSESSMENT INSTRUMENTS OF OTHERS

Another effective approach to judging the worth of the planning system is to review the planning assessment instruments of others. For example, Steiner has developed a five-part questionnaire that includes forty questions by which to evaluate the effectiveness of strategic planning programs.[2] Part A relates to the perceived values of the planning process; Part B assesses the effects of the planning system; Part C contains the benefits of the system; and Parts D and E focus on the process, method, mental attitude, climate, and procedures of the planning pro-

[2] Steiner, *Strategic Planning*, pp. 300–304.

cess. Schaffir has also produced a technique or method by which planners can evaluate their planning systems by identifying clues in ten areas.[3] These are:

1. Does the planning process help the planner to function better?
2. Is there practical commitment to established plans?
3. Does the plan contain sufficient information to help realize the mission?
4. Have plans been produced by reviewing the internal and external environments that have led to the formulation of strategies?
5. Have alternatives been carefully considered and adequately shown in the plans?
6. Does the planning process synthesize solutions from problems, alternatives, and priorities?
7. Is the planning system linked to resources properly?
8. Is paperwork kept to a minimum?
9. Are the planning system and plans applicable to many planning administrative styles and behavior?
10. Is the planning system woven into the fabric of the school organization?

An effective and comprehensive instrument for evaluating the planning system could be developed by considering the contents of this chapter. No prescriptive evaluative instrument can be used by all school districts because the assessment needs of each organization vary.

EVALUATING THE SYSTEM AGAINST ITS OBJECTIVES

The planning manual should state some specific objectives of the planning program. If the planning system is effective, these objectives should be accomplished. The planning program's value is based on how well the objectives were thought through and set.

ASSESSING THE PLANNING SYSTEM AGAINST PITFALLS

Steiner has compiled a list of pitfalls, which has been previously referred to in this chapter. One approach to measure the effectiveness of the planning system is to compare it with this list. Another approach is

[3] Walter B. Schaffir, *Strategic Planning: Some Questions for the Chief Executive* (New York: AMACOM, 1976), pp. 34–40.

for the planning coordinator to produce a list of indicators of a success-ful planning system and compare it with the existing system.

SALIENT POINTS

The effectiveness of the planning process is the responsibility of the superintendent. He or she delegates this responsibility to individual planning unit administrators in order to manage the process in the most effective manner. The chief school administrator is also responsible for assessing whether the central planning unit is having a positive or negative effect on individual planning units as well as on the planning units as a whole. What should be sought is a smoothly and efficiently operating school organization established around effectively operated planning units, so that performance results of the staff are compounded at a reasonable pace to bring forth improvements in all of the major key result areas. It is the superintendent of school's responsibility to main-tain an effective planning system. A productive strategic and opera-tional planning system and school administration are a combination that leads to a sound school district. Ineffective planning will not only lead to wasted time and energy on the part of planning unit administra-tors and staff, but will have a devastating effect on the total school district. The most successful way to implement and improve the plan-ning system is continuously to conduct an assessment of critical aspects of the process.

APPLICATION STRATEGY 17

Unfortunately, no attempt has been made to present a written evalua-tion of how effective planning has been in the field of public education, However, you may look at the following material to determine the degree to which strategic planning has been successful in other areas: Malcolm W. Pennington, "Why Has Planning Failed and What Can You Do About It?" *Planning Review*, November 1975; Kjell A. Ringbakh, "Why Planning Failed," *European Business*, Spring 1971; Harold W. Henry, "Formal Planning in Major U.S. Corporations," *Long-Range Planning*, October 1977; and J. C. Camillus, "Evaluating the Benefits of Formal Planning Systems," *Long-Range Planning*, June 1975.

Develop an instrument for evaluating the effectiveness of strategic planning. Test the instrument for validity and reliability. Request that someone respected in planning review the instrument and revise or modify it if necessary. Use this instrument to study several school dis-tricts that have been engaged in long-range planning, and review the results with the superintendent.

APPENDIX

CLARIFYING THE PLANNING PROCESS

The information in this appendix, with completed forms, should enable any school district to prepare a complete set of strategic and operational plans, state departments of education to develop policies on the planning process, and practicing school administrators to engage successfully in the preparation of viable plans.

A complete set of plans has not been included in the sample because of the limitation of space; however, a complete set of plans for the central planning unit does appear. Some items in both school planning units have been omitted in order to avoid unnecessary duplication.

PREPARING THE CRITICAL ANALYSIS

Description of the Community

The description of the community should be accompanied by a map that also reflects cities and towns bordering the school community. School planning units will usually include in this section a description of the immediate community they serve.

Description of the School District

Usually this description is developed by the central planning unit. A map identifying each school and the geographical area of the school district is also included. An organizational chart is included by the central planning unit and the school planning unit in their individual plans.

In an effort to keep the main planning document short, the central planning unit may not require individual school planning units to submit this section with their plans. It is, however, a good practice for each school planning unit to maintain a complete set of plans for its own use.

Network of Aims

The central planning unit should include in this section the basic purposes and mission statements, as well as the school district's educational goals. Again, in order to limit the volume of the planning document, individual school planning unit statements pertaining to basic purposes, mission, and educational goals and objectives are usually not submitted to the central planning unit for inclusion in the main planning document.

Demographics

Because this section requires too much space in most plans, a simple chart, such as the included sample, should suffice. This information is completed and updated by the central planning unit so that it is included in their plans.

Student Learning and Growth

The student learning and growth profile sheet is an expeditious way to display academic progress. School planning unit administrators usually complete a profile form for their individual schools and submit a copy to the central planning unit, which in turn prepares a composite profile to be included in the main planning document.

Faculty Profile

A copy of each faculty profile sheet is submitted to each school planning unit by the central planning unit.

Financial History

The form used to display the financial history might also include a complete listing of programs and costs as well as major key result areas. The financial history form should be completed by the central planning unit and school planning units. Obviously, school planning units must wait until the central planning unit has completed a financial history statement for the school district to prepare their reports.

Competition Analysis

The central planning unit is responsible for completing the competitive analysis form, although, in rare cases, a school planning unit may do it. The central planning unit is better equipped to conduct this type of study; however, any valuable information or assistance from school planning unit members is welcomed. The results of the competitive analysis should be discussed with all planning unit administrators in a group meeting.

School District Problems

This sample form, used to depict school-related problems, can provide a composite of adverse influences on the district. Individual school planning units should complete this form and submit it to the central planning unit where a composite is prepared for the entire district.

Swop Analysis

The swop analysis is prepared by both the central and school planning units. If an analysis is completed by the central planning unit, the school planning unit usually is not required to prepare one. For example, in the sample a swop analysis was completed by the central planning unit under the major key result area of student learning and growth regarding low SAT scores. A swop analysis does not always have to be completed by the appropriate school planning unit. In fact, every item related to low SAT scores will be initially planned by the central planning unit.

Stakeholder Analysis

The central planning unit is responsible for identifying and analyzing all of the major stakeholders in the school district. The study results should be shared with all planning unit administrators. It may be appropriate to ask individual planning unit administrators to be watch dogs for specific stakeholder groups.

If a school planning unit administrator becomes aware of a new major stakeholder, this information should be reported immediately to the central planning unit, where appropriate action is taken.

Past Performance Results

The individual school planning unit administrator should develop this document to show past performance results, immediately after the annual performance review. This information is then inserted on a similar form to track the outcome of each long-range goal on an annual basis.

STRATEGIC PLANS

Guidelines for Formulating Strategies

A good rule of thumb to identify the planning unit responsible for completing the form for formulating strategies is to associate the strategy with the long-range goal itself. For example, if the long-range goal pertains to an exclusive school planning unit, then the strategy should be formulated by that planning unit. If, however, the long-range goal is the responsibility of a member of the central planning unit, then the strategy should be prepared by that person.

Strategic Planning Package

Whoever formulates the strategy should also complete the strategic planning package. The central planning unit should be responsible for reviewing and approving all strategic planning packages. A corrected copy should be submitted to the central planning unit, where it is filed with the main planning document.

OPERATIONAL PLANS

The planning unit responsible for attaining a specific long-range goal should prepare the operational plans to accomplish that task. For example, in the sample, the assistant superintendent of business affairs is responsible for the long-range goal of establishing a reproduction center. Anything dealing with planning in this area is the responsibility of this administrator. Although math was not a long-range goal set by the central planning units, it was one identified by the planning unit administrator of Alpha Elementary School, who is therefore responsible for developing the operational plan in this area.

Strategic Planning

Planning Unit: _____Central_____ Date: _June 15, 19XX_

Planning Unit Administrator: _Dr. James Wilkinson_ Position: _Superintendent_

Planning Component: _Critical Analysis_ Page __1__ of __5__

Content:

A. Description of community
B. Description of school district
C. Network of aims
D. Demographice
E. Student learning and growth
F. Faculty profile
G. Financial history

H. School district problems
I. Swop analysis
J. Competition analysis
K. Stakeholders analysis
L. Threat analysis
M. Past performance results

A. Description of Community

The Somewhere area is a community with a broad range of socioeconomic levels and ethnic groups. The average market value of a property is among the highest in the southeastern area; one mil of tax is equal to a levy of $186,584. As a result of this relatively high value of property, there is a corresponding low state-aid ratio.

On the other hand, some residential areas of the district reflect the lower end of the socioeconomic continuum and the myriad of problems that accompany such conditions.

The Somewhere area is not sustained by any one industrial, health care, or governmental unit, although many companies are located withing the district's geographical area. Somewhere State College and Nowhere State College, tax-exempt institutions, are also located within the district and employ a large number of people.

The people of this area have traditionally supported the ideals of public education. Their support of public schools is almost as old as public education itself. Growth in the school district has not changed the strength of this support.

The Somewhere School District is located 25 miles west of Utopia in the southeastern portion of Walton County. It includes the seven townships that surround the more urban setting of the Borough of Somewhere. In contrast, the suburban area section includes impressive country estates. Somewhere is the legal and financial center of Waltion County.

B. Description of School District

There are more than 30,000 students enrolled in the 30 elementary schools, 6 junior highs, and 3 secondary schools. Each building is managed by a minimum of 1 principal and 1 assistant principal. Each elementary school is devided into teams, whereas the junior and secondary high schools are organized around departments.

All buildings are in good shape.

The central administration is organized around divisions: Curriculum and Instruction, Business Affairs, Administration and Personnel, and Strategic Planning. Leading the school district is a superintendent with an assistant superintendent for each division. Refer to the following page for an organizational chart of the school district.

C. Network of Aims

Basic Purposes and Mission Statement

School District

Provide the community with high quality, results-oriented and cost-effective education, so that all students will learn and grow intellectually, emotionally, socially, aesthetically, and physically, according to their maximum potential by managing and operating all schools within our geographical area.

Central Administrative Divisions

Maintains adequate accounting of records and books concerning all business activities of the school district. Ensures that proper procedures are carried out involving the receipts and expenditures of revenue. Files required forms in a timely fashion. Directs the operations of facilities, grounds, and security.

Curriculum and Instruction

Ensures that appropriate programs and courses are made available for students so that the school district is in line with the legal requirements of the State Department of Education and the expectations of the community. Assists in the preparation, communication, and dissemination of a results-oriented and humanistic curriculum.

Administration and Personnel

Ensures that all necessary support services are provided to implement, maintain, and improve the instructional program. Makes certain that personnel are hired in a timely manner and that the affirmative action mandate is properly enforced.

Strategic Planning

Provides district-wide plicy, direction, coordination and training, follow-up, and assessment concerning long-range and short-range plans, quarterly reviews, special planning studies. Directs the operations of the Data Processing and Research and Evaluation Services.

Overall, the central administration exists in order to articulate and coordinate all school activities in order to:

Prepare students properly in all areas to assume a productive and satisfactory life.

Involve the community in the affairs of its' schools.

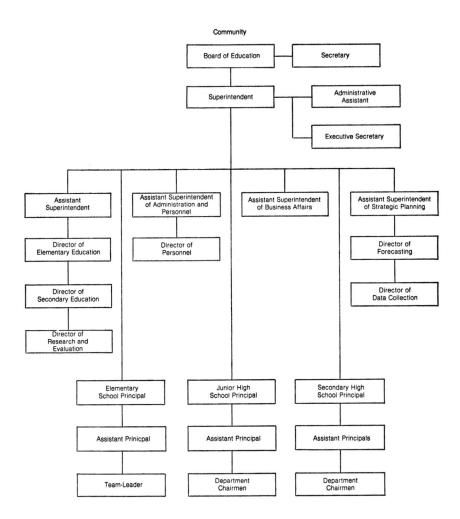

Provide an effective marketing strategy to highlight the activities and programs of the school district.

Ensure cost-effective use of available resources.

Maintain a healthy and goal-oriented environment for both teaching and learning.

Ensure that all staff members are provided with proper performance review and training to avoid obsolescence.

District-Wide Educational Goals

In order to fulfill the basic purposes and mission of the school district, the following nineteen educational goals have been officially adopted by the community and Board of Education.

Every student is required to:

1. Learn how to be a productive member of society.

2. Learn to live in a multi-ethnic community.

3. Learn and understand world events.

4. Develop proficiency in the basic skills.

5. Become computer literate.

6. Learn to love one self.

7. Learn how to retrieve information.

8. Become proficient in family life education.

9. Learn to love others.

10. Develop preventry skills to enter the field of work.

11. Learn to manage one's personal life.

12. Learn the value of understanding the past, present and predicting the future.

13. Learn to use time in an efficient manner.

14. Gain vital information to select and maintain an effective job.

15. Develop pride in self.

16. Develop a purpose for living.

17. Develop a positive self-image.

18. Learn to become a considerate and kind individual.

19. Learn to obey man's laws and the laws of nature.

20. Develop a thirst for knowledge and understanding.

Strategic Planning

Planning Unit: __Central__   Date: __June 15, 19XX__

Planning Unit Administrator: __Dr. James Wilkinson__   Position: __Superintendent__

Planning Component: __Critical Analysis__   Page __1__ of __1__

Demographic Profile

Categories	19 _XX_ Current M	F	Percent of Increase (Decrease) M	F	Projection (5 years) M	F	Percent of Increase (Decrease) M	F
A. Population Age and Sex Adults 35 and over	3,470	5,670						
25 - 34	6,170	9,805						
19 - 24	5,150	6,809						
Children 14 - 18	1,975	2,635						
10 - 13	2,980	3,851						
5 - 9	7,145	11,565						
3 - 4	1,701	2,450						
Sub Total	13,801	20,500						
TOTAL	34,301							
B. Race White	58,000	72,000						
Black	11,600	14,400						
Hispanic	1,450	1,800						
Other	325	410						
Sub Total	71,375	90,610						
TOTAL	161,985							
C. Occupation Professional/ Business Management/ White Collar	14,760	11,010						
Blue Collar	38,170	9,100						
Sub Total	52,930	20,110						
TOTAL	73,040							
D. Family Income Under $4,999/year								
$5,000 - $9,999	4,000	914						
$10,000 - $19,999	37,740	9,600						
$20,000 and over	11,190	7,750						
Sub Total	52,930	18,264						
TOTAL	71,194							
E. Foster Children	1,150	2,975						
Sub Total								
TOTAL	4,125							
F. Social Services Children	2,148	3,750						
Sub Total								
TOTAL	5,898							

Strategic Planning

Planning Unit: ___Central_____ Date:__June 15, 19XX__

Planning Unit Administrator: __Dr. James Wilkinson__ Position:__Superintendent__

Planning Component: _Critical Analysis_ Page __1__ of __2__

Student Learning and Growth

A. Academic Achievement

Title of Test _Stanford Achievement_ Date Administered _Oct. 1, 19XX_

B. State-wide Test Results

Grade Level	19 XX to XX		19___ to___		19___ to___		19___to___		19___to___	
	Verbal	Math	Verbal	Math	Verbal	Math	Verbal	Math	Verbal	Math
3rd Grade	33%	38%								
6th Grade	20%	21%								
9th Grade	25%	26%								
11th Grade	31%	35%								

C. SAT Results

Section	19XX to XX	19___ to ___	19___ to ___	19___ to ___	19___ to ___
Verbal	414	411			
Math	450	449			

D. Placement of Graduates

Item	19XX to XX	19___ to ___	19___ to ___	19___ to ___	19___ to ___
Number. and Percentage Students Entering College	950 (72%)	956 (73%)			
Number and Percentage Students Entering Com. Schools	45 (24%)	39 (24%)			
Number and Percentage Students Entering Armed Services	20 (2%)	22 (2%)			
Number and Percentage Students Entering Other Fields	20 (2%)	14 (1%)			
Total	1,035	1,031			

E. National Awards/Honors

Title of Award/Honor	19 XX to XX	19___ to ___	19___ to ___	19___ to ___	19___ to ___
National Science Award	4	6			
National Merit Award	8	19			
Literary Guild Honors	4	6			

Strategic Planning

Planning Unit: _____ Central _____ Date: June 15, 19XX

Planning Unit Administrator: Dr. James Wilkinson _____ Position: Superintendent

Planning Component: Critical Analysis _____ Page __1__ of __2__

Faculty Profile

Composition of Staff

Classification	19XX to XX		19__ to __		19__ to __		19__ to __		19__ to __	
	T	A	T	A	T	A	T	A	T	A
Male	415	82								
Female	975	12								
Total	1,390	94								
White	1,019	71								
Black	275	19								
Hispanic	14	2								
Oriental	2	2								
Other										

Years of Experience

Classification	1 year		5 years		10 years		15 years		20 years		25+ years	
	T	A	T	A	T	A	T	A	T	A	T	A
Male	20	4	121	45	190	25	98	8	26		10	
Female	31	2	382	7	314	3	175		29		44	
White	41	7	345	40	410	11	100	13	40		83	
Black	10	2	110	10	140	4	15	3				
Hispanic		1	10	1	2		2					
Oriental			4									
Other												

Tenure Profile

Classification	White				Black				Hispanic				Oriental				Other			
	F	M	T	A	F	M	T	A	F	M	T	A	F	M	T	A	F	M	T	A
Non-tenured	65	45	110	10	15	1	16	2	1		1									
Tenured	539	370	909	54	240	19	259	17	13	1	14	1	4		4					

Percentage of Teachers/Administrators Engaging in Additional Training

Grade Level	19 XX to XX		19___ to ___		19___ to ___		19___ to ___		19___ to ___	
	T	A	T	A	T	A	T	A	T	A
Kindergarten	11%	10%								
First	18%									
Second	21%									
Third	11%									
Fourth	9%									
Fifth	13%									
Sixth	10%									
Seventh	6%	5%								
Eighth	5%									
Ninth	3%	1%								
Tenth	1%									
Eleventh	2%									
Twelfth	1%									

Strategic Planning

Planning Unit: ___Central_____   Date:___June 15, 19XX___

Planning Unit Administrator: _Dr. James Wilkinson_____   Position:Superintendent

Planning Component: _Critical Analysis_   Page __1__ of __2__

Summary of Financial History

Major Key Result Areas	19__ to __	19__ to __	19__ to __	19__ to __	19__ to __
	Amount	Amount	Amount	Amount	Amount
1. Financial Resources	1,245,000				
2. Performance Evaluation and Training	150,000				
3. Physical Resources	4,785,410				
4. Student Learning and Growth	2,941,000				
5. Organizational Management	1,745,000				
6. Innovation	875,000				
7. Community Involvement and Relations	50,000				
8. Instructional Programs and Services	54,148,730				
9.					
10.					
Total	65,940,140				
Change Increase/ Decrease					

Anticipated Revenue

Source	19 XX to XX	19 __ to __	19 __ to __	19 __ to __	19 __ to __
	Amount	Amount	Amount	Amount	Amount
1. Local taxes	29,527,140.				
2. State aid	28,740,000.				
3. Title I	1,450,000.				
4. Transportation	4,769,000.				
5. Other	1,454,000.				
Total	65,940,140.				

Strategic Planning

Planning Unit: _____Central_____   Date: _June 15, 19XX_

Planning Unit Administrator: _Dr. James Wilkinson_____   Position: _Superintendent_

Planning Component: _Critical Analysis_   Page __I__ of __1__

Adverse Influences on School District

Description of Influence	19 _xx_ to _xx_	19_xx_ to_xx_	19__ to __	19__ to __	19__ to __
1. Student absentee rate	11%	12%			
2. Faculty absentee rate	10.4%	9.1%			
3. Cost of substitute teachers' salaries	3,740,410	3,010,915			
4. Staff turnover	31:2110	24:2112			
5. Cost of vandalism	650,000	675,000			
6. Number of students assaulted	375	390			
7. Number of faculty assaulted	110	139			
8. Incidents of student accidents	470	498			
9. Incidents of faculty accidents	125	109			
10. Incidents of pregnancy	120	131			
11. Drop-out rate	18%	19%			
12. Students killed	0	7			
13. Faculty killed	0	1			
14. Students enrolling in non-public schools	410	515			

Strategic Planning

Planning Unit: _____Central_____ Date: _June 15, 19XX_

Planning Unit Administrator: _Dr. James Wilkinson_____ Position: Superintendent

Planning Component: Critical Analysis   Page ___1___ of __8__

Swop Analysis: _____

Major Key Result Area:	Student Learning and Growth

Major Strengths/Opportunities	Major Weaknesses/Problems
-Teachers are eager to receive training in reading. -Most teachers would welcome the opportunity to reduce the number of reading programs to 2 or 3. -The pilot reading program revealed that students made "unusually" high gains in reading.	-A large percentage of the elementary teachers have received little or no developmental training in reading in the past 5 years. -Reading is not stressed in the other subject areas, either in the junior high or senior high schools. -More than 7 different reading programs are currently being implemented in the school district.

Action to be taken: Reference

Develop a plan to implement the reading program used in the pilot study on a district-wide level. Provide an orientation program to expose teachers and parents to the mechanics of the reading program by using students. Implement the program on a district-wide level.

Strategic Planning

Planning Unit: _Central_   Date: _June 15, 19XX_

Planning Unit Administrator: _Dr. James Wilkinson_   Position: _Superintendent_

Planning Component: _Critical Analysis_   Page _2_ of _8_

Swop Analysis: _____

Major Key Result Area:	Organizational Management
Major Strengths/Opportunities	Major Weaknesses/Problems
-Superintendent is committed to a program that will reduce teacher illness absences without intimidation. -Bell Telephone Company is willing to assist the school district in implementing an effective program to eliminate or reduce the severity of this problem.	-Staff absenteeism rate is 12 days per teacher, amounting to $3,740,410 per year for substitutes. -Teacher-student contact is reduced by the number of days teachers are absent. -Regular educational program is interrupted. -Most substitute teachers are unable to carry on with the regular educational program. -Any attempt to reduce teacher absenteeism will be met with suspicion by the Teachers' Association.

Action to be taken: Reference

Investigate the Bell Telephone program to reduce teacher illness absenteeism. Extract the best aspects of this program, and design a similar program. Make certain that officials from the Teachers' Association are involved in the program from the onset.

Strategic Planning

Planning Unit: __Central_____   Date: __June 15, 19XX__

Planning Unit Administrator: __Dr. James Wilkinson_____   Position__Superintendent__

Planning Component: __Critical Analysis__   Page ___3___ of __8__

Swop Analysis: _____

Major Key Result Area:	Innovation

Major Strengths/Opportunities	Major Weaknesses/Problems
-A number of members of the community have experienced the assessment center approach for selecting personnel. These members are interested in assisting the school district in this area. -The state-wide association for school administrators is eager to assist the school district with this problem. -Funds are available to implement a viable program for selecting school administrators.	-The success rate in hiring school administrators using the interviewing approach is less than 40%. -The Board of Education is dissatisfied with the school district's current selection process. -The local association for school administrators should be actively involved in the new program at the onset.

Action to be taken: Reference

Take advantage of the members of the community who are familiar
with the assessment center approach for selecting personnel, and
develop a plan for implementing such a program within the school
district.

Strategic Planning

Planning Unit: __Central_____   Date: __June 15, 19XX__

Planning Unit Administrator: __Dr. James Wilkinson__   Position: __Superintendent__

Planning Component: __Critical Analysis__   Page ___4__ of __8__

Swop Analysis: _____

Major Key Result Area: Performance Evaluation and Training	
Major Strengths/Opportunities	Major Weaknesses/Problems
–Assistant superintendent for personnel is the author of several books on staff evaluation.	–Current teacher evaluation program does not meet new state mandate.
–Good relationship exists between teacher union and superintendent.	–Teacher evaluation program has not been validated or tested for reliability.
–For the past few years, superintendent initiated an active program for involving teachers in the decision-making process.	–Current teacher evaluation program evolves around characteristics and traits of teachers.
–State department of education has mandated some major changes in staff evaluation.	–Teacher evaluation program does not improve instruction.
–The new state mandate on staff evaluation presents an excellent opportunity for the school district to overhaul its entire staff evaluation program.	–The time span set by the new mandate poses a serious problem for the school district because of the desegregation ruling by the federal government and the need to modify the desegregation proposal.
–Able leadership exists in central administration and teachers union to perform this task effectively.	

Action to be taken: Reference

Organize a district-wide staff evaluation council to assist in
planning, developing, implementing, and evaluating the teacher
evaluation program. (Include this proposed action as an objective,
performance standard, or activity.) Effective leadership
currently exists in the central administration to spearhead a
move to revamp the teacher evaluation program so that it fulfills
its mission and meets the new mandate on staff evaluation
established by the state department of education.

Strategic Planning

Planning Unit: _____Central_____   Date: ___June 15, 19..

Planning Unit Administrator: _Dr. James Wilkinson_____   Position:_Superintendent

Planning Component: _Critical Analysis_   Page _____5_____ of ___6___

Swop Analysis: _____

Major Key Result Area:	Financial Resources
Major Strengths/Opportunities	Major Weaknesses/Problems
-The board is willing to appropriate funds to establish a position of grants writer. -A number of proposal writing consultants live within the community and would be interested in training a staff person to write proposals. -The superintendent is willing to have the school district compete for funds with the private and nonprofit sectors.	-Because of declining enrollment, state aid is decreasing each year. -Several surrounding school districts are supplementing their budget by as much as $3,000,000. -More than $3 billion is available in grants and contracts, of which the school district currently receives very little.

Action to be taken: Reference

Hire a person to write grant proposals. Develop a format that will give the school district a competitive edge. Subscribe to various publications, such as The Federal Register and Commerce Business Daily, to obtain information on grants.

Strategic Planning

Planning Unit: ___Central_____   Date: June 15, 19XX

Planning Unit Administrator: Dr. James Wilkinson   Position: Superintendent

Planning Component: Critical Analysis   Page ___6___ of ___8___

Swop Analysis: _____

Major Key Result Area:	Community Involvement and Relations
Major Strengths/Opportunities	**Major Weaknesses/Problems**
-Todays's students are more intelligent and emotionally and socially mature than their parents were at the same age, and therefore are able to graduate in less than the standard time. -Fewer staff members may be needed. -Parents seem to be interested in 5-year programs in the senior high school.	-A recent report of the State Departement of Education indicated that many of today's students can graduate from high school in less than four years. -State aid may be affected by a decrease in enrollment due to early release from school. -Special permission may be needed from the State Department of Education and Higher Education to implement the 5-year program.

Action to be taken:	Reference

Organize a committee composed of members of the school and community to study school districts across the nation that have adopted a 3-, 4-, or 5-year educational program on the secondary level. Armed with this information and experience, prepare a plan to institute such a program in the school district.

Strategic Planning

Planning Unit: __Central_____   Date: _June 15, 19xx_

Planning Unit Administrator: _Dr. James Wilkinson_____   Position: _Superintendent_

Planning Component: _Critical Analysis_   Page ___7___ of __8__

Swop Analysis: _____

Major Key Result Area:	Physical Resources

Major Strengths/Opportunities	Major Weaknesses/Problems
-Space is available in the school district to set up a reproduction center.	-Reproduction costs the school district more than $500,000 each school year.
-One of the custodians has extensive experience in printing.	-Reproduction demands will most likely increase in the future.
-Cost for a reproduction center could be offset some by doing outside printing.	-Most contracted printing jobs have not been received on the date promised.

Action to be taken: Reference

Visit several large school districts and organizations to determine the type of equipment used in a contemporary reproduction center. Use the information gained during these visits to prepare and implement a plan to install such a reproduction center in the school district.

Strategic Planning

Planning Unit: ___Central_____   Date: _June 15, 19XX_

Planning Unit Administrator: _Dr. James Wilkinson___   Position: _Superintendent_

Planning Component: _Critical Analysis_   Page ___8___ of ___8___

Swop Analysis: _____

Major Key Result Area:	Instructional Programs and Services
Major Strengths/Opportunities	Major Weaknesses/Problems
-There is a growing interest in the community for students to begin the PSAT in junior high school. -A course is being planned to prepare students to take the SATs. -Some students enroll in outside prep courses on the SAT.	-SAT scores are declining each year. -No prep program is offered to students in the senior high school to prepare them for the test. -The test is administered to seniors only once during the school year.

Action to be taken: Reference

Conduct a research study to determine why SAT scores are declining in the school district. Use this information to implement a program to reverse this trend.

Strategic Planning

Planning Unit: ___Central_____ Date:_June 15, 19XX___

Planning Unit Administrator: _Dr. James Wilkinson_____ Position: _Superintendent_

Planning Component: _Critical Analysis_   Page __1__ of __1__

Competitive Analysis

Name of Competitor: _St. Mary Secondary School_____

What has been the impact of this competitor on the school district?

Students who would ordinarily enroll in the Beta Senior High School are leaving the Delta Junior High School and enrolling at St. Mary Secondary School. This resulted in a loss of state aid amounting to $341,000.

The sports program has also suffered tremendously. Most of the exceptionally talented athletes have also enrolled at St. Mary.

What strategy(ies) has it utilized?

St. Mary has an excellent reputation for quality education. It uses this reputation to market its programs, services, and staff. An elaborate multicolor brochure has been produced for the school. The local newspaper is used to recruit students, and the athletic director is actively involved in recruiting students by promising them an entree to certain colleges and universities.

What are the strengths and weaknesses of this competitor?

Strengths: outstanding educational and athletic programs; highly
          qualified staff; aggressive and articulate director;
          excellent success rate with students; and a large
          number of students enroll in college

Weaknesses: large classroom enrollment; insufficient supervisors
           and support staff; low salary scale when compared with
           public schools; and no vocational program

What action should the school district take to reduce the impact of this competitor?

Hire a person who has both a marketing and public relations background. Prepare long-range marketing strategies to reverse the declining enrollment trend. Base the performance of this person on concrete results.

Strategic Planning

Planning Unit: _____Central_____   Date: June 15, 19XX

Planning Unit Administrator: ___Dr. James Wilkinson_____   Position: Superintendent

Planning Component: Critical Analysis   Page ___1___ of ___1___

Stakeholder Analysis

Stakeholder: _Title I Community Council_____

Attitudes	Expectations	Action to be Taken	Ref.
Antagonistic toward the Board of Education. Suspicious of the Superintendent. Determined to have a firm voice in spending Title I funds.	Expects its decisions concerning the use of Title I funds to be carried out. Will require the school district to demonstrate the effectiveness of Title I program through concrete results.	Establish a policy of meeting with the Title I Community Council on a monthly basis to request their assistance in identifying Title I programs and activities; monitor Title I program on a quarterly basis; and report the program results in writing to the council.	

Stakeholder: Local Teachers' Association_____

Attitudes	Expectations	Action to be Taken	Ref.
Good relationship exists between central administrators and leaders of Teachers' Association. Concerned about the present trait approach for evaluating teachers. Eager to assist in improving the school district.	Continuation of monthly meetings between Superintendent and officers of Teachers' Association.	Continue actively to involve Teachers' Association in all affairs of the superintendent. Continue Superintendent's luncheon meeting with the president of the Association.	

Strategic Planning

Planning Unit: _____Central_____ Date: _June 15, 19XX_

Planning Unit Administrator: _Dr. James Wilkinson_ Position: _Superintendent_

Planning Component: _Critical Analysis_ Page __1__ of __3__

Threat Analysis

Harmful Impact on the School Organization (vertical axis: Catastrophic, High, Moderate, Low, None)

Probability (horizontal axis: 0%, 20%, 50%, 75%, 100%)

| | | Desegregation Plan | Teacher Strike |

Declining Enrollment — Superintendent Dismissal / Defeated School Budget

Threat Analysis

Describe the threat |

Past experience has indicated that the school budget will
be defeated on the first ballot.

Rank its impact on school district |

  1   2   ③   4   5   6   7   8   9

Action to be taken | Reference:

Develop a strategy with the teacher association to provide
transportation and babysitting services to the community.
Establish school events to get parents into the schools
where registration and voting is taking place. Establish
a telephone campaign. Have administrators visit the churches
in the community to make a presentation about voting on the
school budget.

Describe the threat |

The superintendent does not have a majority on the Board.

Rank its impact on school district |

  1   2   3   ④   5   6   7   8   9

Action to be taken | Reference:

Prepare resume and disseminate around the county. Publicize
track record, both in person and through the press.

Describe the threat |

There is a very high probability that there will be a
teachers' strike.

Rank its impact on school district |

  ①   2   3   4   5   6   7   8   9

Action to be taken | Reference:

Continue to impress on the Board that more money and fringe
benefits must be given to teachers this school year. Conduct
a comparative analysis stydy of all school districts within
a radius of 25 miles. Establish a policy of having
breakfast with the association official to discuss school
district problems.

Threat Analysis

| Describe the threat |

There is a high probability that the school district desegregation
plan will not be approved and as a result, federal funds will
be withheld.

| Rank its impact on school district |

| 1 | ② | 3 | 4 | 5 | 6 | 7 | 8 | 9 |

| Action to be taken | Reference: |

Be prepared to send a team of administrators to Washington
to work with federal officials until an acceptable plan is
worked out.

| Describe the threat |

If the enrollment continues to decline at its current rate, in
5 years 3 elementary schools and 1 senior high school will
have to be closed.

| Rank its impact on school district |

| 1 | 2 | 3 | 4 | ⑤ | 6 | 7 | 8 | 9 |

| Action to be taken | Reference: |

Develop a marketing strategy to combat the number of students
enrolling in nonpublic schools. Determine the feasibility of
retaining the services of an advertising agency.

| Describe the threat |

| Rank its impact on school district |

| 1 | 2 | 3 | 4 | 5 | 6 | 7 | 8 | 9 |

| Action to be taken | Reference: |

Strategic Planning

Planning Unit: ___Central_____   Date: June 15, 19XX

Planning Unit Administrator: __Dr. James Wilkinson____   Position: Superintendent

Planning Component: __Critical Analysis____   Page ___1___of __8__

Past Performance Results

Major Key Result Area	Student Learning and Growth
Action Determined by:	

Student learning and growth profile.

Long-Range Goal:	Code: 10		Priority ① 2 3 4 5 6 7 8 9

To increase student achievement in reading from the 17th percentile to the 75th percentile as indicated by Stanford Achievement Test by June 30, 19XX (5 years).

Past Performance:	Year ① 2 3 4 5	OP ☒ AP ☐ BP ☐

Student achievement in reading increased from the 17th percentile to the 68th percentile as indicated by the aggregate results on the Stanford Achievement Test.

Past Performance:	Year 1 2 3 4 5	OP ☐ AP ☐ BP ☐

Past Performance:	Year 1 2 3 4 5	OP ☐ AP ☐ BP ☐

Past Performance:	Year 1 2 3 4 5	OP ☐ AP ☐ BP ☐

Past Performance:	Year 1 2 3 4 5	OP ☐ AP ☐ BP ☐

Strategic Planning

Planning Unit: _____Central_____ Date: _June 15, 19XX_

Planning Unit Administrator: __Dr. James Wilkinson_____ Position: _Superintendent

Planning Component: _Critical Analysis_   Page ___2___of ___8___

Past Performance Results

Major Key Result Area	Organizational Management
Action Determined by:	

Adverse influences on the school district.

Long-Range Goal:	Code: 20		Priority①2 3 4 5 6 7 8 9

To reduce teacher illness absences without intimidation from
9.7 to 4.0 percent by June 30, 19XX (4 years).

Past Performance:	Year① 2 3 4 5	OP ☑ AP ☐ BP ☐

Teacher illness absences on a district-wide level were
decreased from 9.7 to 6.9 percent as indicated by the
collective results of the absentee report.

Past Performance:	Year 1 2 3 4 5	OP ☐ AP ☐ BP ☐

Past Performance:	Year 1 2 3 4 5	OP ☐ AP ☐ BP ☐

Past Performance:	Year 1 2 3 4 5	OP ☐ AP ☐ BP ☐

Past Performance:	Year 1 2 3 4 5	OP ☐ AP ☐ BP ☐

Strategic Planning

Planning Unit: __Central_____   Date: __June 15, 19XX__

Planning Unit Administrator: __Dr. James Wilkinson__   Position: Superintendent

Planning Component: __Critical Analysis__   Page ___3___ of ___8___

Past Performance Results

Major Key Result Area	Innovation
Action Determined by:	

Superintendent.

Long-Range Goal:	Code: 30	Priority 1 2③4 5 6 7 8 9

To replace the current subjective approach to selecting
school administrators and teachers with a more objective
approach by June 30, 19XX (3 years).

Past Performance:	Year① 2 3 4 5	OP ☒ AP ☐ BP ☐

A committee comprised of teachers, administrators, and
psychologists was organized, and a plan has been prepared
to implement the assessment center approach for selecting both
administrators and teachers.

Past Performance:	Year 1 2 3 4 5	OP ☐ AP ☐ BP ☐

Past Performance:	Year 1 2 3 4 5	OP ☐ AP ☐ BP ☐

Past Performance:	Year 1 2 3 4 5	OP ☐ AP ☐ BP ☐

Past Performance:	Year 1 2 3 4 5	OP ☐ AP ☐ BP ☐

Strategic Planning

Planning Unit: _____Central_____ Date: _June 15, 19XX_

Planning Unit Administrator: _Dr. James Wilkinson_____ Position: _Superintendent_

Planning Component: _Critical Analysis_____ Page ____4___of __8___

Past Performance Results

Major Key Result Area	Performance Evaluation and Training
Action Determined by:	

Board of Education and superintendent.

Long-Range Goal:	Code: 40		Priority 1②3 4 5 6 7 8 9

To replace the current subjective approach to staff
evaluation with a results-oriented approach by June 30, 19XX
(3 years).

Past Performance:	Year① 2 3 4 5	OP ☒ AP ☐ BP ☐

A district-wide task force has been organized by the assistant
superintendent for personnel, and an appraisal program is being
developed using school management by objectives. The contents
for this program have been reviewed and approved by the central
planning unit.

Past Performance:	Year 1 2 3 4 5	OP ☐ AP ☐ BP ☐

Past Performance:	Year 1 2 3 4 5	OP ☐ AP ☐ BP ☐

Past Performance:	Year 1 2 3 4 5	OP ☐ AP ☐ BP ☐

Past Performance:	Year 1 2 3 4 5	OP ☐ AP ☐ BP ☐

Strategic Planning

Planning Unit: _Central_____   Date: _June 15, 19XX_

Planning Unit Administrator: _Dr. James Wilkinson_   Position: _Superintendent_

Planning Component: _Critical Analysis_   Page ___5___ of __8__

Past Performance Results

Major Key Result Area	Financial Resources
Action Determined by:	

Competitive analysis (loss of students to nonpublic schools).

Long-Range Goal:	Code: 50		Priority ①2 3 4 5 6 7 8 9

To increase contract and grant awards from state, federal, and private foundations from $485,000 to $2,500,000 by June 30, 19XX (3 years).

Past Performance:	Year ① 2 3 4 5	OP ☐ AP ☐ BP ☒

No additional funds from private foundations were obtained; however, $150,000 was secured from HEW to establish a gifted and talented program. Consideration should be given to hiring a grants person to prepare the school district's grants and contracts.

Past Performance:	Year 1 2 3 4 5	OP ☐ AP ☐ BP ☐

Past Performance:	Year 1 2 3 4 5	OP ☐ AP ☐ BP ☐

Past Performance:	Year 1 2 3 4 5	OP ☐ AP ☐ BP ☐

Past Performance:	Year 1 2 3 4 5	OP ☐ AP ☐ BP ☐

Strategic Planning

Planning Unit: ___Central_____ Date: _June 15, 19XX_

Planning Unit Administrator: ___Dr. James Wilkinson_____ Position: _Superintendent_

Planning Component: __Critical Analysis____ Page __6__ of __8__

Past Performance Results

Major Key Result Area	Community Involvement and Relations
Action Determined by:	

Report from the New York State Department of Education.

Long-Range Goal:	Code: 60	Priority 1 2③4 5 6 7 8 9

To plan a school enlargement (school and college) program
enabling students to graduate in 3, 4, or 5 years, instead of
the current fixed 4 years, by June 30, 19XX (3 years).

Past Performance:	Year① 2 3 4 5	OP ☒ AP ☐ BP ☐

A committee comprised of members of the community, higher
education, and the school district meets monthly to work on
the plan for establishing a Sch-lege Program. The program
is on target as indicated by the action plan.

Past Performance:	Year 1 2 3 4 5	OP ☐ AP ☐ BP ☐

Past Performance:	Year 1 2 3 4 5	OP ☐ AP ☐ BP ☐

Past Performance:	Year 1 2 3 4 5	OP ☐ AP ☐ BP ☐

Past Performance:	Year 1 2 3 4 5	OP ☐ AP ☐ BP ☐

Strategic Planning

Planning Unit: _____Central_____ Date: June 15, 19XX

Planning Unit Administrator: Dr. James Wilkinson Position: Superintendent

Planning Component: Critical Analysis Page __7__ of __8__

Past Performance Results

Major Key Result Area	Physical Resources
Action Determined by:	

Request from the Assistant Superintendent for Curriculum
and Instruction.

Long-Range Goal:	Code: 70	Priority 1 ②3 4 5 6 7 8 9

To establish a comprehensive reproduction center, including
staff in the school district, at a cost not exceeding
$450,000 by June 1, 19XX (2 years).

Past Performance:	Year① 2 3 4 5	OP ☐ AP ☒ BP ☐

Reproduction equipment has been ordered, space has been
allocated for setting up the reproduction center, and staff
is currently being recruited. It appears that this center
will be operational by the middle of the next school year.

Past Performance:	Year 1 2 3 4 5	OP ☐ AP ☐ BP ☐

Past Performance:	Year 1 2 3 4 5	OP ☐ AP ☐ BP ☐

Past Performance:	Year 1 2 3 4 5	OP ☐ AP ☐ BP ☐

Past Performance:	Year 1 2 3 4 5	OP ☐ AP ☐ BP ☐

Strategic Planning

Planning Unit: _____Central_____ Date: June 15, 19XX

Planning Unit Administrator: Dr. James Wilkinson Position: Superintendent

Planning Component: Critical Analysis Page ___8___ of ___8___

Past Performance Results

Major Key Result Area	Instuctional Programs and Services
Action Determined by:	

Student learning and growth.

Long-Range Goal:	Code: 80	Priority ①2 3 4 5 6 7 8 9

To increase the SAT scores of the school district in math from a median of 483 to 575 and verbal from a median of 395 to 525, by November 30, 19XX (3 years).

Past Performance:	Year ①2 3 4 5	OP □ AP □ BP ☒

Only one secondary school met its objective for increasing the SAT scores. Unless additional steps are taken by the remaining secondary schools, this objective will not be achieved as planned. Some consideration should be given to giving the junior high students the PSATs and developing a strategy for beginning improvement efforts on this level.

Past Performance:	Year 1 2 3 4 5	OP □ AP □ BP □

Past Performance:	Year 1 2 3 4 5	OP □ AP □ BP □

Past Performance:	Year 1 2 3 4 5	OP □ AP □ BP □

Past Performance:	Year 1 2 3 4 5	OP □ AP □ BP □

Strategic Planning

Planning Unit: ___Central_____ Date: June 15, 19XX

Planning Unit Administrator: _Dr. James Wilkinson_____ Position: Superintendent

Planning Component: _Critical Analysis_ Page ___1___ of ___2___

Past Performance Results

Major Key Result Area	Performance Evaluation and Training	
Short-Range Objective	Code: 40.1	Priority 1 2 3 4 5 6 7 8 9

To prepare policy and procedures for implementing an objective-oriented program that will be acceptable to the Board of Education by June 30, 19XX.

Performance Outcome	OP ☒ AP ☐ BP ☐

A policy and procedures plan for implementing an objective-oriented program was completed and approved by the Board of Education on May 15, 19XX, as attested by the May minutes.

Major Key Result Area	Financial Resources	
Short-Range Objective	Code: 50.1	Priority 1 2 3 4 5 6 7 8 9

To apply for $1,000,000 in grants and contracts and experience a success rate of 15 percent by June 30, 19XX.

Performance Outcome	OP ☐ AP ☒ BP ☐

Two hundred thousand and fifty dollars were received from competitive grants and contracts secured from the federal government during the current school year.

Major Key Result Area	Community Involvement and Relations	
Short-Range Objective	Code: 60.1	Priority 1 2 3 4 5 6 7 8 9

To prepare a plan for implementing a school enlargement program
by June 30, 19XX.

Performance Outcome	OP ☐ AP ☒ BP ☐

The school enlargement plan was completed by the committee and
found acceptable by the senior high school faculty, community,
superintendent, and Board of Education, as indicated by the
minutes of these groups' meetings.

Major Key Result Area		
Short-Range Objective	Code:	Priority 1 2 3 4 5 6 7 8 9

Performance Outcome	OP ☐ AP ☐ BP ☐

Major Key Result Area		
Short-Range Objective	Code:	Priority 1 2 3 4 5 6 7 8 9

Perfromance Outcome	OP ☐ AP ☐ BP ☐

Strategic Planning

Planning Unit: _____Central_____ Date: June 15, 19XX

Planning Unit Administrator: __Dr. James Wilkinson__ Position: Superintendent

Planning Component: _Guide for Formulating Program Strategy_ Page __1__ of __2__

| 1. Major Key Result Area: | Student Learning and Growth |

| 2. Long-Range Goal: | Code: 10 | Priority 1 2 3 4 5 6 7 8 9 |

To increase student achievement in reading from the 17th percentile to the 75th percentile as indicated by Stanford Achievement Test by June 30, 19XX (5 years).

Strategic Approach:

☒ Emulation ☐ Proactive ☐ Reactive

4. Analyze Alternative Strategies:

Summary of Alternative Strategies	Project Cost	Maximize Strengths	Minimize Weaknesses	Remedy Threat	Stakeholder Expectation	Respond to Competition	Impact	Rank
1. Retrain teachers in the present reading method.	mod.	some	some	no	no	--	mod.	2
2. Require only 3 reading programs instead of 8.	high	no	no	may-be	yes	--	mod.	3
3. Install the validated Action Reading Program.	mod.	yes	yes	yes	yes	--	high	1
4. Individualize the reading program.	mod.	some	some	may-be	no	--	low	4

---

5. Select Appropriate Strategy:

This strategy will be to train all elementary teachers and principals in Action Reading, whereby a 5-day workshop will be conducted incorporating 3 hours of theory and 3 hours of practical application using students. A supervisor will be appointed to provide guidance and directions for teachers. Concrete objects will be used before students learn to respond to abstract symbols. Instructional kits will also be used. Students will sing and dance while learning reading. A systematic process will be devised to monitor both student and program results. Teaching students how to take tests will be a major focus of this reading program.

---

6. Compare Long-Range Goal with Program Strategy:

The results of the pilot study reveal that there is a high probability that the program will help to realize the long-range goal.

---

7. Implementation of Strategy:

a) Who is responsible for completing strategy? <u>Assistant Superintendent for</u>
<u>Curriculum and Instruction</u>

b) When will the strategy be launched? <u>July 1, 19XX-submit monthly reports</u>

c) What support services will be required? <u>clerical and teacher aid assistance</u>

d) What specifically are the key tasks that need to be performed for the strategies to be implemented? <u>(1) develop a plan for implementing</u>
<u>Action Reading; (2) develop in-house materials and secure</u>
<u>kits for each teacher; (3) construct a system for monitoring</u>
<u>progress of both the students and the program; and (4)</u>
<u>implement Action Reading</u>

Strategic Planning

Planning Unit: _____Central_____ Date: June 15, 19XX

Planning Unit Administrator: _Dr. James Wilkinson_ Position: Superintendent

Planning Component: _Guide for Formulating Program Strategy_ Page __1__ of __2__

1. Major Key Result Area: Organizational Management

2. Long-Range Goal:	Code: 20	Priority ① 2 3 4 5 6 7 8 9

To reduce teacher illness absences without intimidation from 9.7 to 4.0 percent by June 30, 19XX (4 years).

Strategic Approach:

☒ Emulation   ☐ Proactive   ☐ Reactive

4. Analyze Alternative Strategies:

Summary of Alternative Strategies	Project Cost	Maximize Strengths	Minimize Weaknesses	Remedy Threat	Stakeholder Expectation	Respond to Competition	Impact	Rank
1. Do not hire substitutes for the first two months of school.	low	no	some	some	no	--	mod.	3
2. Install a long-term incentive program.	high	no	no	some	no	--	mod.	4
3. Use motivational approach and recognize excellent attendance.	low	yes	yes	yes	no	--	high	1
4. Set objectives to reduce teacher illness absences.	low	some	some	some	no	--	mod.	2

5. Select Appropriate Strategy:

Establish a method for recording, collecting, and analyzing staff absences. Use Hertzberg motivational approach to improve behavior. Make use of positive reinforcement and recognize excellent attendance.

6. Compare Long-Range Goal with Program Strategy:

Program strategy seems to be excellent in helping to achieve the long-range goal. Studies with N.Y. Telephone indicate outstanding results.

7. Implementation of Strategy:

a) Who is responsible for completing strategy? Assistant Superintendent for Administration and Personnel

b) When will the strategy be launched? September 1, 19XX

c) What support services will be required? Train clerical staff on how to collect and analyze data

d) What specifically are the key tasks that need to be performed for the strategies to be implemented? (1) develop forms and instructions to collect data; (2) train staff to complete forms; (3) train professional staff in Hertzberg motivational approach, (4) identify a recognition plan; (5) present the plan to the board; (6) implement the plan; and (7) evaluate the plan.

Strategic Planning

Planning Unit: _____ Central _____ Date: June 15, 19XX

Planning Unit Administrator: Dr. James Wilkinson   Position: Superintendent

Planning Component: Guide for Formulating Program Strategy   Page 1 of 2

---

1. Major Key Result Area: Innovation

2. Long-Range Goal: | Code: 30 | Priority 1 2 ③ 4 5 6 7 8 9

To replace the current subjective approach to selecting school administrators and teacher with a more objective approach by June 30, 19XX (3 years).

Strategic Approach:

☒ Emulation   ☐ Proactive   ☐ Reactive

4. Analyze Alternative Strategies:

Summary of Alternative Strategies	Project Cost	Maximize Strengths	Minimize Weaknesses	Remedy Threat	Stakeholder Expectation	Respond to Competition	Impact	Rank
1. Establish screening team.	low	no	no	yes	yes	--	mod.	2
2. Use outside recruitment agency.	high	no	no	--	no	--	low	3
3. Implement assessment center approach.	high	yes	yes	yes	yes	yes	high	1

---

5. Select Appropriate Strategy:

Organize a team composed of members of the community who are
employed in recruitment types of jobs, teachers, administrators,
psychologists, and a consultant familiar with the assessment
center approach to selecting personnel, and prepare a plan to
establish such a program. Pay professional staff during the
summer months to develop materials, such as games and
questionnaires. Install the program on a trial basis first,
make the necessary adjustments, and fully implement.

---

6. Compare Long-Range Goal with Program Strategy:

Program stratey accommodates the long-range goal adequately.
Funds may be a problem in terms of locating a suitable space,
staffing the center, and paying the professional staff for
developing materials.

---

7. Implementation of Strategy:

a) Who is responsible for completing strategy? _Assistant Superintendent for_
   Administration and Personnel

b) When will the strategy be launched? _July 1, 19XX_
   ~~Use of reproduction center when~~

c) What support services will be required? _organized and of several secretaries_
   and graphic artist

d) What specifically are the key tasks that need to be performed for the
   strategies to be implemented? _(1) allocate funds; (2) organize a_
   committee; (3) provide adequate training; (4) prepare plan;
   (5) implement plan; (6) establish the center on a trial
   basis; (7) adapt the program; and (8) operate the center
   fully

Strategic Planning

Planning Unit: ___Central_____ Date:_June 15, 19XX_

Planning Unit Administrator: _Dr. James Wilkinson_____ Position: _Superintendent_

Planning Component: _Guide for Formulating Program Strategy_ Page __1__ of __2__

1. Major Key Result Area: Performance Evaluation and Training

2. Long-Range Goal: | Code: 40 | Priority 1 ② 3 4 5 6 7 8 9

> To replace the current subjective approach to staff
> evaluation with a results-oriented approach by June 30,
> 19XX (3 years).

Strategic Approach:

☐ Emulation   ☒ Proactive   ☐ Reactive

4. Analyze Alternative Strategies:

Summary of Alternative Strategies	Project Cost	Maximize Strengths	Minimize Weaknesses	Remedy Threat	Stakeholder Expectation	Respond to Competition	Impact	Rank
1. Prepare behavioral objectives for students and use these to assess teacher performance.	high	no	--	some	no	--	mod.	3
2. Use the prescriptive job description and the indicators for conducting an objective assessment.	low	no	some	some	no	--	mod.	2
3. Implement school management by objectives.	low	yes	yes	yes	yes	--	high	1

---

5. Select Appropriate Strategy:

Organize a committee of teachers to be trained to use school management by objectives, for the purpose of developing and implementing a plan to utilize this approach for conducting a performance approach program.

---

6. Compare Long-Range Goal with Program Strategy:

The program stratey seems to be compatible with the long-range goals; however, the individual teachers in the community should present the concept to the staff. It is assumed that the president of the Teachers' Association is an active member of this committee.

---

7. Implementation of Strategy:

a) Who is responsible for completing strategy? Assistant Superintendent for Administration and Personnel

b) When will the strategy be launched? February 1, 19XX

c) What support services will be required? Use of reproduction center if organized and several secretaries

d) What specifically are the key tasks that need to be performed for the strategies to be implemented? (1) organize committee; (2) train committee members in school management by objectives; (3) develop performance appraisal plan; (4) implement plan on a trial basis; (5) revise plan to accommodate needs cited by the trial run; (6) establish performance appraisal plan district-wide

Strategic Planning

Planning Unit: _____Central_____ Date:_June 15, 19XX_

Planning Unit Administrator: _Dr. James Wilkinson_ Position:_Superintendent_

Planning Component: _Guide for Formulating Program Strategy_ Page __1__ of __2__

1. Major Key Result Area: Physical Resources

2. Long-Range Goal: | Code: 70 | Priority 1 ② 3 4 5 6 7 8 9

To establish a comprehensive reproduction center, including staff in the school district, at a cost not exceeding $450,000 by June 1, 19XX (2 years).

Strategic Approach: |

☐ Emulation   ☒ Proactive   ☐ Reactive

4. Analyze Alternative Strategies: |

Summary of Alternative Strategies	Project Cost	Maximize Strengths	Minimize Weaknesses	Remedy Threat	Stakeholder Expectation	Respond to Competition	Impact	Rank
1. Lease equipment.	mod.	yes	yes	--	yes	--	high	1
2. Purchase equipment.	high	yes	yes	--	yes	--	mod.	3
3. Lease and purchase equipment.	mod.	yes	yes	yes	--	yes	mod.	2
4. Lease-contract out.	low	yes	no	--	yes	--	low	4

---

5. Select Appropriate Strategy:

Locate a central location in the school district. Prepare a year plan for locating equipment and offices. Lease all equipment with an option to purchase.

---

6. Compare Long-Range Goal with Program Strategy:

Program strategy accommodates the long-range goal quite well. Since reproduction equipment will most likely change in 3 to 5 years, it was decided that all equipment should be leased, as opposed to purchased.

---

7. Implementation of Strategy:

a) Who is responsible for completing strategy? Assistant Superintendents for Business Affairs and Curriculum and Instruction

b) When will the strategy be launched? January 1, 19XX

c) What support services will be required? Hire adequate personnel to accommodate the reproduction center

d) What specifically are the key tasks that need to be performed for the strategies to be implemented? (1) prepare plan; (2) allocate budget; (3) hire director; (4) locate suitable location; (5) lease equipment; (6) hire additional staff; (7) set up reproduction center; (8) prepare and implement policies and procedures

---

Strategic Planning

Planning Unit: _____Central_____ Date:_June 15, 19XX_

Planning Unit Administrator: _Dr. James Wilkinson_____ Position:_Superintendent_

Planning Component: _Guide for Formulating Program Strategy_ Page __1__ of _2__

1. Major Key Result Area:	Instructional Programs and Services

2. Long-Range Goal:	Code: 80	Priority① 2 3 4 5 6 7 8 9

To increase SAT scores of the school district in math from a median of 483 to 575 and verbal from a median of 395 to 525, by November 30, 19XX (3 years).

Strategic Approach:

☐ Emulation   ☐ Proactive   ☒ Reactive

4. Analyze Alternative Strategies:

Summary of Alternative Strategies	Project Cost	Maximize Strengths	Minimize Weaknesses	Remedy Threat	Stakeholder Expectation	Respond to Competition	Impact	Rank
1. Hires outside consultant to teach a class in each senior high school.	high	no	no	may-be	no	--	mod.	2
2. Establish a comprehensive testing/tutoring program.	high	yes	yes	yes	yes	--	high	1
3. Provide after-school training for tutoring students taking the SATs.	low	no	no	no	no	--	mod.	3
4. Rewrite the curriculum to emphasize elements of the SATs.	low	yes	no	no	yes	--	low	4

5. Select Appropriate Strategy:

The strategic thrust here is to develop a comprehensive plan to
increase the SAT scores by familiarizing junior high students
with the PSAT and SAT; reviewing the curriculum for strengthening
SAT elements; and requiring students to take the PSAT once in the
7th grade and twice in the 8th grade, and three times in the
9th grade. Establish SAT tutorial classes in senior high school.
In addition, all junior and senior high students will be required
to take 6 years of English and 4 years of math in order to
graduate.

6. Compare Long-Range Goal with Program Strategy:

This comprehensive plan should enable the school district to
raise SAT scores. This program strategy seems to be compatible
with the long-range goal.

7. Implementation of Strategy:

a) Who is responsible for completing strategy? _Assistant Superintendent for_
Curriculum and Instruction

b) When will the strategy be launched? September 28, 19XX

c) What support services will be required? clerical services

d) What specifically are the key tasks that need to be performed for the
strategies to be implemented? (1) insist on new basic education
requirements; (2) revamp the curriculum to include SAT
elements; (3) require all junior high students to take the
PSAT; and (4) establish SAT tutorial classes in each high
school

Strategic Planning Package

Planning Unit: _____Central_____ Date: June 15, 19XX

Planning Unit Administrator: _Dr. James Wilkinson_____ Position Superintendent

Planning Component: _____ Page __1__ of __2__

Major Key Result Area:	Student Learning and Growth

Long-Range Goal	Code: 10

To increase student achievement in reading from the 17th percentile to the 75th percentile as indicated by Stanford Achievement Test by June 30, 19XX (5 years).

Strategy Selected	Train all elementary teachers and principals in Action Reading in a 5-day workshop that incorporates

3 hours or theory and 3 hours of practical application using students. Appoint a supervisor to provide guidance and direction for teachers. Concrete objects will be used before students learn to respond to abstract symbols. Students will sing and dance while learning reading. A systematic process will be devised to monitor both the student

Results Expected	and program results. The major focus of the program will be to teach students to take tests.

It is expected that within a 5-year period, 75 percent of the student body will be reading on grade level.

Monitoring Responsibility

Assistant Superintendent for Curriculum and Instruction

Monitoring Efforts and Dates

Monthly reading achievement reports to begin on November 1, 19XX.

Budget:

Code	Programs	19 XX to XX		19 to		19 to		19 to		19 to	
		Objective Budget		Objective Budget		Objective Budget		Objective Budget		Objective Budget	
		Program Budget		Program Budget		Program Budget		Program Budget		Program Budget	
1105	English/ Language Arts	374,940									
		374,940									

Code	Programs	19___ to ___	19___ to___	19___ to ___	19___ to___	19___ to___
		Objective Budget	Objective Budget	Objective Budget	Objective Budget	Objective Budget
		Program Budget	Program Budget	Program Budget	Program Budget	Program Budget

Totals Past Performance Results

Code	Program	19XX to XX			19___ to ___			19___ to ___			19___ to ___			19___ to ___		
		OP	AP	BP	OP	AP	BP	OP	AP	BP	OP	AP	BP	OP	AP	BP
1105	English/ Language Arts		x													

Indicate what corrective action will take place to improve all performances achieved below plan

OP - On Plan
AP - Above Plan
BP - Below Plan

Strategic Planning Package

Planning Unit: _____Central_____ Date: June 15, 19XX

Planning Unit Administrator: Dr. James Wilkinson Position: Superintendent

Planning Component: _____ Page __1__ of __2__

Major Key Result Area:	Organizational Management
Long-Range Goal Code: 20	

To reduce teacher illness absences without intimidation from 9.7 to 4.0 percent by June 30, 19XX (4 years).

Strategy Selected

Establish a method for recording, collecting, and analyzing staff absences. Use Hertzberg motivational approach to improve behavior. Make use of positive reinforcement and recognize excellent attendance.

Results Expected

Teacher absenteeism due to illness will decrease; and as a result, morale will improve, and the school budget will have a surplus.

Monitoring Responsibility

Assistant Superintendent for Administration and Personnel

Monitoring Efforts and Dates

Quarterly reports beginning January 1, 19XX; April 1, 19XX; July 1, 19XX; and October 1, 19XX.

Budget:

Code	Programs	19XX to XX Objective Budget / Program Budget	19 to Objective Budget / Program Budget	19 to Objective Budget / Program Budget	19 to Objective Budget / Program Budget	19 to Objective Budget / Program Budget
2309	General Administration	4,810 / 195,456				

Code	Programs	19___ to ___		19___ to___		19___ to ___		19___ to ___		19___ to ___	
		Objective Budget	Program Budget	Objective Budget	Program Budget	Objective Budget	Program Budget	Objective Budget	Program Budget	Objective Budget	Program Budget

Totals Past Performance Results

Code	Program	19 XX to XX			19___ to ___			19___ to ___			19___ to ___			19___ to ___		
		OP	AP	BP	OP	AP	BP	OP	AP	BP	OP	AP	BP	OP	AP	BP
2309	General Administration		x													

Indicate what corrective action will take place to improve all performances achieved below plan

OP - On Plan
AP - Above Plan
BP - Below Plan

Strategic Planning Package

Planning Unit: _____ Central _____ Date: June 15, 19XX

Planning Unit Administrator: Dr. James Wilkinson _____ Position: Superintendent

Planning Component: _____ Page __1__ of __2__

Major Key Result Area:	Innovation
Long-Range Goal Code: 30	

To replace the current subjective approach to selecting school
administrators and teachers with a more objective approach by
June 30, 19XX (3 years).

Strategy Selected | Organize a team composed of members of the community
who are employed in recruitment types of jobs, teachers,
administrators, and psychooogists, and a consultant familiar with
the assessment center approach to selecting personnel, and prepare a
plan to establish such a program. Pay professional staff during the
summer months to develop materials. Install the program on a trial
basis first, make the necessary adjustments, and implement.

Results Expected

A more effective and objective process will be employed to
select school administrators, thereby decreasing the attrition
rate in this area.

Monitoring Responsibility

Assistant Superintendent for Administration and Personnel

Monitoring Efforts and Dates

Quarterly reports beginning three months after the program is
installed.

Budget:

Code	Programs	19 XX to XX	19 to	19 to	19 to	19 to
		Objective Budget	Objective Budget	Objective Budget	Objective Budget	Objective Budget
		Program Budget	Program Budget	Program Budget	Program Budget	Program Budget
2309	General Administration	28,000				
		195,456				

Code	Programs	19__ to __		19__ to __		19__ to __		19__ to __		19__ to __	
		Objective Budget	Program Budget	Objective Budget	Program Budget	Objective Budget	Program Budget	Objective Budget	Program Budget	Objective Budget	Program Budget

Totals Past Performance Results

Code	Program	19 XX to XX			19__ to __			19__ to __			19__ to __			19__ to __		
		OP	AP	BP	OP	AP	BP	OP	AP	BP	OP	AP	BP	OP	AP	BP
2309	General Administration	x														

Indicate what corrective action will take place to improve all performances achieved below plan

OP - On Plan
AP - Above Plan
BP - Below Plan

Strategic Planning Package

Planning Unit: _____Central_____ Date: June 15, 19XX

Planning Unit Administrator: Dr. James Wilkinson _____ Position: Superintendent

Planning Component: _____ Page __1__ of __2__

Major Key Result Area:	Performance Evaluation and Training

Long-Range Goal	Code: 40

To replace the present subjective approach to staff evaluation
with a results-oriented approach by June 30, 19XX (3 years).

Strategy Selected

Organize a committee of teachers to be trained to use school
management by objectives, for the purpose of developing and
implementing a plan to utilize this approach for conducting
a performance approach program.

Results Expected

A shift away from the trait approach to the objective approach for
evaluating teachers will help produce a more objective way of
determining development needs.

Monitoring Responsibility

Assistant Superintendent for Administration and Personnel

Monitoring Efforts and Dates

Quarterly reports three months after the program is implemented.

Budget:

Code	Programs	19XX to XX	19 to	19 to	19 to	19 to
		Objective Budget	Objective Budget	Objective Budget	Objective Budget	Objective Budget
		Program Budget	Program Budget	Program Budget	Program Budget	Program Budget
2309	General Administration	15,450				
		195,456				

Code	Programs	19___ to ___		19___ to ___		19___ to ___		19___ to ___		19___ to ___	
		Objective Budget		Objective Budget		Objective Budget		Objective Budget		Objective Budget	
		Program Budget		Program Budget		Program Budget		Program Budget		Program Budget	

Totals Past Performance Results

Code	Program	19XX to XX			19___ to ___			19___ to ___			19___ to ___			19___ to ___		
		OP	AP	BP	OP	AP	BP	OP	AP	BP	OP	AP	BP	OP	AP	BP
2309	General Administration		x													

Indicate what corrective action will take place to improve all performances achieved below plan

OP - On Plan
AP - Above Plan
BP - Below Plan

Strategic Planning Package

Planning Unit: _____Central_____ Date: June 15, 19XX

Planning Unit Administrator: Dr. James Wilkinson ____ Position:Superintendent

Planning Component: _____ Page __1__ of __2__

Major Key Result Area:	Community Involvement and Growth
Long-Range Goal	Code: 60

To establish a program whereby students can graduate in 3 or 4 years, earning a diploma, or in 5 years, earning an associate degree, by June 30, 19XX (3 years).

Strategy Selected

Organize a committee to study and plan the school enlargement program.

Results Expected

Students who are able to graduate from senior high school in 3, 4, or 5 years will be allowed to do so, while those who would like to enroll in the school enlargement program can do so to receive an associate arts degree.

Monitoring Responsibility

Principal

Monitoring Efforts and Dates

Quarterly report, beginning December 1, 19XX.

Budget:

Code	Programs	19XX to XX		19 to		19 to		19 to		19 to	
		Objective Budget		Objective Budget		Objective Budget		Objective Budget		Objective Budget	
		Program Budget		Program Budget		Program Budget		Program Budget		Program Budget	
10.4	English/ Language Arts	71,000									
		237,400									

Code	Programs	19___ to ___		19 ___ to ___		19 ___ to ___		19 ___ to ___		19 ___ to ___	
		Objective Budget		Objective Budget		Objective Budget		Objective Budget		Objective Budget	
		Program Budget		Program Budget		Program Budget		Program Budget		Program Budget	

Totals Past Performance Results

Code	Program	19XX to XX			19___ to ___			19___ to ___			19___ to ___			19___ to ___		
		OP	AP	BP	OP	AP	BP	OP	AP	BP	OP	AP	BP	OP	AP	BP
10.4	English/ Language Arts	x														

Indicate what corrective action will take place to improve all performances achieved below plan

OP - On Plan
AP - Above Plan
BP - Below Plan

Strategic Planning Package

Planning Unit: _____Central_____ Date: June 15, 19XX

Planning Unit Administrator: __Dr. James Wilkinson__ Position: Superintendent

Planning Component: _____ Page __1__ of __2__

Major Key Result Area:	Physical Resources

Long-Range Goal	Code:	70

To establish a comprehensive reproduction center, including
staff in the school district, at a cost not exceeding $450,000
by June 1, 19XX (2 years).

Strategy Selected

Locate a central location in the school district. Prepare a
year plan for locating equipment, offices, and the like. Lease
all equipment with an option to purchase.

Results Expected

It is anticipated that an in-house reproduction center will
save the school district money, and will help to generate
more timely media productions.

Monitoring Responsibility

Assistant Superintendent for Business Affairs

Monitoring Efforts and Dates

Quarterly reports beginning after the program is installed.

Budget:

Code	Programs	19XX to XX Objective Budget / Program Budget	19 to Objective Budget / Program Budget	19 to Objective Budget / Program Budget	19 to Objective Budget / Program Budget	19 to Objective Budget / Program Budget
2500	Business Administration	110,585 495,615				

Code	Programs	19___ to ___ Objective Budget / Program Budget	19___ to ___ Objective Budget / Program Budget	19___ to ___ Objective Budget / Program Budget	19___ to ___ Objective Budget / Program Budget	19___ to ___ Objective Budget / Program Budget

Totals Past Performance Results

Code	Program	19 XX to XX			19___ to ___			19___ to ___			19___ to ___			19___ to ___		
		OP	AP	BP	OP	AP	BP	OP	AP	BP	OP	AP	BP	OP	AP	BP
2500	Business Administration	x														

Indicate what corrective action will take place to improve all performances achieved below plan

OP - On Plan
AP - Above Plan
BP - Below Plan

Strategic Planning Package

Planning Unit: _____ Central _____   Date: June 15, 19XX

Planning Unit Administrator: __ Dr. James Wilkinson _____   Position: Superintendent

Planning Component: _____   Page __1__ of __2__

Major Key Result Area:	Instructional Programs and Services

Long-Range Goal	Code:	80

To increase SAT scores of the school district in math from a
median of 483 to 575 and verbal from a median of 395 to 525, by
November 30, 19XX (3 years).

Strategy Selected | The strategic thrust here is to develop a comprehensive
plan to increase SAT scores by familiarizing junior
high students with PSAT and SAT, reviewing the curriculum for
strengthening SAT elements, requiring junior high students to take
PSATs once in 7th grade and twice in 8th. Establish SAT tutorial
classes in senior high school. In addition, all junior and senior
high students will be required to take 6 years of English and 4 of

Results Expected | math to graduate.

As a result of improved SAT scores, students! chances of being
accepted into their college of choice will be enhanced.

Monitoring Responsibility |

Assistant Superintendent of Curriculum and Instruction

Monitoring Efforts and Dates |

On the 28th of each month after this program is established.

Budget: |

Code	Programs	19 XX to XX		19 to		19 to		19 to		19 to	
		Objective Budget		Objective Budget		Objective Budget		Objective Budget		Objective Budget	
		Program Budget		Program Budget		Program Budget		Program Budget		Program Budget	
1105	English/ Language Arts	374,940									
		374,940									
1111	Mathematics	285,141									
		285,141									
1131	Test Taking	70,145									
		70,145									

Code	Programs	19___ to ___		19___ to ___		19___ to ___		19___ to ___		19___ to ___	
		Objective Budget		Objective Budget		Objective Budget		Objective Budget		Objective Budget	
		Program Budget		Program Budget		Program Budget		Program Budget		Program Budget	

Totals Past Performance Results

Code	Program	19 xx to xx			19___ to ___			19___ to ___			19___ to ___			19___ to ___		
		OP	AP	BP	OP	AP	BP	OP	AP	BP	OP	AP	BP	OP	AP	BP
1105	English/ Language Arts	x														
1111	Mathematics	x														
1131	Test Taking			x												

Indicate what corrective action will take place to improve all performances achieved below plan

OP - On Plan
AP - Above Plan
BP - Below Plan

OPERATIONAL PLAN

Planning Unit: _____ Central _____

Planning Unit Administrator _____ Dr. James Wilkinson _____

Major Key Result Area: _____

Date: _June 15, 19XX_

Position: _Superintendent_

Page _1_ of _3_

Programs	Action to be Taken (Performance Objectives)	Performance Standards (This objective is satisfactorily achieved when . . .)	Performance Outcome
Performance Evaluation and Training	40.1 To prepare policy and procedures for implementing an objective-oriented program that will be acceptable to the Board of Education by June 30, 19XX.	40.10 The assistant superintendent for administration and personnel receives adequate training in school management by objectives. 40.11 Objective-oriented performance appraisal programs are collected from school districts around the nation. 40.12 A committee of teachers and administrators is organized to prepare an objective-oriented performance appraisal program using relevant books and materials received from other school districts. 40.13 The program is approved by the superintendent of schools. 40.14 The objective-oriented program is developed and clarified to the staff. 40.15 A system is established to monitor results and make changes in the program one year after it has been instituted.	A policy and procedures plan for implementing an objective-oriented program was completed and approved by the Board of Education on May 15, 19XX as indicated by the May minutes.

OPERATIONAL PLAN

Planning Unit: ___Central___

Planning Unit Administrator ___Dr. James Wilkinson___

Major Key Result Area: _____

Date: ___June 15, 19XX___

Position: ___Superintendent___

Page ___2___ of ___3___

Programs	Action to be Taken (Performance Objectives)	Performance Standards (This objective is satisfactorily achieved when . . .)	Performance Outcome
Financial Resources	50.1 To apply for $1,000,000 in grants and contracts and experience a success rate of 15% by June 30, 19XX.	50.10 A Director of Resource Development is hired.	Two hundred thousan and fifty dollars were received from competitive grants and contracts secured from the federal government during the current school year.
		50.11 The Director of Resource Development is properly trained in at least 3 approaches to writing grants.	
		50.12 Guidelines on writing proposals are developed for the staff to participate in grantsmanship.	
		50.13 Administrative policy and procedures are approved by the superintendent and clarified to the staff.	
		50.14 An assortment of printed materials has been identified and secured to assist in locating leads and relevant information.	
		50.15 A capabilities perspective is prepared and disseminated to the Department of Education Office to familiarize them with the capabilities of the school district.	
		50.16 The Director of Resource Development maintains a contact with the Department of Education.	

OPERATIONAL PLAN

Planning Unit: _____ Central

Planning Unit Administrator _____ Dr. James Wilkinson

Major Key Result Area: _____

Date: _____ June 15, 19XX

Position: Superintendent

Page _____ 3 _____ of _____ 3

Programs	Action to be Taken (Performance Objectives)	Performance Standards (This objective is satisfactorily achieved when . . .)	Performance Outcome
Community Involvement and Relations	60.1 To prepare a plan for implementing a school enlargement program by June 30, 19XX.	60.10 The assistant superintendent for curriculum and administration establishes a committee composed of members of the school district, higher education, and community in order to establish the school enlargement program. 60.11 Contact is made with those school districts implementing similar programs, and materials are collected. 60.12 Several selected school districts are selected and visited to observe their programs in action. 60.13 Armed with relevant materials and experience, the committee prepares the school enlargement whereby some students can graduate in 3, 4, or 5 years and earn a high school diploma or an associate arts degree. 60.14 The school enlargement program is discussed with the staff and community.	The school enlargement program was completed by the committee and found acceptable by the senior high school faculty, community, superintendent, and Board of Education, as indicated by the minutes of these various groups' meetings.

Strategic Planning

Planning Unit: ___Central_____ Date:_June 15, 19xx_

Planning Unit Administrator: _Dr. James Wilkinson_____ Position:_Superintendent

Planning Component: _Long-Range Goals_ Page ____1____ of ___3___

Major Key Result Area:	Student Learning and Growth
Action Determined by:	

Student learning and growth profile.

Long-Range Goal	Code: 10	Priority① 2 3 4 5 6 7 8 9

To increase student achievement in reading from the 17th percentile to the 75th percentile as indicated by Stanford Achievement Test by June 30, 19XX (3 years).

Major Key Result Area:	Organizational Management
Action Determined by:	

Adverse influences on the school district.

Long-Range Goal	Code: 20	Priority① 2 3 4 5 6 7 8 9

To reduce teacher illness absences without intimidation from 9.7 to 4.0 percent by June 30, 19XX (4 years).

Major Key Result Area:	Innovation
Action Determined by:	

Superintendent

Long-Range Goal	Code: 30	Priority 1 2 ③ 4 5 6 7 8 9

To replace the current subjective approach to selecting school administrators with a more objective approach by June 30, 19XX (3 years).

Strategic Planning

Planning Unit: _____Central_____ Date:_June 15, 19XX_

Planning Unit Administrator: _Dr. James Wilkinson_ Position:_Superintendent_

Planning Component: _Long-Range Goals_ Page __2__ of _3_

Major Key Result Area:	Performance Evaluation and Training
Action Determined by:	

Board of Education and Superintendent.

Long-Range Goal	Code: 40	Priority 1 ②3 4 5 6 7 8 9

To replace the present subjective approach to staff evaluation with
a results-oriented approach by June 30, 19XX (3 years).

Major Key Result Area:	Financial Resources
Action Determined by:	

Competitive analysis (loss of students to nonpublic schools).

Long-Range Goal	Code: 50	Priority①2 3 4 5 6 7 8 9

To increase contract and grant awards from state, federal, and
private foundations from $485,000 to $2,500,000 by June 30, 19XX
(3 years).

Major Key Result Area:	Community Involvement and Relations
Action Determined by:	

Report from the New York State Department of Education.

Long-Range Goal	Code: 60	Priority 1 2 ③4 5 6 7 8 9

To plan a school enlargement (school and college) program enabling
students to graduate in 3, 4, or 5 years, instead of the present
fixed 4 years, by June 30, 19XX (3 years).

Strategic Planning

Planning Unit: __Central_____   Date:_June 15, 19XX__

Planning Unit Administrator: __Dr. James Wilkinson____   Position: _Superintendent_

Planning Component: _Long-Range Goals_   Page ___3___ of ___3___

Major Key Result Area:	Physical Resources
Action Determined by:	

Request from the Assistant Superintendent for Curriculum and Instruction.

Long-Range Goal	Code: 70	Priority 1 ②3 4 5 6 7 8 9

To establish a comprehensive reproduction center, including staff in the school district, at a cost not exceeding $450,000 by June 1, 19XX (2 years).

Major Key Result Area:	Instructional Programs and Services
Action Determined by:	

Student learning and growth profile.

Long-Range Goal	Code: 80	Priority① 2 3 4 5 6 7 8 9

To increase the SAT scores of the school district in math from a median of 483 to 575 and verbal from a median of 395 to 525, by November 30, 19XX (3 years).

Major Key Result Area:	
Action Determined by:	

Long-Range Goal	Code:	Priority 1 2 3 4 5 6 7 8 9

STRATEGIC PLANNING PROCESS

Planning Unit: ____Central_____   Date: _Sept. 30, 19XX_

Planning Unit Administrator: __Dr. James Wilkinson_____   Position: Superintendent

Planning Component: ___Planning Exception Report_____   Page __1____of ___1_

Change Requirement: ☒ Planning Assumption   ☐ Long Range Goal   ☐ Short Range Objective
                       ☐ Performance Standard   ☐ Action Plan   ☐ Budget

---

1. Reason for the exception/s present and/or anticipated:

All incumbents lost their seats on the Board of Education.

---

2. Impact of change (present or anticipated):

Superintendent's contract was renewed for 5 years.

---

3. Corrective action to be taken:

All planning units will proceed with strategic plans as planned.

---

4. Impact of change on goal(s) and/or objective(s):

Projected improvements should result as planned.

---

5. Expected results before the change: ☐ On plan   ☐ Above plan   ☒ Below plan
   Comments:

Enthusiasm for initiating strategic plans was low--there was a high probability
that most plans would be achieved below plan.

Approved by: _____   Submitted by: Dr. James Wilkinson_____

Position: _____   Position: ___Superintendent_____

STRATEGIC PLANNING PROCESS

Planning Unit: _____Central_____   Date: November 1, 19XX

Planning Unit Administrator: _Dr. James Wilkinson_____   Position: Superintendent

Planning Component: ___Planning Exception Report_____   Page ___1___ of _1___

Change Requirement: ☐ Planning Assumption ☐ Long Range Goal ☐ Short Range Objective
                     ☐ Performance Standard ☐ Action Plan   ☒ Budget

---

1. Reason for the exception/s present and/or anticipated:

Desegregation plan was not approved by the federal government.

---

2. Impact of change (present or anticipated):

All anticipated federal funds will be withheld until an acceptable
desegregation plan is submitted to the federal government.

---

3. Corrective action to be taken:

Send an administrative team to Washington and have them remain there until
an acceptable desegregation plan is finalized and approved.

---

4. Impact of change on goal(s) and/or objective(s):

Cash flow may become a problem; interest income will be reduced, and some
staff may have to be laid off temporarily.

---

5. Expected results before the change: ☐ On plan   ☒ Above plan   ☐ Below plan
   Comments:

Approved by: _____   Submitted by: Dr. Paul Willie

Position: _____   Position: _Assistant Superintendent of_
                                                     Business

Strategic Planning

Planning Unit: _____Central_____   Date: July 1, 19XX

Planning Unit Administrator: __Dr. James Wilkinson_____   Position: Superintendent

Planning Component: _Scenarios_   Page __1__ of __1__

Topic: __Financial Resources_____

Strategic Planning Period: 19_____ to _____

Planning Assumption

Most Probable Scenario	Pessimistic Scenario	Optimistic Scenario	Ref.
1. Teahers' strike will occur and last for less than a week.	1. Teachers' strike will last for 3 months.	1. Teachers' strike will be averted.	
2. School budget will be passed on the third attempt.	2. Austerity budget will be utilized throughout the full school year.	2. School budget will be passed on the first attempt.	
3. Superintendent will not receive an extended contract.	3. Superintendent will be fired before his term expires.	3. Superintendent will receive a three-year extended contract.	
4. State aid for transportation will be reduced from 100% to 90%.	4. State aid for transportation will be reduced below the 90% level.	4. State aid for transportation will not be reduced.	
5. School budget will be increased by 9%.	5. School budget will be increased by 6%.	5. School budget will be increased beyond the 9% level.	
6. One school will be closed as a result of declining enrollment.	6. Two schools will be closed as a result of declining enrollment.	6. No schools will be closed as a result of declining enrollment.	
7. Enrollment will decrease by 237 students.	7. Enrollment will decrease by 269 students.	7. Enrollment will decrease by 160 students.	
8. Five teachers will be laid off because of declining enrollment.	8. Eight teachers will be laid off because of declining enrollment.	8. No teachers will be laid off because of declining enrollment.	
9. The school district desegregation plan will not be acceptable to the federal government.	9. The federal government will deny federal funds to the school because of an unacceptable desegregation plan.	9. The school district desegregation plan will be acceptable to the federal government with minor revisions.	
10. Energy costs will increase by 30%.	10. Energy costs will increase beyond 30%.	10. Energy costs will increase by less than 20%.	
11. Additional funds amounting to $200,000 will be secured from the federal government and private foundations.	11. No additional funds will be secured from the federal government or private foundations.	11. Additional funds amounting to $500,000 will be secured from the federal government and private foundations.	

Strategic Planning

Planning Unit: ___Alpha Elementary School___   Date: June 15, 19XX

Planning Unit Administrator: _Dr. Paul West_   Position: Principal

Planning Component: Critical Analysis   Page __1__ of __2__

Content:

A. Description of community   H. School district problems
B. Description of school district   I. Swop analysis
C. Network of aims   J. Competition analysis
D. Demographic   K. Stakeholders analysis
E. Student learning and growth   L. Threat analysis
F. Faculty profile   M. Past performance results
G. Financial history

A. Description of Community

More than 18,000 people reside within 3 miles of the school. Twenty percent of these are unemployed. The school services a predominently Black and Hispanic community.

B. Description of the School District

The school is administered by a principal and an assistant principal. The school is organized around a program of individualized instruction and team teaching. The six team leaders coordinate the activities of the team. A school advisory council is organized and meets to assist the school to plan programs and other related activities.

C. Network of Aims

Basic Purposes and Mission Statement

Alpha Elementary School

Contribute to the Somewhere School District's effots to ensure that every elementary student receives a meaningful learning and growth experience and to properly equip them for success in school. To this end the Alpha Elementary School will provide all students with the following:

> Instructional activities in Math, Reading-Language Arts, Science, Home Economics, Industrial Arts, Music, Social Studies, Spanish, French, Career Education, Guidance, Arts, Health, and Talented and Gifted Education.

> Physical activities in physical education, outdoor survival, swimming, tennis, golf, and bowling.

The Alpha Elementary School exists to:

1. Prepare students adequately to achieve success in the junior and senior high schools.

2. Ensure cost-effective use of available resources in pursuit of the basic purposes and mission of the school.

3. Create and maintain a learning environment that will enhance students' learning and growth.

4. Help students to become productive members of society.

Upon completion of the kindergarten program, students:

develop a working vocabulary and understanding of concepts zero to ten

as measured by scoring 12 out of 16 on a checklist.

By the end of the third grade, students:

master the addition and subtraction of two- or three-place numerals with regrouping, the multiplication of two one-digit numerals less than or equal to six, and the division of numerals less than or equal to six with no remainder.

demonstrate proficiency in the areas of measurement and geometry.

display knowledge of number concepts.

display competence in problem solving.

as measured by attaining 80% on teacher-made tests and 75% on the Silver Burdett Achievement Tests.

At the end of the fifth grade, students:

compute basic mathematical operations using whole numbers and fractions (addition and subtraction of like fractions and mixed numbers).

understand number and operation.

solve word problems.

evaluated by scoring 75% or better on teacher-made tests.

Strategic Planning

Planning Unit: <u>Alpha Elementary School</u>   Date: <u>June 15, 19XX</u>

Planning Unit Administrator: <u>Dr. Paul West</u>   Position: <u>Principal</u>

Planning Component: <u>Critical Analysis</u>   Page <u>1</u> of <u>1</u>

<u>Student Learning and Growth</u>

A. Academic Achievement

(Month Growth in Reading)

(Grade Level)

Title of Test <u>Stanford Achievement</u>   Date Administered _____

B. State-wide Test Results

Grade Level	19 XX to XX		19__ to __		19__ to __		19__ to __		19__ to __	
	Verbal	Math	Verbal	Math	Verbal	Math	Verbal	Math	Verbal	Math
3rd Grade	54%	61%								
6th Grade	42%	55%								
9th Grade										
11th Grade										

Strategic Planning

Planning Unit: _____Alpha Elementary School_____ Date:_June 15, 19XX___

Planning Unit Administrator: _Dr. Paul West_____ Position:_Principal____

Planning Component: _Critical Analysis_   Page ___1___ of ___2____

Faculty Profile

Composition of Staff

Classification	19XX to XX		19__ to __		19__ to __		19__ to __		19__ to __	
	T	A	T	A	T	A	T	A	T	A
Male	7	1								
Female	38	1								
Total	45									
White	28									
Black	15	1								
Hispanic	2									
Oriental										
Other										

Years of Experience

Classification	1 year		5 years		10 years		15 years		20 years		25+ years	
	T	A	T	A	T	A	T	A	T	A	T	A
Male	1		2	1	4							
Female	4		8		12	1	12		2			
White	4		1	1	13		8		2			
Black			8		3	1	4					
Hispanic	1		1									
Oriental												
Other												

Tenure Profile

Classification	White				Black				Hispanic				Oriental				Other			
	F	M	T	A	F	M	T	A	F	M	T	A	F	M	T	A	F	M	T	A
Non-tenured	5		5						1		1									
Tenured	18	5	23		13	2	15	1	1		1									

Percentage of Teachers/Administrators Engaging in Additional Training

Grade Level	19XX to XX		19___ to ___		19___ to ___		19___ to ___		19___ to ___	
	T	A	T	A	T	A	T	A	T	A
Kindergarten	10%									
First	5%									
Second	20%									
Third	15%									
Fourth	10%									
Fifth	25%									
Sixth	10%									
Seventh										
Eighth										
Ninth										
Tenth										
Eleventh										
Twelfth										

Strategic Planning

Planning Unit: _____ Alpha Elementary School _____   Date: June 15, 19XX

Planning Unit Administrator: __Dr. Paul West__   Position: Principal

Planning Component: Critical Analysis   Page ___1___ of ___1___

Summary of Financial History

Major Key Result Areas	19 XX to XX	19___ to ___	19___ to___	19___ to___	19___ to___
	Amount	Amount	Amount	Amount	Amount
1. Financial Resources	1,000				
2. Performance Evaluation and Training	5,185				
3. Physical Resources	15,500				
4. Student Learning and Growth	17,150				
5. Organizational Management	117,000				
6. Innovation	75,800				
7. Community Involvement and Relations	2,900				
8. Instructional Programs and Services	1,227,750				
9.					
10.					
Total	1,462,285				
Change Increase/ Decrease					

Strategic Planning

Planning Unit: __Alpha Elementary School_____ Date:__June 30, 19XX__

Planning Unit Administrator: __Dr. Paul West_____ Position:__Principal__

Planning Component: __Critical Analysis__ Page __1__ of __1__

Adverse Influences on School District

Description of Influence	19XX to XX	19XX to XX	19__ to __	19__ to __	19__ to __
1. Student absentee rate	5.5%	4.9%			
2. Faculty absentee rate	13.7%	9.9%			
3. Cost of substitute teachers' salaries	102,750.	80,190.			
4. Staff turnover	2:40	3:42			
5. Cost of vandalism	2,150.	3,905.			
6. Number of students assaulted	4	12			
7. Number of faculty assaulted	0	1			
8. Incidents of student accidents	14	76			
9. Incidents of faculty accidents	2	3			
10. Incidents of pregnancy	0	0			
11. Drop-out rate	0	0			
12. Students killed	1	0			
13. Faculty killed	0	1			
14. Students enrolling in non-public schools	12	45			

Strategic Planning

Planning Unit: ___Alpha Elementary School_____ Date: June 15, 19XX

Planning Unit Administrator: ___Dr. Paul West_____ Position: Principal

Planning Component: __Critical Analysis__   Page __i__ of __1__

Swop Analysis: _____

Major Key Result Area:	Student Learning and Growth
Major Strengths/Opportunities	Major Weaknesses/Problems

-Many teachers realize that they are not properly trained to teach math effectively.	-Too many students are achieving below grade level in math.
	-No system has been implemented to monitor student achievement.
	-Many teachers lack the necessary skills to teach math adequately.
	-A supervisor is needed to provide proper supervision for teachers of math.
	-The textbook approach to teaching math is not supplemented with games, concrete items, kits, and the like.

Action to be taken: Reference

Research information on validated math programs. Identify one
that has been successful in a similar school district. Consider
implementing it on a trial basis, and if the response is
favorable, develop a comprehensive training program for both
teachers and administrators.

Strategic Planning

Planning Unit: _____Alpha Elementary School_____   Date: June 15, 19XX

Planning Unit Administrator: ___Dr. Paul West___   Position: Principal

Planning Component: Critical Analysis   Page __1__ of __2__

Past Performance Results

Major Key Result Area	Student Learning and Growth	
Short-Range Objective	Code: 10.1	Priority①2 3 4 5 6 7 8 9

To increase student achievement in reading from the 22nd to 35th percentile as indicated by Stanford Achievement Test by June 30, 19XX (first of five years).

Performance Outcome	OP ☒ AP ☐ BP ☐

Student achievement in reading was increased from the 22nd to the 36th percentile as attested by the results of the Stanford Achievement Test as well as the state-wide reading test.

Major Key Result Area	Organizational Management	
Short-Range Objective	Code: 20.1	Priority①2 3 4 5 6 7 8 9

To reduce teacher illness absences, without intimidation, from a rate of 12.1 to 9.7 by June 30, 19XX (first of four years).

Performance Outcome	OP ☐ AP ☒ BP ☐

Teacher absences due to illness were drastically decreased from a rate of 12.1 to 8.5 as attested by the May absentee report submitted to the central planning unit.

Major Key Result Area	Student Learning and Growth	
Short-Range Objective	Code: 10.2	Priority 1②3 4 5 6 7 8 9

To ensure that 100 percent of the students required to attend kindergarten programs are properly innoculated against the state-prescribed childhood diseases, as indicated by the school nurse's report, by December 31, 19XX.

Performance Outcome	OP ⊠ AP ☐ BP ☐

Working with the attendance officer, all students required to attend kindergarten were properly innoculated either by our or the child's physician by December 31, 19XX, as indicated by the records in the nurse's office.

Major Key Result Area	Student Learning and Growth	
Short-Range Objective	Code: 10.3	Priority 1②3 4 5 6 7 8 9

To increase student achievement in math from the 30th to the 45th percentile as indicated by Stanford Achievement Test by June 30, 19XX (first of five years).

Performance Outcome	OP ⊠ AP ☐ BP ☐

Student achievement in math was increased from the 30th to 46th percentile as indicated on the Stanford Achievement profile sheet.

Major Key Result Area		
Short-Range Objective	Code:	Priority 1 2 3 4 5 6 7 8 9

Perfromance Outcome	OP ☐ AP ☐ BP ☐

Strategic Planning

Planning Unit: ___Alpha Elementary School_____ Date: June 15, 19XX

Planning Unit Administrator: ___Dr. Paul West_____ Position: Principal___

Planning Component: __Guide for Formulating Program Strategy__ Page __1__ of __2__

---

1. Major Key Result Area: Student Learning and Growth

---

2. Long-Range Goal: | Code: 20 | Priority 1 ② 3 4 5 6 7 8 9

To increase student achievement in math from the 30th percentile
to the 75th percentile as indicated by Stanford Achievement
Test by June 30, 19XX (5 years).

Strategic Approach:

☒ Emulation   ☐ Proactive   ☐ Reactive

---

4. Analyze Alternative Strategies:

Summary of Alternative Strategies	Project Cost	Maximize Strengths	Minimize Weaknesses	Remedy Threat	Stakeholder Expectation	Respond to Competition	Impact	Rank
1. Retrain teachers and administrators in the present math program.	low	some	some	no	no	--	low	2
2. Identify and use a different math test.	mod.	no	no	no	no	--	low	3
3. Install a new math program using mini calculators.	mod.	no	no	no	no	--	low	4
4. Implement the validated Dale Avenue Math Program.	low	yes	some	some	yes	--	mod.	1

---

5. Select Appropriate Strategy:

Capitalize on the track record of the Dale Avenue Math Program
by: using teachers already trained in the program to train other
staff; requesting that they attend seminars during the summer
months; and appointing a teacher to supervise the program. A
major strategic emphasis will be to provide practical experience
to the teachers, which should be backed up with supervisory
consultation right in the classroom.

---

6. Compare Long-Range Goal with Program Strategy:

Based upon the track record of the Dale Avenue Math Program, this
program strategy seems to be compatible with the long-range goal.

---

7. Implementation of Strategy:

   a) Who is responsible for completing strategy? ___Principal_____

---

   b) When will the strategy be launched? __September 1, 19XX_____

   c) What support services will be required? __Teacher's aid for each team___

   d) What specifically are the key tasks that need to be performed for the
      strategies to be implemented? __(1) appoint Dale Avenue Supervisor;___

      (2) train all teachers and administrators; (3) secure___

      necessary supplies and materials; (4) construct a
      monitoring system

Strategic Planning Package

Planning Unit: _____ Alpha Elementary School _____ Date: June 15, 19XX

Planning Unit Administrator: __Dr. Paul West__ Position: **Principal**

Planning Component: _____ Page __1__ of __2__

Major Key Result Area:	Student Learning and Growth

Long-Range Goal	Code: 20

To increase student achievement in math from the 30th percentile to the 75th percentile as indicated by Stanford Achievement Test by June 30, 19XX (5 years).

Strategy Selected	Capitalize on the track record of the Dale Avenue Math Program by; using teachers already trained in

the program to train other staff; requesting that they attend seminars in the summer months; and appointing a teacher to supervise the program. A major strategic emphasis will be to provide practical experience to the teachers, which should be backed up with supervisory consultation right in the classroom.

Results Expected

If the track record of the Dale Avenue Math Program prevails with this school district, the math problem should be resolved in 3 to 5 years.

Monitoring Responsibility

Assistant Principal

Monitoring Efforts and Dates

Begin monitoring results on a quarterly basis, starting on January 1, 19XX.

Budget:

Code	Programs	19 XX to XX		19 to		19 to		19 to		19 to	
		Objective Budget		Objective Budget		Objective Budget		Objective Budget		Objective Budget	
		Program Budget		Program Budget		Program Budget		Program Budget		Program Budget	
1111	Math	17,150									
		210,000									

Code	Programs	19___ to ___		19___ to ___		19___ to ___		19___ to ___		19___ to ___	
		Objective Budget		Objective Budget		Objective Budget		Objective Budget		Objective Budget	
		Program Budget		Program Budget		Program Budget		Program Budget		Program Budget	

Totals Past Performance Results

Code	Program	19 XX to XX			19___ to ___			19___ to ___			19___ to ___			19___ to ___		
		OP	AP	BP	OP	AP	BP	OP	AP	BP	OP	AP	BP	OP	AP	BP
1111	Math	x														

Indicate what corrective action will take place to improve all performances achieved below plan

OP - On Plan
AP - Above Plan
BP - Below Plan

OPERATIONAL PLAN

Planning Unit: _Alpha Elementary School_

Planning Unit Administrator _Dr. Paul West_

Major Key Result Area: _____

Date: _June 15, 19XX_

Position: _Principal_

Page _1_ of _3_

Programs	Action to be Taken (Performance Objectives)	Performance Standards (This objective is satisfactorily achieved when . . .)	Performance Outcome
Student Learning and Growth	10.1 To increase student achievement in reading from the 22nd to 35th percentile as indicate by the Stanford Achievement Test by June 30, 19XX (first of five years).	10.10 The pilot reading program results are explained to both teachers and parents. 10.11 Guidelines have been developed to implement the Action Reading program, and it contains content for teaching comprehension, interpretation, and so on. 10.12 Sufficient reading kits have been received for each teacher. 10.13 All administrators and teachers have received 5 days of training in the Action Reading program incorporating 3 hours of theory and 3 hours of practical application using students. 10.14 Profile sheet is on file and updated weekly on each student. 10.15 Students are tested on a weekly basis and progress is charted.	Student achievement in reading was increased from the 22nd to 36th percentile as attested by the results of the Stanford Achievement Test as well as the state-wide reading test.

OPERATIONAL PLAN

Planning Unit: ___Alpha Elementary School___

Planning Unit Administrator: ___Dr. Paul West___

Major Key Result Area: ___

Date: ___June 15, 19XX___

Position: ___Principal___

Page ___2___ of ___3___

Programs	Action to be Taken (Performance Objectives)	Performance Standards (This objective is satisfactorily achieved when . . .)	Performance Outcome
Student Learning and Growth	10.2 To ensure that 100% of the students required to attend kindergarten programs are porperly inoculated against the state-prescribed diseases, as indicated by the school nurse's report, by December 31, 19XX.	10.21 Letters are sent home to parents to request them to have their children immunized against certain childhood diseases. 10.22 Announcements are made on the local radio and television stations informing parents about the inoculation laws regarding school children. 10.23 The school district's mobile inoculation unit circulates the community inoculating those students who have not been previously treated. 10.24 Children who do not show up for school after 5 days are monitored by the school district attendant officer who follows up with a telephone inquiry.	Working with the attendance officer, all students required to attend kindergarten were properly inoculated either by the school or child's own physician by December 31, 19XX as indicated by the records in the nurse's office.

OPERATIONAL PLAN

Planning Unit: _____ Alpha Elementary School_____

Planning Unit Administrator _____ Dr. Paul West_____

Major Key Result Area: _____

Date: _____ June 15, 19XX_____

Position: _____ Principal_____

Page _____ 3_____ of _____ 3_____

Programs	Action to be Taken (Performance Objectives)	Performance Standards (This objective is satisfactorily achieved when . . .)	Performance Outcome
Student Learning and Growth	10.3 To increase student achievement in math from the 30th to the 45th percentile as indicated by Stanford Achievement Test by June 30, 19XX (first of five years).	10.31 A plan is developed for implementing the Dale Avenue Math program. 10.32 All teachers and administrators received 5 days of training incorporating 3 hours of theory and 3 hours of practical application with students. 10.33 All necessary equipment and materials are received in a timely manner in order to implement the program. 10.34 Student profile sheets designed to monitor performance are completed for each student.	Student achievement in math was increased from the 30th to 46th percentile as indicated on the Stanford Acheivement profile sheet.

Strategic Planning

Planning Unit: _____Alpha Elementary School_____   Date: _June 15, 19XX_

Planning Unit Administrator: _____Dr. Paul West_____   Position: _Principal_

Planning Component: _Long-Range Goals_   Page __1__ of __1__

Major Key Result Area:	Student Learning and Growth
Action Determined by:	

Central planning unit

Long-Range Goal	Code: 10	Priority ①2 3 4 5 6 7 8 9

To increase student achievement in reading from the 22nd percentile
to the 75th percentile as indicated by Stanford Achievement Test
by June 30, 19XX (5 years).

Major Key Result Area:	Organizational Management
Action Determined by:	

Central planning unit

Long-Range Goal	Code: 20	Priority ①2 3 4 5 6 7 8 9

To reduce teacher illness absences without intimidation form 12.1
to 4.0 percent by June 30, 19XX (4 years).

Major Key Result Area:	Student Learning and Growth
Action Determined by:	

Latest math test results on the Stanford Achievement Test, as well
as recommendations from the staff.

Long-Range Goal	Code: 10	Priority 1 ②3 4 5 6 7 8 9

To increase student achievement in math from the 30th percentile to
the 75th percentile as indicated by the Stanford Achievement Test
by June 30, 19XX (5 years).

Strategic Planning

Planning Unit: ___Beta Senior High School___   Date: June 15, 19XX

Planning Unit Administrator: ___Dr. Mary North___   Position: Principal

Planning Component: Critical Analysis   Page ___1___ of ___2___

Student Learning and Growth

A. Academic Achievement

Title of Test _Stanford_ Date Administered_____
Achievement

B. State-wide Test Results

Grade Level	19XX toXX		19__ to__		19__ to__		19__ to__		19__ to__	
	Verbal	Math	Verbal	Math	Verbal	Math	Verbal	Math	Verbal	Math
3rd Grade										
6th Grade										
9th Grade										
11th Grade	55%	61%								

C. SAT Results

Section	19XX_ toXX	19 XX to XX	19___to___	19___to___	19___ to ___
Verbal	421	419			
Math	465	461			

D. Placement of Graduates

Item	19XX_ toXX	19 XX to XX	19___to ___	19___ to ___	19___to___
Number. and Percentage Students Entering College	301 (85%)	330 (82%)			
Number and Percentage Students Entering Com. Schools	21 (6%)	33 (9%)			
Number and Percentage Students Entering Armed Services	12 (4%)	19 (5%)			
Number and Percentage Students Entering Other Fields	19 (5%)	16 (4%)			
Total	353	371			

E. National Awards/Honors

Title of Award/Honor	19XX toXX	19XX_ to XX	19___ to ___	19___to___	19___to ___
National Science Award	4	6			
National Math Award	10	21			
Literary Guild Award	4	7			

Strategic Planning

Planning Unit: ___Beta Senior High School___ Date: _June 15, 19XX_

Planning Unit Administrator: _Dr. Mary North_ Position: _Principal_

Planning Component: _Critical Analysis_ Page ___1___ of ___2___

Faculty Profile

Composition of Staff

Classification	19 XX to XX		19 __ to __		19 __ to __		19 __ to __		19 __ to __	
	T	A	T	A	T	A	T	A	T	A
Male	70	3								
Female	20	1								
Total	90	4								
White	60									
Black	27									
Hispanic	3									
Oriental										
Other										

Years of Experience

Classification	1 year		5 years		10 years		15 years		20 years		25 + years	
	T	A	T	A	T	A	T	A	T	A	T	A
Male	9		20	3	30		6		2		3	
Female	2		10	1	3		5					
White	2		22		22		6				3	
Black	3		7		10		5		2			
Hispanic	1		1		1							
Oriental												
Other												

Tenure Profile

Classification	White				Black				Hispanic				Oriental				Other			
	F	M	T	A	F	M	T	A	F	M	T	A	F	M	T	A	F	M	T	A
Non-tenured	4		4		4		4		1		1									
Tenured	12	44	56			23	23			2	2									

Percentage of Teachers/Administrators Engaging in Additional Training

Grade Level	19 XX to XX		19___ to ____		19___ to___		19___ to____		19___ to ____	
	T	A	T	A	T	A	T	A	T	A
Kindergarten										
First										
Second										
Third										
Fourth										
Fifth										
Sixth										
Seventh										
Eighth										
Ninth										
Tenth	--	10%								
Eleventh	5%	10%								
Twelfth	2%	10%								

Strategic Planning

Planning Unit: _____Beta Senior High School_____ Date: June 15, 19XX

Planning Unit Administrator: _Dr. Mary North_____ Position: _Principal___

Planning Component: _Critical Analysis_ Page __1__ of __1__

Summary of Financial History

Major Key Result Areas	19 XX to XX	19__ to __	19__ to __	19__ to___	19__ to___
	Amount	Amount	Amount	Amount	Amount
1. Financial Resources	3,750				
2. Performance Evaluation and Training	8,175				
3. Physical Resources	31,890				
4. Student Learning and Growth	14,450				
5. Organizational Management	178,000				
6. Innovation	46,000				
7. Community Involvement and Relations	8,700				
8. Instructional Programs and Services	2,415,000				
9.					
10.					
Total	2,705,965				
Change Increase/ Decrease					

Strategic Planning

Planning Unit: _____ Beta Secondary School _____ Date: June 30, 19XX

Planning Unit Administrator: Dr. Mary North _____ Position: Principal

Planning Component: Critical Analysis _____ Page __1__ of __1__

Adverse Influences on School District

Description of Influence	19XX toXX	19 XX to XX	19__ to __	19__ to __	19__ to __
1. Student absentee rate	11.4%	12.2%			
2. Faculty absentee rate	12.1%	9.8%			
3. Cost of substitute teachers' salaries	453,750.	367,500.			
4. Staff turnover	12:155	19:155			
5. Cost of vandalism	65,010.	71,140.			
6. Number of students assaulted	25	37			
7. Number of faculty assaulted	14	18			
8. Incidents of student accidents	65	51			
9. Incidents of faculty accidents	10	11			
10. Incidents of pregnancy	30	44			
11. Drop-out rate	19%	22%			
12. Students killed	0	7			
13. Faculty killed	0	0			
14. Students enrolling in non-public schools	20	34			

Strategic Planning

Planning Unit: _____ Beta Senior High School _____ Date: June 15, 19XX

Planning Unit Administrator: _____ Dr. Mary North _____ Position: Principal

Planning Component: Critical Analysis _____ Page __1__ of __1__

Swop Analysis: _____

Major Key Result Area:	Student Learning and Growth
Major Strengths/Opportunities	Major Weaknesses/Problems
-The instructional materials' center is well stocked with an assortment of books related to English/Language Arts. -One of the English teachers is an expert on individualized learning.	-A large segment of the student body is failing English/Language Arts. -Teachers are complaining that more individualized instruction is needed, but they don't have the time. -Members of the Board of Education view this area as a serious problem in the senior high school. -Few students are able to write a simple letter or to fill out a job application. -The verbal results of the SAT and Stanford Achievement are testimonies that English/Language Arts is a serious problem in the senior high school. -Some of the teachers need training to upgrade their English/Language Arts skills.

Action to be taken: Reference

Identify space in the senior high school to install an English laboratory center. Use a committee composed of eight teachers and students to develop a plan for implementing and maintaining the center. Staff will have to be hired to develop relevant English/ Language Arts materials.

Strategic Planning

Planning Unit: _____Beta Senior High School_____ Date: June 15, 19XX

Planning Unit Administrator: Dr. Mary North _____ Position: Principal

Planning Component: Critical Analysis   Page ___1___ of ___2___

Past Performance Results

Major Key Result Area	Student Learning and Growth	
Short-Range Objective	Code: 10.1	Priority 1 2 3 4 5 6 7 8 9

To develop a plan for providing diagnostic-prescriptive
instruction in English/Language Arts to senior high school
students by June 30, 19XX.

Performance Outcome	OP☒ AP ☐ BP ☐

A plan was developed by the senior high faculty, superintendent,
and Board of Education to install an English/Language Arts
laboratory center in the senior high school on June 15, 19XX.

Major Key Result Area	Organizational Management	
Short-Range Objective	Code: 20.1	Priority 1 2 3 4 5 6 7 8 9

To reduce teacher illness absences from a rate of 12.1% to 9%
per teacher, without intimidation, by June 30, 19XX.

Performance Outcome	OP☒ AP ☐ BP ☐

Staff illness absences were reduced from a rate of 12.1% to 8.9%
per teacher, without intimidation, as attested by the May
attendance report.

Major Key Result Area	Instructional Programs and Services	
Short-Range Objective	Code: 80.1	Priority 1 2 3 4 5 6 7 8 9

To increase the median SAT scores from 495 in verbal to 520 and from 510 in math to 530, by June 30, 19XX.

Performance Outcome	OP ☒ AP ☐ BP ☐

Median SAT scores rose from 495 to 522 in verbal and from 510 to 529 in math, as attested by the SAT profile sheet.

Major Key Result Area		
Short-Range Objective	Code:	Priority 1 2 3 4 5 6 7 8 9

Performance Outcome	OP ☐ AP ☐ BP ☐

Major Key Result Area		
Short-Range Objective	Code:	Priority 1 2 3 4 5 6 7 8 9

Perfromance Outcome	OP ☐ AP ☐ BP ☐

Strategic Planning

Planning Unit: _____Beta Senior High School_____ Date:_June 15, 19XX_

Planning Unit Administrator: _Dr. Mary North_____ Position:_Principal_

Planning Component: _Guide for Formulating Program Strategy_ Page ___1___ of ___2___

1. Major Key Result Area: Student Learning and Growth

2. Long-Range Goal: | Code: 10 | Priority 1 2 3 4 5 6 7 8 9

To establish an English/Language Arts laboratory center to individualize instruction by June 30, 19XX (3 years).

Strategic Approach: |

☐ Emulation   ☐ Proactive   ☒ Reactive

4. Analyze Alternative Strategies: |

Summary of Alternative Strategies	Project Cost	Maximize Strengths	Minimize Weaknesses	Remedy Threat	Stakeholder Expectation	Respond to Competition	Impact	Rank
1. Use educational learning packets.	mod.	some	some	some	no	--	mod.	3
2. Implement computerized assisted instruction.	high	some	some	no	no	--	mod.	4
3. Establish English/Language Arts laboratory center.	mod.	some	some	yes	yes	yes	high	1
4. Install nongraded concept.	low	some	some	may-be	yes	--	mod.	2

---

5. Select Appropriate Strategy:

A major strategic thrust will be to locate an English laboratory
in the senior high school, which will be staffed by an English/
Language Arts specialist who will assist students to complete
their individually prescribed learning tasks and/or activities.
After the learning exercise has been successfully completed, the
students will return to their class to continue the learning
process. All students will be expected to keep up with their
regular assignments.

---

6. Compare Long-Range Goal with Program Strategy:

This strategy appears to be the best alternative to assist
students to close learning gaps, thereby meeting the long-
range goal.

---

7. Implementation of Strategy:

a) Who is responsible for completing strategy? ___Principal_____

_____

b) When will the strategy be launched? _September 1, 19XX_____

c) What support services will be required? _clerical and reproduction_____

d) What specifically are the key tasks that need to be performed for the
strategies to be implemented? _(1) hire an English/Language Arts____

_specialist on the secondary level; (2) locate space to_____
accommodate the center; (3) develop a plan for implementing
the center; and (4) implement the plan and monitor the
results of student performance.

Strategic Planning Package

Planning Unit: ___Beta Senior High School_____ Date: June 15, 19XX

Planning Unit Administrator: ___Dr. Mary North_____ Position: Principal

Planning Component: _____ Page ___1___ of ___2___

Major Key Result Area:	Student Learning and Growth

Long-Range Goal	Code: 10

To establish an English/Language Arts laboratory center to
individualize instruction by June 30, 19XX (3 years).

Strategy Selected

Set up an English/Language Arts lab to provide opportunities
for students to complete individually prescribed learning tasks
or activities, assisted by a specialist in the area.

Results Expected

As a result of the lab experience, students should be able to
close certain learning gaps because of the prescriptive and
individualized approach to mastering needs.

Monitoring Responsibility

Principal

Monitoring Efforts and Dates

Quarterly effort reports, beginning September 1, 19XX.

Budget:

Code	Programs	19XX to XX		19 to		19 to		19 to		19 to	
		Objective Budget		Objective Budget		Objective Budget		Objective Budget		Objective Budget	
		Program Budget		Program Budget		Program Budget		Program Budget		Program Budget	
10.4	English/ Language Arts	48,500									
		237,400									

Code	Programs	19___ to ___	19___ to___	19___ to ___	19___ to ___	19___ to ___
		Objective Budget	Objective Budget	Objective Budget	Objective Budget	Objective Budget
		Program Budget	Program Budget	Program Budget	Program Budget	Program Budget

Totals Past Performance Results

Code	Program	19XX to XX			19___ to ___			19___ to ___			19___ to ___			19___ to ___		
		OP	AP	BP	OP	AP	BP	OP	AP	BP	OP	AP	BP	OP	AP	BP
10.4	English/ Language Arts	x														

Indicate what corrective action will take place to improve all performances achieved below plan

OP - On Plan
AP - Above Plan
BP - Below Plan

OPERATIONAL PLAN

Planning Unit: __Beta Senior High School__

Planning Unit Administrator __Dr. Mary North__

Major Key Result Area: ____

Date: __June 15, 19XX__

Position: __Principal__

Page __1__ of __3__

Programs	Action to be Taken (Performance Objectives)	Performance Standards (This objective is satisfactorily achieved when . . .)	Performance Outcome
Student Learning and Growth	10.1 To develop a plan for providing diagnostic-prescriptive instruction in English/Language Arts to senior high school students by June 30, 19XX.	10.10 An English/Language Arts specialist has been hired on the secondary level. 10.11 Space for a new English/Language Arts laboratory has been located within the senior high school. 10.12 A plan for establishing the lab has been developed and approved by the superintendent. 10.13 The plan is clarified to the staff and community. 10.14 The plan is implemented. 10.15 A system is established to monito student progress and the effectiveness of the laboratory.	A plan was developed by the senior high faculty, superintendent, and Board of Education to install an English/Language Arts laboratory center in the senior high school on June 15, 19XX.

OPERATIONAL PLAN

Planning Unit: ___Beta Senior High School___

Planning Unit Administrator ___Dr. Mary North___

Major Key Result Area: ___

Date: ___June 15, 19XX___

Position: ___Principal___

Page ___2___ of ___3___

Programs	Action to be Taken (Performance Objectives)	Performance Standards (This objective is satisfactorily achieved when...)	Performance Outcome
Organizational Management	20.1 To reduce teacher illness absences from a rate of 12.1% to 9% per teacher, without intimidation, by June 30, 19XX.	20.10 The director of personnel is properly prepared in the Bell Telephone approach for reducing staff illness absences. 20.11 A system is developed to record, collect, and analyze data pertaining to staff attendance. 20.12 All administrators are properly trained to implement the program. 20.13 Selected clerical staff are properly trained to record pertinent data. 20.14 A program for recognizing "good attendance" records has been developed and approved by the Board of Education. 20.15 A system is installed to monitor results. 20.16 Each planning unit administrator includes, within the operational plan, a short-range objective to reach a long-range goal.	Staff illness absences were reduced from a rate of 12.1% to 8.9% per teacher without intimidation, as attested by the May attendance report.

OPERATIONAL PLAN

Planning Unit: ___Beta Senior High School___

Planning Unit Administrator ___Dr. Mary North___

Major Key Result Area: ___

Programs	Action to be Taken (Performance Objectives)	Performance Standards (This objective is satisfactorily achieved when . . .)	Performance Outcome
Instructional Programs and Services	80.1 To increase the median SAT scores from 495 in verbal to 520 and from 510 in math to 530 by June 30, 19XX.	80.10 A teacher is hired to conduct a class on preparing for the SAT. 80.11 Junior and senior high schools begin to incorporate elements of the SAT within the English/Language Arts and Math programs. 80.12 A study is conducted on the senior hgih level to determine the specific areas where students are experiencing difficulties on the SAT, and the curriculum is altered to stress these areas. 80.13 Teachers on the junior high school levels are introduced to the PSAT and SAT and are encouraged to include relevant content in their lessons. 80.14 Students are required to take the PSAT once in the 7th, twice in the 8th, and three times in the 9th grade.	Median SAT scores rose from 495 to 522 in verbal and from 510 to 529 on math as attested by the SAT profile sheet.

Strategic Planning

Planning Unit: __Beta Senior High School__   Date:_June 15, 19XX_

Planning Unit Administrator: __Dr. Mary North__   Position:_Principal_

Planning Component: _Long-Range Goals_   Page ___1___ of __1__

Major Key Result Area:	Community Involvement and Relations
Action Determined by:	

A recent report of the State Department of Education.

Long-Range Goal	Code: 60.3	Priority 1 2 3 4 5 6 7 8 9

To establish a program whereby students can graduate either in 3 or 4 years, earning a diploma, or in 5 years, earning an associate degree, by June 30, 19XX (3 years).

Major Key Result Area:	Student Learning and Growth
Action Determined by:	

Student learning and growth profile.

Long-Range Goal	Code: 10	Priority 1 2 3 4 5 6 7 8 9

To establish an English/Language Arts laboratory center to individualize instruction by June 30, 19XX (3 years).

Major Key Result Area:	
Action Determined by:	

Long-Range Goal	Code:	Priority 1 2 3 4 5 6 7 8 9

INDEX